THE PRIVATE WORLD OF
OTTOMAN WOMEN

Women having fun on the Great Wheel, early seventeenth century (F. Taeschner, *Alt-Stambuler . . .*, Hanover, 1925)

Godfrey Goodwin

The Private World of
Ottoman Women

Saqi
Essentials

To Gillian

British Library Cataloguing-in-Publication Data
A catalogue record for this book is available from the British Library

ISBN 0-86356-745-2
EAN 9-780863-567452

First published in hardback in 1997 by Saqi Books

This edition published 2006

SAQI
26 Westbourne Grove
London W2 5RH
www.saqibooks.com

I shall die this autumn. My tasks are finished now
I have washed in the brook, climbed the walnut-tree, frightened birds
Been kidnapped. Born twelve children. Cradled, watched
Married a son, lost a daughter, lived to be thirty.

From 'Autumn' by the female Turkish poet Gülten Akın (b. 1933). Translation by Nermin Menemencioğlu (from *The Penguin Book of Turkish Verse*, edited by N. Menemencioğlu).

Contents

Illustrations

Illustrations

A Note on Pronunciation

The spelling adopted here is based on modern Turkish but I have even taken liberties with that. All Turkish letters are pronounced as in English except for the following:

c pronounced *j* as in *jam*
ç pronounced *ch* as in *child*
ğ not pronounced; lengthens the preceding vowel
ı akin to the pronunciation of *u* in *radium*
ö pronounced *ö* as in the German *König*
ş akin to the *sh* in *shark*
ü pronounced *u* as in the French *tu*

Genealogy of the House of Osman

including all the sultans and some of their wives and children who are mentioned in the text

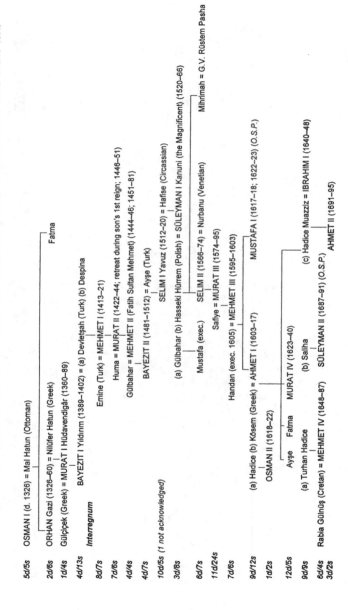

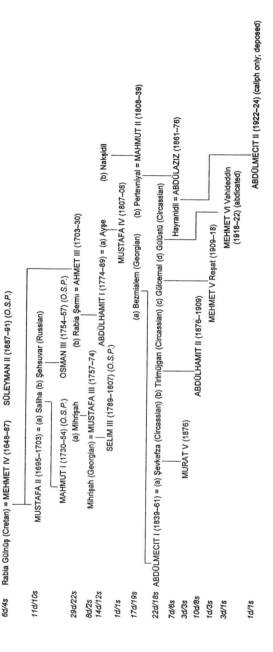

Acknowledgements

This book was born of many invaluable conversations, including those with the late Mme Emin Pasha, the late Aliye Berger-Boronai and the late Princess Fahrülnissa Zeyd-ül-Huseyn, among other members of the Şakir Pasha family. Şirin Devrim is still very much alive. The sections on costume owe much to the authoritative publications of Dr Jennifer Scarce from whose works I do not quote directly; indeed, she may feel that she had no influence at all.

It would be impossible to list all the Turkish women – and men – who have helped me with information, nor can I include all the people who, although not Turkish, have a deep knowledge of the country. They include: Dr Sina and Tulin Akşın, Professor Gülen Aktaş, the late Bay Tahir Alangu, Professor Metin And, Professor R. Arık, Professor Nurhan Atasoy, Professor Esin Atıl, Mrs Dorin Axel, Dr Margaret Bainbridge, Professor Oya Başak, Professor Michele Bernadini, Professor Faruk Birtek, Lady Burrows, Dr Filiz Çağman, Dr Cevat Capan, Professor John Carswell, Lady Daunt, the late Bay Emin Divanı-Kibrizli, Elmas Hanım, Dr Jale Erzen, Andrew and Dr Caroline Finkel, Mrs Minnie Garwood, Bayan İlin Gülensoy, Professor Haldun Gürmen, Professor Fahir İz, Professor Özer Kabaş and the sadly missed late Ayma Kabaş, Mrs Evelyn Kalças, Dr Denise Kandioti, Professor Cemal Kavadar and Professor Gülru Necipoğlu, Professor Geoffrey and Mrs Lewis, Mrs Arlette Melaart, the late Mrs Nermin Menemencioğlu-

Streeter, Mr Sedat Pakay, the late Mehmet Ali Pazarbaşı, Dr Helen Philon, Professor André Raymond, Professor J. M. Rogers, Bayan Kereme Senyücel, Dr Ezel Kural Shaw, in particular the late Dr Susan Skilliter, Bay Artun Ünsal, Mrs Gillian Warr, Bay Balı and Angela Yazıcı.

I have to thank Bayan Mary Berkmen for her hospitality and support and the librarians of Boğazıcı Üniversitesi; Michael Pollock, Librarian of the Royal Asiatic Society in London, and its conservationist Graeme Gardiner; the staff of the British Library; and, in particular, Dr Tony Greenwood, Director of the American Research Institute in Arnavutköy.

My wife has been an invaluable critic and has survived the intrusion of the manuscript into her life.

As always, my publisher André Gaspard has been continually protective and encouraging while Jana Gough has again been the most humane of editors. With this book she has taken quite exceptional pains and I am deeply indebted to her.

The Wedding (F. Taeschner, *Alt-Stambuler . . .*, Hanover, 1925)

Foreword

We Must Walk Where No Aircraft Flies

It is important to make clear from the start that the great problem in writing this book has been the paucity of letters by Turkish women, let alone diaries. I have therefore had to resort to contemporary accounts – these are mainly by European travellers who were often poor or spasmodic witnesses. There is, however, another source: the growing evidence gathered and evaluated by modern economic and social historians such as Inalcık and Faroqhi in particular.

The scope of the book has been restricted else it would have grown out of all proportion. It is for this reason that Syrian and Egyptian women have been ignored: although, strictly speaking, they were Ottomans for several centuries, they belong to their own respective cultures. I also decided to stop at 1924 when Atatürk founded the Republic. The period requires a second volume in which to record the achievements of women in the last seventy years. Nor would I be able to write it. It is for that reason that the book is restricted to the period of the sultanate. Even this has had to be cut ruthlessly because the Ottoman empire nurtured many disparate societies.

∾   ∾   ∾

Anyone who has lived and travelled in modern Turkey, and who cares a jot for the human race, can only be impressed by the hardship of village life even today. This includes that of the extended villages which form the suburbs of cities and towns. For a great many people, life is a condition that must be endured. Yet there are moments of relaxation, of pleasure and of festivities while the earth still bears fruit, however grim the future may be with the dwindling harvests from forests and sea. It is gossip which keeps a community alive – that great game that notices the slightest gesture that is out of place, hesitation before a familiar door, the late arrival at the washing place that is the club to which all village women belong. It comes from acute observation and a shared store of knowledge beside which the skills of poker, bridge and meddling with micro-chips appear singularly commonplace.

The Republic legalized the liberation of women in spite of all the prejudices nurtured through generations which recede into the dark ages before recorded history. Women now direct major museums and are professors in the universities. They are beginning to be a force in the politics of the democracy. This change from the past to the future is not confined to the educated but is perceptible among the young in spite of reaction and this heartens older generations who battled for liberation. It should be remembered how recently equality for women has evolved in the richer countries of Europe and America. Even today, a woman has never been elected president of the United States or appointed editor of a great newspaper. Such things will come.

It is important to recognize that the nineteenth century was just as much a period of social and political turmoil in Istanbul as it was in the rest of Europe. It did not come to the rescue of Ottoman women immediately but the first schools for girls bred the first suffragettes. It was to be long before the villager could enjoy the privilege of reading and writing. Besides the schools, a secret revolution occurred when governesses came into fashion among wealthy families. These women came from England, France and Germany, sometimes all at the same time. Some were not very clear in their own minds about the future of women as they saw it. They were unlikely to evangelize their charges except by osmosis and by endowing them with the eye-widening pleasures of commanding several languages and their imported cultures.

If at the end of the journey, the palsied hand of romanticism has been amputated, that will have been worth attempting. To be tough is not enough. A life is futile if it has not taken one step on its own, unhandicapped by sex or impoverishment. Some steps were taken and the footprints are worth finding.

Not all that has resulted from the great advances in women's lives since the Republic has been beneficial to country life. A determination to educate their children has meant parents' sending them away to towns in order to attend secondary school. Success results in recruitment by universities in both Istanbul and the provinces. The graduates do not return other than to make affectionate visits. The result is that a father who, before the age of 50, could formerly have looked forward to handing over heavy work to a son, now continues to work the land. He can no longer become the pundit of the teahouse. Moreover, his society is destabilized by television. The women are equally hard hit. This may be true of the suburbs of the cities, which are merely new forms of village: the young are missing from an early age. But this is material which belongs to another book. Here it is enough to consider the period of the sultanate.

∿   ∿   ∿

What I originally set out to prove was the strength of will of the women of the Ottoman period as natural and human disasters followed one upon the other. Looking back, I now see this to have been a simple-minded view that made it hardly worth the telling of the story. Fortunately, I rapidly discovered that I was not writing about the self-evident tough spirit of Ottoman women but of something quite other, something at once more tragic and of far greater importance than a recognition of the force of the inevitable. I hope that what is written here will lead to my real point; a point which a reader anywhere will readily understand as the book progresses.

Young woman carrying a pitcher from the fountain, Levni, 1720–25
(T.S.M.K.)

Introduction

Heiresses of Eve

The Ottomans came out of Asia to rule from the Danube to the Nile. They had settled first in Anatolia and married the women of the villages. Some remained nomads and were faithful to their clans: and there were the sultans and their central government who married slaves. Peasants continued to toil as they had always done under their old masters while townsfolk sought prosperity through crafts and trade. Whatever the man might do, it was the woman who cared for the family and worked long hours as well. Without her there could have been no future. This was equally true of Europe.

Apart from the life of the wealthy in Istanbul, this book concentrates on the people of the Balkans, Thrace and Anatolia. In these provinces ordinary women endured 600 years of hardship and trouble, raised their children, mourned their dead and, in doing so, developed those courageous personalities which dominate this account.

It is with an ever-growing awareness of the mercilessness of the struggle to survive that one can understand what it meant to be alive, to marry and to give birth. One is not surprised that superstition made more sense than reason in the loneliness of the country but it also flourished in the noise and strife of great cities. Wherever she might be, the mother developed the republic of the home, achieving family love out of the conflict around her, the equal of any man. And this, with their enduring respect for her, her sons well knew.

On high were the princesses and the great ladies who achieved political power. Many of them had personalities so strong that, intellectually, they are still alive. Much more is recorded about life in the palace than in humble homes, but even from these much can be deduced: and yet more as the research moves into the nineteenth century and reveals a plethora of conflicting accounts of what it meant to be alive in the last years of the Ottoman empire. Veils come and go, our heroines are stricken and dumbfounded, homes are burnt and crops are pillaged: but there was no one who could forsake the struggle. It was just as well, because without them there would have been no Ottomans at all.

In neither the medieval east nor west was there a place for individuals except for symbolic heroes and heroines and gilded figures of power. Later these became people with a history who, if they spoke, had their speeches rewritten for them by biased partisans or nineteenth-century historians and poets. As for the common herd, they remained the common herd. They were not thought of as personalities but as loiterers on the road of life, formed by circumstance and subject to circumstance. The women in this book lived, suffered, achieved, failed and most certainly died: as did most of their children before reaching adulthood. Some of them were born into fortunate homes and very few achieved a place in history because they had beauty and wit.

In village terms, marriage for women had some of the characteristics of a guild in the sense that women worked like a clan to achieve its consummation. With the implacable approach of maturity, it was essential for a girl to be taught needlework and possibly spinning and weaving. She would already know how to cook, tend animals and garden. At about the age of 15 this meant that the burden or, if she were fortunate, the pleasure of marriage and its fulfilment were at hand; in spite of learning about sex as if by eavesdropping rather than explanation in physical terms. There were three periods in a woman's life – childhood, maternity and widowhood. This meant that she had a sense of place and a socially necessary duty within a relatively simple society. Badly paid child weavers can also be seen as students of older women and as having a humble place within the social structure.

No one could escape the destiny of disciplines without which a community could not survive let alone develop. And such a destiny was as true of one sex as another. The struggle to survive left little time to develop a questioning mind: it was easier to consult the past, real or imaginary. There is a self-evident difference between a society living in the present and the past and one that is aware of, and ponders, the forces of change and danger: still more so when the sexes have achieved equality. Moreover, villages declined and towns and cities grew. The village was no longer a unity when there were strangers in the next street or even in one's own apartment. The sense of unity was further disrupted by the need to travel to work with people of like skills but with no communal or family relationships. Moreover, life was no longer seasonal and working hours never varied.

The lives of most wealthy Ottoman women are only recorded on gravestones as fighters for the Faith and little else. Their names repeat themselves. Their headstones may be pretty with flowers but they are dumb. Dumber still are the rough stones that marked a common peasant grave and the man fared no better than his wife. If a number of men loved their wives and felt impoverished without them, many accounts agree that far more of them only felt the loss of a worker, a nurse, a cook and a pillow. This was because they had sought company with fellow men and not with other women than the wives who served them. That they were unaware of their deprivation did not make it any the less. This deprivation was an intellectual arthritis which was reflected all over life in the Ottoman world and no less in central and western Europe at the time.

Criticism of Ottoman society should be seen in the context of the times. This was more than some western travellers could achieve. One grows weary of the carping of even so great an archaeologist as Sir William Ramsay. The intellectual chauvinist personified could not understand why his wife got on so well with people in Anatolia whom he saw as near savages and who interfered with his work, which he had not thought of explaining to them. Travellers often appear to have had no knowledge of their own countries so that their condemnation of the galleys or brutal punishments in Turkey in the seventeenth or eighteenth century ignores the hulks in Britain or that discipline in the British army or navy was maintained by flogging. The seventeenth-century historian Evliya Çelebi, who was an inveterate traveller, was horrified by the cruelty of justice in Iran: what he would have said to the hanging of 10-year-olds for theft in England before the nineteenth century can only be left to the imagination.

Then there were books which concocted myths such as the 'tragedy' of Sultan Abdülhamit II's (1876–1909) daughter – which never happened, since she was alive and entertaining friends in the 1920s, long after her supposed murder. There was the redoubtable Aimée, cousin (or even sister in one account) of Josephine, the first wife of Napoleon. She was said to have been captured by pirates and married to the sultan, becoming the mother of Mahmut II (1808-39) and the inspiration behind his reforms: the truth is that the inspiration came from Selim III (1789-1807). We have to thank the misuse and falsification of evidence for this weird story by the romantic writers Hervé and Morton among others. Aimée's signature on the marriage register shows, however, that she was home in France two years after her supposed son was born, which would have been impossible if she was incarcerated in the Harem.[1] As for the palace at Topkapı, derivative accounts for the fires of fancy brewed tureens of nonsense.

Inönü in the 1960s, virtually unchanged since the end of the nineteenth century (author)

Village woman . . . (author)

CHAPTER 1

The Coming of the Nomads

In the Beginning

Anatolia is as big as Germany and France put together. Even today, distances are great although roads have transformed the country during the last forty years and vehicles travel speedily. It is still wise to think of a night's break when travelling by car from Istanbul to Dıyarbekir let alone by bus, however luxurious this means of transport has become. A hundred years ago, only the Tatar (Tartar) mounted post could ride 300 kilometres in one day in a crisis. A dispatch from the governor of Dıyarbekir could rarely reach Istanbul in less than ten days. The army might take almost as many weeks. All this was after a military route was established, with depots for revictualling, in the tracks of the Seljuks (Selcuks), Byzantines and Romans before them.

Anatolia is a harsh plateau girdled by a kind coastline and the population needed, and still needs, to be tough to survive the hot summers and bitter winters. The Hittites, Hurrites and Uratu, among the many people who came after the hunter-gatherers and the earliest settlers of the plains of Greater Syria, were indeed tough. They produced leaders, and therefore rivals, who added war to the catastrophes of the climate. The gods had to be placated or enlisted, if possible, and the remains of divine symbols cover large areas of the plateau. They have nothing to do with love but are the entreaties of humanity. There are no statistics to draw on and one may only guess at the numbers of these settlers, the fertility of their wives and how many children survived into adolescence (seen as maturity then because life was short). We do know that they stayed in a harsh terrain for so long because there were no cities to escape to: Constantinople had no name and not even Byzans had been imagined.

Later it was to be different. Other people invaded the pastures and benefited from past husbandry. Eventually, these predators were to include the Romans. Many of the administrators of the Eastern Roman empire had never seen Italy but were educated in the Balkans and Thrace. It was even less likely that many of their troops were Italian-born. Where did the Hittites come from, for that matter?

It is a strange army which leads a celibate life and rare troops who travel with their wives and families. Thus the stock of the plateau embraced some alien blood and some of the children survived. What the Romans did bring with them was their legal code, the father of both Byzantine and Ottoman land laws,[1] which were just benevolent enough to reduce the impulse to escape even when the land was poor. It was an agricultural system based on the family holding. Small farms were held by free peasants whose main crops were the wheat and barley which were vital to subsistence. Since land varies in fertility, the measure was linked to the amount of land that could be ploughed by one yoke of oxen. This was the most efficient economic and political system because the family as a whole supplied the labour and good husbandry increased loyalty to imperial rule. Direct rule from Rome ended when lines of communication became too stretched and the empire was divided into two. The Byzantines in the east were more often of Greek or Balkan origin than Italian and it was rational to be rid of Latin as the twin language by the sixth century when Greek became paramount. The Byzantines accepted the principles of the Roman agrarian system but this did not prevent the growth of large estates when imperial authority dwindled or showed no interest. Many smallholders came to be no better than serfs. The peasants struggled on. They lived in such poverty and remoteness that their mores and ways of living changed little over the centuries, especially where generations were rooted in the same area.

Older Gods

These people clung to their superstitions and pagan beliefs related to the demons of nature, since a terrain so harsh and a climate so unattractive bred very few kindly spirits. Natural phenomena took on their old importance. A great mountain like Erciyas (Mount Argeus) which ennobles Kayseri clearly had to be one of divine importance. It stands overlooking the plain, in an atmosphere which has the gift of transforming this beautiful extinct volcano into a mystery. The only dispute was which deity was enthroned on the summit. Any beautiful stream with its life-giving water would achieve the same importance. Trees in particular were regarded with awe, and in the villages elders met under the finest to discuss local problems in the shade of its invisible wisdom. If it were so old that it showed signs of falling, everything would be done to prop it up. Plane trees were the most revered and the Rev. Walsh, who was chaplain to the British embassy in Istanbul in the 1820s, reported that they were sometimes planted on the birth of a child. In the early 1960s, when the coast lane from Istanbul to Rumeli Hısar was widened, the new road was split to run either side of such a tree rather than that it should be cut down. It is either because of educational progress or municipal power that it has since been felled.

Trees, rocks and springs were so important that new religions, when they reached Anatolia, could not – or were wise enough not to – interfere with primitive beliefs. There are many sites which are equally sacred to Christians and Moslems just as there are the tombs of shared saints. The sacred tree on the Milas to Bodrum road still flaunts its coloured rags above the whitewashed adobe tomb of a holy man, in order to attract his attention in heaven; their number and that of the stones stacked against his monument attest to his sanctity although his name is unknown. He continues to intercede on behalf of the innocent for the cure of diseases, the relief of suffering and to awaken life in a barren womb. It was the women who had the greatest sense of their ancestry, as well they might since they, and they alone, ensured the continuation of a family with the help of benevolent spirits. So tombs were especially precious for women and to worship there was particularly comforting. The worst tyrant among husbands had no right to prevent his wife seeking solace in such places any more than he could forbid her going to the *hamam*, or bath.[2] Ancestor worship was just as important as in Cairo, where the families of the deceased still picnic on the graves of their forebears and even sleep there. This practice was pursued on a more modest scale in Ottoman cemeteries.

For the intellectuals of the Greek Orthodox Church, Anatolia was a place of exile. The great bishops, Fathers of the Church though they may have been, dreaded such sees as Caesaria (Kayseri) with its icy winters and mud-sodden springs, despite Roman engineering. The local clergy were as superstitious as their flocks and often as illiterate.[3] It was barely possible to find any priest who was prepared to live in a village of mean crofts far from a town and there perform the duties of Christ's Vicar. The humbler monks offered far more to a peasantry from whom many had sprung, but although there were many monasteries, the country was too large for them to have much influence outside their immediate neighbourhood. Moreover, some monks resorted to centres like Cappadocia to adorn self-dug caves with unsophisticated frescoes of remarkable brilliance just as a few continue to seek refuge on Mount Athos, the holy mountain of Thrace. In Ottoman times, the same problem of finding scholarly *imams*, or prayer leaders, who would work in outlying places continued and again the situation was sometimes ameliorated by dervish *tekkes*, or Sufi monasteries. The tomb of the founder became a place of supplication. The dervish movement was mystical and offered an entanglement of spiritual paths. It followed that the many sects held different tenets, but they were brotherhoods akin in their belief that from God we come and to God we shall return.

Such brotherhoods could be widespread and some had *tekkes* in Central Asia which then branched out and spread all over the Ottoman dominions. In Central Asia, they were influenced by shamanism and it was there that the Turkish *babas*, or holy men, emerged as leaders. They brought with them antlers and other symbols of the past. While the beliefs of some orders remained simple, others were highly sophisticated, such as those of the Mevlevi order whose vision of the universe was as vivid as it was intellectually rewarding. Its founder, Celalettin Rumi (d. 1273), who was the greatest poet of his age, taught the unity of all reality in God and called on his followers to recognize the place of sin in this unity. The concept is expressed in the choreography of the famous dance of the Mevlevi, where one hand is raised heavenwards and the other points down to the earth.

It was not long before the convents of the brotherhoods attracted the women of the villages because of their humanity.[4] The Bektaşi even admitted women into their order: women *şeyhs*, or masters, have been reported. The historians Hasluck and (a century later) Kafadar are open-minded on this claim. More certainly, there were groups of women mystics who met in each other's houses and were affiliated to a Bektaşi *tekke* where they might observe the ceremonies.

The Iconoclastic movement of the seventh century grew up among the educated Byzantine clergy because it was obvious that the humble prayed to the image instead of God and were therefore idolatrous. Hence the attempt to suppress icons – but the monks, who had far more sympathy for and friendship with the simple villagers, prevailed. The icons even included those of the Virgin Mary, the Queen of Heaven, who was of foremost solace to all women. She was the supreme intercessor because she was the Matriarch. When the Iconoclasts were defeated, hers was the first mosaic to be set up in the apse of the basilica of Hagia Sophia. Cybele was reborn.

Conquering Sheep

By the eleventh century, climatic changes had deprived the Mongol hordes of their grazing lands in Central Asia which supported their horses and their flocks. This deracinating revolution resulted in a planned and devastating cataract of invasions. First, the settled peoples of the region fled before their advance and then the Mongols went on to sack and burn Baghdad and their Seljuk successors to take Isfahan. Conquest usually begins with looting and ends with settling, and restoring, a devastated city and the farmland which feeds it; but the advance from Asia was different. The Mongols had no affinity with settled lands and cities and therefore no use for them. What they, and the Seljuk Turks after them, wanted was grazing land.

A flock of sheep was not a matter of a few hundred head but of tens of thousands. In Spain, the migration of the Berbers from the Atlas mountains and Morocco threatened the farms and set routes had to be enforced when they moved their flocks from summer to winter pastures else crops would have been obliterated. But the Mongol rulers had no use for gardens because they had lived, in so far as their memories could stretch, like cowboys in the saddle and had no need of crops.

Memory is of two natures. There is that which does or does not recall a grandparent and that which feeds on legends of astonishing times when heroes were magical. One such hero ran away from a giant who was hurling mountains at him (could this be a way of describing an earthquake or volcano?) and mounted a convenient horse. What else would a tribesman do? The horse sped off as only a Mongol pony could speed but the giant soon caught up with the hero, who dismounted, stuck the horse in his pouch and was happily ignored as a worthless peasant.[5]

Mongol women were just as used to horses as they were to babies.[6] They were treated with respect and as near equals by men – except in councils of war since they were not Amazons. In this is a rooted inequality. Think how Florence Nightingale's intervention in the Crimean war was seen as an affront to the generals: she would have had less difficulty with Chingis Khan. By the nineteenth century, women went completely covered in the streets of Turkistan and divorce by the man was common.[7] The Russians claimed to have freed 25,000 slaves when they captured Khiva in 1873. These girls were regularly culled by the Turcoman (Türkmen) in raids on Persian villages.[8] In the past, no Mongol would ever marry a slave, unlike the Ottomans, but they could be brutally punished and mutilated. Moser, exploring Central Asia in the latter half of the nineteenth century, contrasted this with the customs of the Khirgiz Turks, among whom the beautiful 20-year-old wife of a chieftain went unveiled in the guest tent. Shamanism had no use for veils.[9]

Out of Arabia

Immediately after the death of the Prophet, the forces of the new religion of Islam achieved spectacular conquests. Syria and Egypt were taken and Persia absorbed its conquerors. Anatolia followed. The province was in distress, under Byzantine rule, due to over-taxation and unpoliced disorder. Whatever may have been the causes – corruption at all levels of government and a greed for property which the authorities made little effort to restrain – the Byzantine empire was in decline. The frontiers were poorly guarded so that Turkish nomads, in search of grazing when they were driven out of their old pastures by the approaching Mongols, infiltrated Byzantine territories. These were ideal for them because they had plains by the sea for winter grazing and the slopes of foothills up narrow valleys in summer time. When the emperor Romanus was defeated at Manzikirt in the north-east of the province in 1067, the Turkish tribes flowed into the country and they had no inclination to live a sedentary life for which they had no training. The women had the most to lose because they enjoyed a way of life which, like the Mongols', was freer than that of any villager under Byzantium.

The life of the Turcoman nomads is the first to be considered in this book because, although they pre-dated the Ottomans, they remained under their bureaucracy since they had nowhere to flee but the sea. Other tribes entered Iran and were of military importance once the Persians had wooed the Mongols and the Seljuk Turks with luxury and the comforts of the city. These tribes were valiant and, as the Kızılbaş (Red Heads, so named because of their turbans), some were dangerous to the future Ottoman government because they were religious fanatics following the Shia heresy. The Ottomans were followers of the strictly orthodox Sunni schools against whom these rebellious nomads were pitted, heart and soul.

The Seljuk Turks who defeated the emperor Romanus were the foremost of a brotherhood of tribes from Asia who established their capital at Caesarea. They repaired the Roman roads and in pursuit of trade added new ones, for which they built bridges and *kervansarays* (caravanserais), thus bringing prosperity back to Anatolia. Their relationships with the Byzantines varied – they even fought as allies when it was advantageous – and they cultivated Byzantine court practices. This civilized state was to fragment when it fell under Mongol overlordship. Whereas the Seljuks accepted the established system of land tenure, Mongol agrarian policy came from a dark age.[10] Like the grand Byzantine landowners, their lords were only interested in immense estates and invested fortunes in land, unlike the more modest Seljuks. These lands were so vast and so diverse that they had to be farmed out to peasants. Thus in the thirteenth century one Rashid ud-Din had 3,000 horses distributed between Iran and Anatolia – as were his 50 flocks of sheep which had 500 head each, making 25,000 in all. This is a number that only such feudal lords as the Hungarian or the Spanish Knights of Calatrava could rival. There were also 10,000 camels, half of them brood camels, and the same number of geese and ducks along with 20,000 hens. The animals provided manure for fuel, clarified butter from the sheep, goatskins for tents and rope, and wool for carpets. As for the harvest of eggs, one hesitates to guess or to suggest who ate them. It is worth remembering that bad eggs were used in tanning. But we do know that each flock was looked after by 2 contracted shepherds and 2 sheepdogs with a ration of 740 grams of barley flour a day.[11] The Mongols considered 1,000 head to be the maximum number of a flock or herd if there were to be enough grazing.

However overweening the feudal lordships may have been, the fourteenth-century Hispano-Arab traveller Ibn Battuta had much to praise when he visited the Mongol royal encampment.[12] The Hatun, or queen, sat in a wagon covered with rich blue woollen cloth and kept the windows and doors of her tent open. The reference to doors and windows indicates both the size and luxury of this tent. She was attended by 4 exquisitely dressed girls of great beauty, followed by 300 more in other wagons.[13] Mongols never wore veils and Ibn Battuta could talk freely to this great lady. It was not a caravan that the traveller had encountered but a city on the move. In the afternoon, there was no difficulty in lifting tents, mosques and shops off their wagons because they were so light.[14] Later, Ibn Battuta was able to watch the Hatun's stately walk – her robes were furnished with loops with which to lift them off the ground. Her conical headdress was decorated with precious stones and surmounted with peacock feathers. Merchants' wives were similarly dressed although more modestly adorned. The freedom of Mongol women was related to the natural freedom of nomadic life.

The Seljuks became sedentary when they settled in Anatolia. They retained some of their tribal customs, however, and their respect for women was exemplified in the tombs of Hatuns who founded charities and mosques as grand as any prince's. In the past, some women had even gone to war alongside their men. Even under Islam, women of strong character remained all but the equals of their husbands: and sometimes more. Their misfortune was widowhood, when politics dictated that they should be married to some *vezir*, or minister of state, as part of the usual system of dynastic alliances.[15]

The Flocks of Ertuğrul

With the collapse of Seljuk and Mongol rule, Anatolia owed only nominal allegiance to any ruler. Many Turkish groups carved out states for themselves, including the lords of Karamania and the Menteşe pirates of the Mediterranean coast. At the end of the twelfth century the future Ottomans appear. Whether they were of the Kaya tribe or other descent is undocumented but, like the rest of the migrants, they were nomadic and their northern route led, implacably but unintentionally, to Constantinople. Their first recorded leader, Ertuğrul,[16] was allegedly accompanied by 400 followers and reached a hamlet, now Söğut, where he may have built a tiny mosque. It was rebuilt in the nineteenth century by Abdülhamit II for propaganda purposes. It still can scarcely hold 16 men at prayer. This may give an idea of the modesty of the encampment. Ertuğrul was succeeded by Osman (who gave his name to the dynasty) in about 1280, when he was some 22 years of age. He still followed a semi-nomadic life, grazing his flocks over a considerable tract of grassland on the plain in winter and ascending to mountain pastures in summer. He was on good terms with his Christian neighbours and, in particular, the lord of Bilecik whose little town was walled. So good was their relationship that when Osman was harassed on his way to his summer camp, he left his treasure in the citadel at Bilecik for safe keeping. It was the women who loaded the treasure on oxen and also gifts of carpets, rugs and cheese together with several head of sheep.[17]

This was an idyllic way of life since the pastures were rich and the innumerable flocks grew in value. The Ottoman love of the camp as opposed to palaces was expressed in the concept of the tent, or 'permanent tent' of brick or stone. In summer the *saray*, or palace, at Manisa was abandoned for the princely, permanent *yayla*, or camp, in the foothills above the town. There both Selim II and Murat III were born in the sixteenth century, which is proof that the women accompanied the men![18]

Osman's handful of followers grew because he was clearly a man of personality. Certainly, some Byzantine Greek families were attracted to him and thus began the religious, as opposed to racial, loyalty which was soon to admit an astonishing number of peoples into the government of the Ottomans. When Osman's followers were sufficient, the temptation to capture Bursa was irresistible. The town was the most prosperous in Anatolia and had its own mint. Osman was not to take it himself but his son, Orhan, succeeded in doing so on 6 April 1326, perhaps before his father died. It was under his rule that the names of two Ottoman women appear on a signed document (dated March 1324) for the first time: one signature is that of Orhan's sister, Fatma Hatun, and the other is of Maik Hatun, daughter of Ömer Bey – she may have been Osman's wife and the daughter of the legendary dervish Edebalı.

Orhan was said to be the lord of 400 castles (which meant small towers and guard posts) although they were probably many less in number. He spent much time in inspecting them and left his formerly Christian wife Nilüfer Hatun, daughter of the lord of Yarhisar, in charge of his capital. This typically nomadic appointment was accepted by his followers most of whom, but by now by no means all, were the sons or grandsons of Turcoman. Nilüfer was clearly a woman of considerable personality. Although she was a loyal follower of Islam, it would appear that this loyalty was sustained by her mystic leanings. Christian converts were often attracted by the dervishes. Nilüfer built one major monument, which still stands in Iznik (Nicaea of the Creed). It is a fine *zaviye*, or dervish monastery, and it was large for its times. She would have needed to endow it: this would have called for a large investment in property in order to pay the wages of servants and the charitable kitchen for travellers and sustain the very poor.

∾   ∾   ∾

Nomadic life had to be democratic and a tribal chief had to be a leader. He had to be approachable by anybody and anywhere: one measure of the woeful times in the fifteenth century was that the sultan no longer walked in the streets. What had gone wrong? The simple answer is that a town cannot be a nomad camp but needs a string of executive officials to deal with day-to-day problems and set a pattern of rules. Thus the leader had become the ruler and an autocrat.

Until the founding of the Republic in 1924 this was the most important of the Ottoman revolutions because the restless nomads, such as they themselves had been, were seen as hostile to the settled state which, under their rule, was to spread rapidly. It was as if the sultans, as opposed to *beys* and emirs, had no further use for their roots. By 1402, when the ever victorious Timur the Lame (Timur Lang) defeated Bayezit I at Ankara, repressive laws were being enforced on the nomads whose loyalty withered until they deserted the sultan. The status of women regressed: they were no longer in earshot of an egalitarian council of elders but shut in their homes if they were the wives of notables. As so often, ordinary folk were freer.

These, then, were the remnants of the first Ottomans, who were but a small clan among many forced to leave Central Asia because of the changes in climate. They had not only brought their sheep with them. Their *babas* conserved a store of legends in their heads with which to inspire the warrior shepherds since no society can live without a past, real or imaginary. The migration was symbolized as a victorious invasion under *gazis*, or heroic leaders, who took little inspiration from Islam. The beloved spouse of such a warrior had to have her own heroic characteristics if she were to survive in a turbulent era. Thus the *kral kizi*, or royal lady, is buried beside her husband, the mighty but mythical Seyyid Battal Gazi, in his 7-metre-long sarcophagus, a measure of his heroism. Another hero, Melik Danişmend, was joined by the noble Artuhi, who brought his beloved Efromiya with him. Like Nilüfer, she was a Greek who converted to the easy-going Islam of the time and place. She rode into battle and on one occasion, after a fearful fight with an enemy hero whom she finally killed, proceeded to slaughter twenty lesser men. Such a woman never stayed out of male company nor did she wear a veil.[19]

Now the living fragments of such a past were to submit clan by clan to the sedentary rule of a bureaucracy. But the Turcoman were tenacious of their past.

Nomads in the Atlas Mountains (author)

CHAPTER 2

The Wanderers

In Search of Pasture

The Turcoman tribes found rich pastures in Anatolia but the Mongols were their first oppressors. They were harsh masters and, when their power declined, the Turcoman had every reason to walk on over the Anatolian plateau in search of grasslands and freedom. There was no ideological motivation. Freedom meant getting on with their own lives. It was not a policy of conquest but of filling up the crevices. The damage that their beasts did to the farmland was ruinous, but it was not done out of malice. Their freedom was that of movement and this determined the comparative freedom of their women. They have survived as Yürüks into the present in spite of repressive legislation, but their numbers have dwindled.

Over the years these Turcoman have never lost that culture which they brought with them from Turkish Asia. Names, for example, were important. The Ahmedli were named after a forebear, others often after a place like the White Mountain and still others after their character-istics or occupation like the Runners or the Men of the Yellow Goats. They became known as Yürüks from the Turkish word *yürümek* – to wander – or so Mrs Garnett, who at the end of the nineteenth century became an authority on Ottoman life and folklore, believed. It must be remembered, however, that it was the name of a Turkish tribe, a branch of the Samayids, once settled north of the Urals.[1]

The individual groups of Turcoman were not lawless[2] because their *aǧa*, or chief, settled all disputes with the approval of the elders who would prevent deviation from the code of the tribe and, therefore, any injustice.[3] The relationship was that of the first among equals. However, the lack of any form of central authority over the various tribes could lead to hostilities.[4] These disputes were rarely territorial but were often due to the abduction of brides by young men when there was no girl available among their own people, particularly when the size of a tribe diminished. There was so fierce a sense of tribal loyalty, as there had to be in order to survive, that the stealing of a bride was acceptable only as a last resort. Divorce and 'temporary marriages' (the latter is legal among the Twelver Shia; see also p. 76) were prohibited partly because of the shortage of girls but mainly because both practices were seen as an insult to women and damaging to the structure of a tribe. In theory, a man might have three wives but not four. However, monogamy was almost universal. Garnett[5] found the tribes firmly endogamous and they still only raided a sister tribe in despair. Two or three young men would raid together and each would help the other in due course. The tribes were well organized and they were hard to tame until, at last, the great confederations were broken up in the seventeenth century.

Turcoman life in Anatolia was one of raids and rampage and they were unable to grasp a bourgeois concept of property and theft.[6] On the other hand, they reclaimed land in the forests and swamps, even the malaria swamps of Cilicia where they grew wheat, cotton and rice for themselves and sometimes for the town market. Originally, they were spared military service because they were so unreliable but later some volunteers were lured into local patrols and were made guardians of bridges and highways while others were craftsmen but did not join a guild.[7] It would have been difficult for life to be harder. It was inevitable that a nomadic people should flee in the face of Timur, who sacked Skopje (probably in 1390). By 1500 some 50 per cent of the Ottoman Balkans were Turcoman but this was partly due to the enforced resettlement of fractious tribes, such as the Black Sea nomads who were sent to Albania.[8] These wanderers were victims of far greater misfortunes than those of the villagers and it is astonishing that any of them survived, but numbers of their descendants are still living the same primitive existence today. Their stubborn pride was, of course, part of the universal enmity between the man of the steppe and the sower of the seed.

Originally, the Turcoman were feared by both the Moslem and the Christian villagers.[9] Settled Turks called them Satans. Before the establishment of Ottoman rule in Anatolia, the Karamanids went to war with the nomads and defeated them at Kavala. Their leaders were paraded through the streets of Konya, insulted and tortured by the inhabitants; their bodies were strung from trees in front of the palace for target practice. The towns were walled against them – and not some possible foreign invader. Yet these nomads were to join the Karamanids when they had to defend their province against the army of the then Ottoman sultan, Murat I (1360–89), and went down with them in defeat.[10]

Once the Ottomans had control in Anatolia, they antagonized the wealthy nomad chiefs whom the Iranian Shah Ismail cultivated. Later, known as the Kızılbaş, and incited by fanatical agents of ambitious shahs, these rebellious tribes of eastern Anatolia were restless even when they were at peace; for such was the nature of their lives. They suffered pitiless subjection by Selim I (1512–20) at the start of the sixteenth century.[11] They had already supported Cem, the most romantic figure of the Ottoman dynasty, against Selim's father, Bayezit II (1481–1512). Once again they were defeated by organized troops who were well led.[12]

The Ottoman government proceeded to organize recognized routes along which the nomads drove their flocks from summer to winter pastures and back. It must be remembered that the vast number of animals involved could ruin a province if their movements were not strictly controlled. The Umayyads in Spain had long since established this rule, but there it had been achieved through negotiation between the nomads and the farmers, whereas the Ottomans attempted to enforce a rule that transhumance should only take three days. Nomads on the move have always to be sensitive to small changes in the weather and maximize access to good water and grazing. Authoritarian edicts inevitably lead to conflict and deceit on the part of the victims.[13] The process of developing stable relationships between the nomads and the state could only be slow but it was implacable and predatory in terms of taxes.

The Mongols had also been ruthless in collecting money as they were parsimonious in spending it on anyone but themselves. It was they, however, who took only 1 head from each 100 sheep or cattle, a rule that, in theory, the Byzantine government was to pursue. They were unable to control tax-collector or tax-payer at all by the eleventh century, which partly accounts for the impoverished state of the province. The Otttomans retained the tax.

By the middle of the sixteenth century most of the tribes were settled gradually and then taxed as if they were peasants .[14] Such an enforced settlement brought with it bevies of fines and taxes.[15] In 1523 there were thirty settled villages in one province but there were still seventy nomadic groups. However, the herds had dwindled to half their number in 1500.[16] The policy was simply one of punishing in order to pacify. In the seventeenth century, the population was 15 per cent nomadic with the addition of 12 per cent Yürük auxiliaries in the Ottoman army, making a total of 27 per cent. The enlistment of nomads was a more effective way of dealing with the problem than any other but obviously could not be universally applied.

The collapse of the control of central Anatolia was because of the discontent of jobless students and soldiers disbanded without pay who had to rob if they were to live. These *celali* mobs and small armies had mixed but usually hostile relationships with the Turcoman, who migrated in such large numbers into western Anatolia that the population increased by 50 per cent. Their flight caused grave damage to the farmlands which lay on their broad routes to Kütahya. They brought great misery to the villages that they pillaged for food, which resulted in a flight from the country to the town, thus littering Anatolia with villages where only the dogs spoke. In eastern Anatolia the Armenian farmers suffered as much brutality as the Moslem and the troubles were compounded by Turcoman hatred for the Kurds. This hatred was partly caused by rivalry over the scarce pastures, whether in the lowlands or the uplands of the present frontier region. It was also due to the rapaciousness of the Kurdish lords, who wrung out dues and paid little for the services which they enforced on the nomads. Their greed had nothing to do with the well-defined areas of winter and summer pasturage.

The Home and its Mistress

Even today the typical nomad *yurt*, or hut, is built of wickerwork within a wooden frame with only a single room for all the family. This is because nomadic life creates an interior where the family is grouped round the fire for warmth. Raised on rough foundations, these homes are mere sheds with thatched roofs and are aligned to conform with sunshine and shade. They have to be small enough for a pack animal to carry. Because, for the most part, they are made of wickerwork they are raised on stones as a precaution against damp, insects and animals.

On the plain, reeds grew in abundance.[17] In some areas these homes were permanent and built of stones with black bedouin tents for roofs. From long in the past, summer *yurts* consisted of black tents with the camels' high wooden pack-saddles arranged round the walls. There was rarely more than one wife; but if there were, then each had her own tent and occupation. It was significant that the *yurts* had neither communal buildings nor spaces.[18]

Throughout Ottoman history, the emphasis on male dominance was challenged by the importance of the matriarch, whose presence is overt among the Turcoman tribes.[19] Descriptions of these women are remarkably alike. They were strong as they were tall although the huge women of Karahisar were exceptional. (They were much admired by Mrs Scott-Stevenson, the devoted wife of a nineteenth-century British officer, whose sense of comedy matched remarkable perception.)[20] Big-limbed, sturdy, dark-haired and white-skinned, they left their faces without heightened complexion. They traditionally wore a form of cushion on the head with a cloth over it which did not cover their faces.[21] Scott-Stevenson also reported that in the region of Aleppo, Turcoman men wore grey and the dresses of the women were red while in Anatolia the colours were reversed.

Because they had nowhere to go but home, at the end of the day the husband's friends came in to taste his wife's bread and drink her coffee without even a curtain to divide the *harem*, or women's area, from the *selamlık*, or men's area. But such alien divisive concepts did not occur to people living in so confined a space. The women's intelligence and knowledge were not wasted and they joined in the conversation without restraint. A woman of strong character might even dominate it.[22] The autocratic position of men was reduced to rational equality except in time of war. The reverse was true in Turkic Siberia, where the indolent husband let his wife do all the work and cared for his horse more than he did his home. But then he lived the life of a predator and so may be said to have earned his living.[23]

The Turcoman woman in Anatolia was responsible for the well-being of the family and the animals as well. From these responsibilities she gained an experience which was too valuable to be ignored on the grounds of sex. In a village, by contrast, the sofa of the headman and sometimes a coffee-house lured the men away. Berbers were typical nomads and had ideas in common with the Turcoman people. For them the wife was seen as the 'tent pole' because she supported the home; it was the world outside which belonged to men.[24] The house was the woman's universe, and the navel of the house was the mother. In addition, the interior of the house was the mirror image or reflection of the external world which had been turned inside out. For the Turcoman, the world was never inside out: his wife had as much right to the sky as he had to the hearth.

Long before Islam, the hearth in Central Asia was the most potent symbol of the family where libations of *kumiss*, or fermented mare's milk, were poured to assuage or beg help from ancestors in times of trouble. It was the unity of the Turcoman's hearths, and therefore their common ancestry, which lead back to their supposed origins on the Mountain by the Pool in the shelter of the Tree of Life.[25] These beliefs mattered more than shaman practices, which also had their importance. The nomad world was one of noise: from the bleating of sheep, birdsong and barking of dogs to the growling or roaring of wild beasts or grass rustling and trees creaking. It is obvious that in such an environment spirits were always abroad, sometimes committed but more often disinterested. Some nomadic Turkish tribes believed that a mystical hound had led them out of Asia to new territories in which they could survive and prosper. As soon as they reached this haven, the invisible spirit was silent and heard no more.[26] The tribe was, so to speak, on its own and both sexes had only one shared task: to keep their family alive. Their work was strictly shared, including shepherding the flocks, and this is likely to have been true when Hittite sheep grazed Anatolia.[27]

Fifty sheep might keep a family on subsistence level but the flocks were often much larger. When pasture was enclosed, however, fifty sheep were in no way sufficient and this was an important reason why the nomads were forced to settle or to starve. A flock of broad-tailed Karamanian sheep needed two or three women to look after them and milk them.[28] A flock of Angora goats needed only one. In the lambing season, the lambs were so numerous as to make a flock of their own and needed another woman's attention. Another woman looked after the camels and another the fuel and water. Yet another was responsible for the butter and cheese and, finally, there was the weaver with a portable, narrow loom on which she wove kilims – tapestry weave, narrow rugs and saddle-bags. If a man had too many daughters, he prepared for hard times: but since children rarely survived early childhood, perhaps only two might reach adulthood and marry. This meant that there were few hands to look after the duties of a household so two or three families would work together and portion out the tasks.

The men were responsible for camel-breeding and also made a living by letting them out for transport, including themselves with their beasts. They bred their animals with care and developed the Toulon camel which was a cross-breed of the Bactrian and Syrian. It withstood the cold of the mountains and the heat of the plain. Some of the men were skilled as woodcutters but others had to sell their services – even to the Kurds although their relationships with them were so bad. When the men let themselves out with their Toulon camels, their wives might be left alone for months during which they were responsible for all the family possessions. This duty made for even longer daily work. Without a sense of family among her neighbours – and everybody was related – a lone woman would have had difficulty in surviving.

Horses were also bred and cross-bred and all the foals were sold at the end of the breeding season, when only the mares were retained.[29] Their visitors have left some idea of the trading of the nomads.[30] Sheep and goat dealers came to their camps as did the wool merchants. One is confronted with the picture of one woman shearing sixty fleeces at the least and sometimes many more. Tinkers were sometimes of nomadic stock.

It is clear that the Turcoman had some ready money, besides being self-sufficient, but could hope for no lasting wealth from the sixteenth century onwards. Things have changed more recently although they now have to pay for their grazing and they keep even closer to themselves.[31] Cattle tax-collectors in the past were trained for the difficult job of the annual collection of their dues. Herds and flocks gradually diminished since they were already vulnerable to disease and wolves. The nomads could only hide as many animals as they dared.

Dairy products were abundant, from milk to yoghurt, butter and cream.[32] A milk soup was flavoured with wild grass. Cheese was made in sheepskins while the Turcoman were on the transhumant routes; the mild cheeses were mixed with a herb not unlike an onion. When Scott-Stevenson visited one *yurt*, the housewife not only baked bread but delicious scones were buttered. Baking was not necessarily done far ahead since unleavened bread cooks rapidly on the hot dome of a beehive-shaped oven. In most places, the oven was the one communal possession. Meat was rarely eaten although there was no prohibition on pork. There were wild berries and occasional fruit or olives according to the particular province in which the tribe had settled their summer and winter *yurts*. There were also the crops of farmers which were raided after dark in spite of the watchdogs; but then the Turcoman were used to fierce dogs of their own. Whatever else the Turcoman took, they ignored cabbages. Living legend explains their distaste for this vegetable. God wrote his laws on the leaves of a cabbage — shortly afterwards they were eaten by a donkey. This was why it was believed that the Turcoman had neither a religion nor a god of their own.[33]

The Turcoman's earnings were partly spent on coffee beans, which were a great luxury; their coffee was made bitterly strong and drunk in large quantities. If the nomads stole, they were themselves robbed in the nineteenth century and before by Circassian refugees from the Crimea fleeing the tsar's troops. Settled in Anatolia wherever land was made available by a benevolent government, the Circassians were soon cursed as bitterly as the Turcoman had been in the past. In Ereğli in the nineteenth century, for example, the Circassians robbed the shops and cut down the fruit trees for firewood. They roamed and ravaged where they could and left towns like Karapınar deserted.[34] Five hundred years before, Ibn Battuta had admired them precisely because of their respect for their own women, even holding them in higher esteem than men.[35]

When the Turcoman celebrated, it was (and had always been) with abandon. Marriage was a great occasion. After the betrothal, the camp feasted on roasted lambs while tambourines played and muskets were fired into the air. The bride-to-be and her groom exchanged embroidered handkerchiefs and, in their regard for a handworked trousseau, nomad and villager were alike. The wedding itself lasted for several days with music, dancing and wrestling. Wrestling was much more than a sport because it had religious significance, as is demonstrated by the very large wrestling ground of the Süleymaniye complex at Istanbul which is now a car park: new gods for old has always been the rule. The bride-price was paid in corn or cattle. When the bride was married she wore a veil for a year: this was, perhaps, an echo of the customs practised in Siberia, where after two or three days bride and groom were separated for a year.[36]

Other Tribes in Anatolia

The Turcoman have become law-abiding unlike the Kurds. The Tatars were also refugees coming from the Russian steppes and from the Crimea but they were great horsemen and so became the riders of the sultan's post. This meant that they left their wives to loneliness but also to authority over all their children and such possessions and farmland as they might have acquired. There is an account of the arrival of the Tatars in Armenian Anatolia centuries before from Grigor of Akanc.[37] The first Tatars, he records, were not like men but had heads as big as buffaloes'. Their snub noses were more like a cat's, their snouts like dogs' and their loins were as narrow as an ant's. They had the strength of lions and voices shriller than the eagle's. The women, we learn, wore beautiful hats crowned at the top with a head shawl of brocade. (Perhaps the Ottomans were to copy this model.) Their broad Tatar faces were plastered with a promiscuous mixture of gums. They gave birth to children like snakes and ate like wolves. Death did not appear amongst them for they lived for 300 years. They did not eat bread at all. Like their descendants, they took children captive from each and every country.

The Avshas like the Circassians, according to Mrs Garnett,[38] were still rough, mannerless and even uncivilized. They continued their nomadic traditions when they reached eastern Anatolia, and were possibly of Mongol descent because they were beardless and had almond-shaped eyes but some ethnographers place them with the Kurds. Their womenfolk tended to fatness and in their tribal dress could be gorgeous in *şalvar* (baggy trousers) and embroidered coats. Corsages of coins were matched with gold earrings. A great tail of false hair, made of cotton and silk, was dyed to match their own. Avshas were industrious and experienced bee-keepers, using hollowed-out logs for hives in the manner of the Turcoman; they made a special cake of honey and wax boiled together.[39] Their guard dogs were thought to be the most ferocious of all yet they were fed on buttermilk. Their huts had two rooms, not one, with a byre for calves between them. With the huts plastered and limewashed, the women amused themselves by adding henna patterns to the bare walls.

The Question of God

Officially, the Turcoman were Moslem. But they disdained both mosque and *hoca* (religious teacher) and worshipped in the open. Pagan customs survived and many men were uncircumcised[40] (like the Yakuts of eastern Siberia who recognize that there must be a God but do not worship something about which they know nothing).[41] Theirs was a mixed religion: so mixed that an Armenian could act as a godparent in some tribes. Some of the women were even called by Christian names. God was one and indivisible and there could be no son. Yet for some Ali was God Incarnate, and so identical with Christ. The contradictions arising from the fusion or confusion of religions was the greater because of the visits of Bektaşi *şeyhs* to tribes, in particular in the Aydın region. Both sexes united in worship in the open and they fasted for only twelve days in the year.[42]

Magic was associated with the graves of great warriors. One example was the grave of a heroic nephew of Osman I which sprouted a mysterious tree. Belief in feminine sacred trees was the same as that in much of Asia and Anatolia.[43] Anatolian tribes buried their dead in shallow graves under stones, to keep off wild animals and dogs, and they were dug near a path so that passers-by might pray for the peace of the deceased.

As for the Turcoman sorcerers, they were direct descendants of the shaman magicians of Central Asia and they performed magic rites, using divining twigs to lead them to lost sheep, for example. They hung garlic in their tents for a charm against the universal evil eye and they were scrupulous about the disposal of the placenta[44] but less so, if at all, about the disposal of human debris such as fingernails.[45] They also believed in *peris*, or fairies, who were as harmless as sprites and who particularly liked to live in streams. Nobody believed in ghosts. They kept a few of their traditions but lost their legends, which is the fate of wanderers: although, in the past, Turkish Asia was a plantation of stories.

Life in the village, near Tokat (G. T. M. Goodwin)

CHAPTER 3

Home and the Peasant

Leasing from the Crown

The Ottoman definition of a peasant, like Romans and Byzantines before them, was a man who was the son of a peasant, reported as such officially and who lived in a village. Peasant life was based on the tenure of land belonging to the state. A peasant might also be a tenant of the landlords, including the sultans and charitable foundations. Retired military of rank, who were themselves tenants for life, might also sublet. But lessees of state lands predominated and these were usually inheritable by sons: under this system (*tapu*)[1] the peasant leased or owned his land in return for taxes. There was, therefore, an incentive to improve his property as much as climate and misfortunes would allow. Since the family supplied their own labour, this meant that everyone in it worked, including women and children at an early age.[2] Even the old could be given simple tasks to do: after that it was time for them to rejoin the earth.

One typical village recorded by Inalcık housed 258 adult males:[3] 11 owned farmsteads, 44 had smallholdings, 32 more had mere plots which could hardly produce enough for sustenance, and there were 59 landless labourers for hire and 12 households unaccounted for. Only the rich had horses; 5 of them had buffalo as well. Half the households had neither ox nor ass and there were few cows. Goats were also rare but there was a common flock of sheep in which one woman, presumably a widow, had a share. Eighteen of the peasants had primitive carts: otherwise these could be rented if there was money to pay, but there were always the backs of the women. (This recalls an island in the Marmara[4] where one wily widower imported the only ox wagon and proceeded to make his fortune, which meant that there had to be a lock and bolt on his door at night: not only against theft.) Crofts were so valueless, and home-made, that only 3 men were without one.[5] The 2 richest men had a slave each who would be cheaper than one bought to work in the town but who would have no skills: they could cost less than a coat.

In 1815 the traveller and scholar Walpole visited Bornabaşı,[6] which was then a Greek village near Alexander's Troy. It consisted of 70 land-owners and farmers, 30 labourers and a shopkeeper under a rapacious *ağa*. Young women spun cotton for practically nothing, except perhaps for a kilo of kidney beans or some other pulse. When potatoes and hops had to be harvested, whole families left their village for the cotton harvests of the Izmir region[7] (a system that was repeated in Britain and all over Europe). This was why large estates developed there just as they had done under the Byzantines. Today one landowner in the Menderes valley still employs 7,000 peasants picking cotton. In Cilicia, men came down from remote mountain villages, mounted and on foot, 100,000 strong to enrich the landowners of the Adana plains where estates ran from some 100 to 2,000 hectares. Today they arrive by truck. The old and lame were and still are left to look after the village.

Lack of fertilizers meant that half the land had to lie fallow because, even if a peasant owned a pair of oxen, there was still insufficient manure. This lack affected gardens as well. Their products were mostly for home supply since only the rich, who even employed casual labour, could reach a market town. On average, the few rich were immensely rich compared with the many poor. However, the life of a villager was not usually as harsh as that of a nomad – except for the destitute, when Ottoman loyalties at least saw that no one starved.

Villages differed simply because of the amount of water that was available after the landlord had taken the biggest share. One (recorded by Inalcık), which had an ample water supply, enjoyed good vegetables but there were no woods or orchards because of the stony soil. The villagers could raise enough corn to feed themselves but they had little if anything to sell. The winters were harsh and the lake froze over so that men and children became good at skating in boots with narrow wooden soles.

This cycle of seasons dictated to the whole family. Men and women had to harvest and thresh together[8] although older children could help with both. Sometimes a boy sat on the threshing board, which was studded with flints, driving the ox in a continual circle. The village flock was tended by older girls since women were responsible for the care of all animals. Hired shepherds were used from time to time but were often kept waiting for their pay.[9] The flock was driven to pasture before dawn and back home again at nightfall because in parts of the country there were wolves, bears and even mountain lions besides predatory nomads. The tradition continues even where there is now none of these hazards.

But if the landowner had too many sheep for the local pastures to feed, the flocks would travel considerable distances. Inalcık recorded one prosperous village as having 40 flocks of 1,200 sheep, for example. The shepherds were given dried soup for rations and took whatever else they could find. From time to time, that proved to be a sheep. Once killed, it was easy to have the sheepdog tear at the fleece to prove that a wolf had been the predator. The dogs wore huge iron spikes in their collars to protect their throats, and were trained to be half-brothers of their owners. While still puppies they grew to know all the village to which they were totally loyal.

Central government attempted to protect the peasantry from forced labour and the abuses of greedy military tenants, whose rapacious exploitation included the requisitioning of carts, demands for loads of hay and the enforcement of extra dues including a hog tax.[10] Moreover, there were judges who toured villages with their bailiffs, judging wrongdoers or performing some other legal task, and then requisitioned sheep, chicken, oil, honey, barley, straw and wood without payment. Central government always put revenue before benevolence. After the earthquake of September 1684, an official was sent to seize the effects of those who had died intestate under the rubble: for the treasury. That peasants who worked the rice paddies of Niksar, on which the local economy depended, were dispersed was of no interest to a short-sighted administration.[11]

Jobless men hunted birds and hares, although the latter were protected by myth (see p. 68). A lone girl, possibly an unfortunate orphan earning her keep, might go to the forest and gather mushrooms, sweet briar, hips and rose-scented mountain apples.[12] Originally, a village owned both common land and forest rights but in the nineteenth century all woods were taken over by the state or else they would have been stripped.[13]

The extortions of land and the state created impossible situations which drove the peasants into debt. The worst *ağas* enclosed the common grazing land and levied dues on forays to the communal woods. Yaşar Kemal has written of the brutality of Kurdish landlords, which has already been noted in respect of the Turcoman nomads.[14] Apart from the *ağa* of a particular village who might supply seed corn and take his interest in kind, usury flourished in the towns. The Manisa court records show that in 1650–51, for example, there were eighty-five cases heard of which ten concerned usury. The sums involved must have been considerable for it to be worth either side taking the matter to court. Litigation has never been cheap. Peasant quarrels with usurers over modest amounts must have been far more common. It is interesting to discover that of the many victims brought to court, there were women who would have been vulnerable on many counts.[15]

The same was not true of those with means and probably powerful family connections. Numerous women did indeed have recourse to the courts and the fact that these were kept busy in the towns indicates a degree of public faith in them and their rulings.[16] In Kayseri and Ankara, in particular, widows owned property, including houses bought for them by their husbands, thus escaping the cruelty of the property laws, which, as we shall see in the Balkans (see pp. 160ff), left widows in reduced circumstances or even desperately poor. Women's wealth was more usually held in valuables[17] or money rather than real estate from which to draw rents. This accounts for a number of women acting as usurers. It is unlikely that many of them had ever hoed a field or dug other than in their private garden. For the despairing peasant whose crop had failed because of drought or storms, it hardly mattered of which sex the money-lender might be.

The problems and hardships were similar in the Balkans – and all over Europe at the time. In the dependency of Wallachia conditions were so bad that serfdom continued until abolished by Mavrocordato, effective ruler of independent Greece, in the late eighteenth century. Peasants were driven to a primitive slash-and-burn farming cycle and lived hidden in the hills for safety.[18] In Bulgaria and Macedonia the loss of woods and common lands ruined the peasants, who were reduced to contracting out their labour to the large landowners[19] in order to survive. In Greece, where the landowners were mostly Moslem, the villagers paid a half to two-thirds of their crops in rent. To this was added corvée labour for building fortresses during the wars between 1748 and 1758. The only relief was smuggling and piracy. In the Morea

(Peloponnese), the common occupation of the women was searching for wild herbs since there was too little water to keep a garden alive. But there were olives, garlic, maize bread, goats' cheese, onions and sour wine.[20] One recalls the old Caucasian folk-tale whose hero said that all a man needs is a thumb and an onion.

Taxes

The Ottomans kept careful registers of landholdings[21] and the roll of such was the responsibility of the *muhtar*, or headman, of each village, who was elected by men over 18, but not by women. Frequently he was one of the oldest men, but not always. Even night-watchmen were elected.[22] The register was of families and the taxes had to be paid by their head. Very rarely, this might be a woman – in this case, she was likely to be a widow with young sons who could not yet inherit. Nonetheless, women did own and sell property as the court records show. The *muhtar* also recorded births and deaths, drew up lists of youths due for military service and made a profit from certificates and affidavits.

In 1930 one audacious *muhtar* held up the groom's procession to fetch his bride because she was legally under age. She was, indeed, only 11 years old. After the fellow had been given money, coffee and sugar, the bride suddenly grew up and the wedding was celebrated. *Muhtars* often misused their seals – sometimes even out of compassion: or out of greed and compassion as when they delayed military service by falsifying a youth's date of birth. But they had to keep open house (except to women) where village business was conducted and stories told.[23] In some villages there were rooms for youths to meet in and they were given specific tasks such as welcoming travellers. Girls of this age could not go out at all, and on no account to a hall full of youths.

His tax was the basic revenue of the state but,[24] like the nomad, the peasant evaded it as best he could although there was little that he could do about his holding or, if a Christian, his poll tax.[25] This tax applied to 12- to 15-year-olds in rural areas if they were able to work. It was in lieu of military service and had its advantages. The relationships between Kurds and Armenians in the nineteenth century were poisoned by it: while the son of a Kurdish farmer might waste years away on military service, just when he was at his strongest, the son of an Armenian was at work on his father's farm which could not help but prosper, poll tax notwithstanding.[26]

As with land tenure, the Ottomans took over the Byzantine tax system with all its blemishes. There were taxes on animals, beehives, hemp, hashish, cotton and vineyards and, in the Ladik region, walnuts.[27] The hardest tax was that on the harvest, which was officially 8 per cent, although if the produce was due to a rapacious landowner he could charge more, pay the real tax and keep the balance for himself. In theory, no peasant could be made to pay more than one third of his income in taxes,[28] which were regulated by price control over grain and other foods.[29] In reality, there were many burdens. For example, the harvest was at the mercy of flocks of birds and wet weather until inspected by the tithe collector. It was the landlord who collected the best sheaths and the best seed corn.

There was also a military tax: this was paid largely in kind in time of war by villages near the military highways. But peasants increasingly fled the demands of the army, which, in spite of the legal levy, included forage raids by troops. Finally, in 1579, the route of the army had to be changed because there were no settled villages left along the old route. On top of all this, payment for forage was either late or not forthcoming at all.[30] This was apart from the burden of delivering legal grain levies to designated camp sites even if it meant the expense of hiring a cart. The only escape from these and many other taxes was for a village to be responsible for guarding bridges and passes. Another exemption was for all new towns, which paid no taxes for the first years after their foundation. Nevertheless, when the Ottomans conquered Cyprus in 1572, the 50,000 peasants were unmolested and their property untouched. Asked if they wished to continue under Latin law, they were thankful to adopt Ottoman law and be rid of the serfdom of the Venetians.

Life was brutal but, unlike Egypt, there was no theft let alone the raids on neighbouring villages for plunder which were common in Palestine[31] although elopement – or, even more, abduction – created an undying canker of revenge.[32] The villagers' impulse to escape to find work in the nearest town never wavered and it has become more and more intensive. During the first half of the sixteenth century, however, before corruption set in throughout provincial governments in imitation of the capital, the population of Anatolian towns and villages increased markedly. The economic problems following on the discovery of America, which resulted in a silver glut, were common to all Europe; but continuing inflation hit the Ottoman treasury worse than most and affected property values in Anatolia and the Balkans. Large estates fell from 15 to 6 per cent of the total and the towns fared as badly. The influx of peasants into Istanbul had been a plague in pre-Ottoman times and successive governments issued decrees ordering the closure of the gates against the peasantry. The frequency with which this edict was reissued indicates a singular lack of success in solving the problem – and the population explosion at the end of the twentieth century has exacerbated it beyond belief.

In the abandoned villages in both Anatolia and the Balkans, wealthy landowners broke down old boundaries so that if peasants did return they were denied all right of access. In villages from which only the men had emigrated, the tragedy lay with the womenfolk who had been left behind to toil in the fields with young boys and daughters because there were no young men left for them to marry or, if there were any, then the impossibility of paying taxes prevented them setting up on their own. The population of the countryside could only fall, causing tax receipts also to fall, with the result that those who remained faced increases that they could not meet.[33] Life was made worse in the seventeenth century by a little Ice Age when the longer, colder winters meant spring was late and the roads impassable for even longer.

Wasteland and Wastrel

Worse was to come. The drop in revenue in the latter half of the sixteenth century led to mutinies of unpaid troops, especially the elite *sipahi* (feudal cavalry) and janissary corps. These mutinies were more or less contained in Istanbul but in the provinces, as we have seen, discharged soldiers and jobless students roamed at will. The important provincial governors raised bands against the outlaws but then ran out of money to pay them and so discharged them with nothing to do but join the rebellion. Retired officers trained their own companies of followers which, when they acted cohesively, threatened the state.[34] The countryside was devastated and trade came to a halt. Not only were caravans robbed but towns and villages were attacked and looted, the latter of food since their possessions were not worth taking. The prosperous villages of the Sardeli area, for example, with 2,200 inhabitants in some 50 hamlets, were helpless and ruined.[35] Whole villages fled in some areas, especially if they were isolated and defenceless against the *celalıs*. Famine was everywhere. There was nowhere that the desperate could go except to abandoned villages elsewhere. They even sold themselves and their families as slaves.[36] In deserted villages, they hoped to lie low so that no tax-collector would come: since there were some 5,000 such villages in Anatolia, their gamble was reasonable.

Other peasants were braver and dug and guarded fosses around their villages and even walled them like the towns. By the mid-seventeenth century, the worst of the *celalı* bands had been defeated but the old stability and security of Anatolia and the Balkans were never recovered. There was to be trouble of the same magnitude in the Balkans at the end of the eighteenth century. These troubles led to the building of palisades and towers, and villagers were officially allowed to be armed for the first time.

Women led bitterly deprived lives, due to the ravaging of crops and destruction of livelihood that left families destitute and weakened social ties. Villages fought for possession of arable land and pastures.[37] It had taken a lifetime to be able to buy a horse which was now ridden by an outlaw. Men were gone not to return or were killed, leaving widows and families to a grief that could be masked by the need to redouble their labours.

The Daily Grind, the Common Task

The women of strong character held power not only because the hand that wields the ladle rules the world. It was because husbands were often absent that all responsibility fell on matriarchal shoulders, including surviving natural disasters like floods or earthquakes let alone outlaws and tax-collectors. Even if the men were at home nothing could be achieved without a certain equality and veils were left to townswomen. Men depended on women to look after the animals and the garden if there were one. Hives were vital to the cook. Young girls could fetch the water, which has that magic quality that is the tent pole of existence and so particularly sacred to woman.

Washing clothes and pots was minimal since the plates were unleavened bread, and eaten. Everyone was needed at harvest time because the fear of debt was real and every grain valuable. If a peasant were forced to eat seed corn, he would certainly be in debt to the *ağa* and never be able to escape his thraldom. Janissaries grew rich in the town through usury – at 30 per cent a month in Tokat – and seized the vineyards and the houses of their debtors if they were in arrears. Nature was as implacable as the money-lenders. Viciously cold winters and summer droughts may not have been exceptional, and were more frequent than earthquakes. In 1697 an earthquake killed 1,228 people in Kanakert and every single cat, dog and chicken.[38]

Different though Alike

In most villages there was a meeting-room where only the men foregathered in the evenings; if they had young children, the women had to stay at home. But during the day they met and talked about this, that and marriages while, for example, making thin bread by slapping dough on the outside of beehive ovens. If the *ağa* or some other landowner were humane, and the wives hospitable, then women would gather in their courtyard.[39] At night in humble homes all the family lay huggermugger on their palettes spread on the ground[40] in the inner room, which was what served as a *harem*. It was home as opposed to the other, public, room where guests could be received and fed. More prosperous families slept on *divans*, or fitted sofas, with two mattresses and a cushion for a pillow under a sheet sewn onto a quilted coverlet (the forerunner of the modern duvet). For the rest, the bed was a matter of sheepskins.

Village hospitality by day was the responsibility of the *muhtar* but by night there was usually a one-room croft where a traveller was lent mattresses and pillows. An effort was made to feed guests well with fresh bread, yoghurt and butter and a homemade cheese.[41] A dish of hot vegetables might be served and, if available, a spoonful of cherry or other jam, the fruit concentrated to the intensity of toffee. This the male guests would eat together with their host. The women served and watched and were happy to gossip about the newcomers and their peculiarities, even within earshot. When the present author visited the house of a great landowner at Aydın, the several serving women joined in the conversation while standing looking on. They were cheerful because they would retire to the inner room and have their own feast when the men were satiated.

In the early nineteenth century, the perceptive traveller Sir Charles MacFarlane arrived in the village of Seradam near Çeşme when the husband was away[42] from the house to which the traveller had been directed. He was received by the wife who, since she could not entertain a man on her own, called in her brother. They went inside to the reception room where, when seated, MacFarlane was given a *naghile*, or hubble-bubble pipe,[43] to smoke. The floor was raised 1 metre along two sides of the room to make a *divan* which was covered in cushions. Above these were shelves, along which were a basin, cups, dishes and a new copper coffee pot which, with other older cooking pots, was for show, not use. An immense harvest of apples, pears and grapes hung by tassels from the ceiling to be preserved in the open all winter long.

Supper was served on a three-legged stool while MacFarlane sat on the floor. There was a good pilaff, fowl nicely steamed with gourds cut up into very small pieces, fine olives and bread of an excellent flavour, wheat mixed with maize. A young Turk waited attentively while the hostess brought a basin and poured water over MacFarlane's hands from an *ibrik*, or slender spouted metal jug, for him to wash; to dry his hands, he used a long towel embroidered at either end with tinsel and coloured wool. The wife's veil slipped down to reveal a fair face which he much admired except that her eyebrows had been trained to meet in the old Persian style. MacFarlane drank his coffee and smoked his pipe cross-legged on the *divan* while his admiration for his hostess produced twenty blushes. She had often seen Europeans so was not inquisitive and troublesome like other village women.[44] Her voice was musical when she spoke Turkish, which he found to be a melodious language unlike Arabic. A little girl peeping from the inner room overcame her bashfulness and approached wearing a fez hung with small coins over her remarkably long hair which tumbled over her shoulders.

The young brother took the bedding from a cupboard at the end of the room and laid two mattresses on top of each other on the floor, covering them with clean coarse sheets and thick coverlets. MacFarlane was clearly pleased and surprised to find no bugs. The husband reached home at midnight and spread his travelling mattresses beside his guest. The wind approached hurricane force and the little wooden house creaked and trembled while the jackals at the door howled. MacFarlane paid the woman for his food but she would accept nothing extra for her trouble and when he attempted to slip a coin into the small girl's hand, it was given back to him.

MacFarlane was equally well received in another hamlet after a long ride.[45] The hut consisted of one divided room in which the wife was cooking at a fire in the middle: round this hearth sat three children and a rough little colt. Two wicker stools and a kettle were all the furniture but Sir Charles sat on the ground to enjoy a baby lamb roasted whole with bulgur (wheat hearts) and yoghurt, *helva* (a sweet made of sesame flour, butter and honey) and unsweetened coffee. Two neighbours dropped in while the family pitched a tent and emptied a bag of sheep-skins for his bed. This hospitality was given as a matter of course and any member of any village would expect the same treatment. The tax-collector was the worst guest of all but was likely to repay the hospitality by turning a blind eye to the surplus of this crop or the other. By the end of the sixteenth century, he was no longer paid by the state but employed by a tax-farmer, greedier than any government official: and his agent, who was paid by results, was greedier still. No wonder then that the tax man's arrival was watched for and, when espied, girls were sent off to the woods with sheep and cattle. Like the wealthy farmer Abu Shaduf in Egypt, men were known to hide among their women where no stranger might go.[46]

Into the nineteenth century, villages had flat roofs and a traveller arriving from eastern Anatolia would exclaim at the sight of the red tiles of Bursa. Village houses had little value and the French visitor Thevenot reported at the end of the seventeenth century that they had no doors – he thought this might be the cause of good health and long lives (though he also mentioned honey in the medicine as an additional reason). In 1674 Richard Chandler[47] found little flat-roofed cottages at Miletus sheltering several Turkish families among the ruins where cut stone was plentiful. Other villages were also clean and dry even when they were not discernible because their bricks were the colour of the soil.[48] The use of the past is exemplified by the quarrying of Seljuk ruins. Great *kervansarays* can look as though a million mice had nibbled away at their foundations as if they were ripe cheese. Rocks were also gathered from the beds of rivers or brooks.

But the basic adobe croft had mud walls which were roofed with as heavy beams as the friable walls could support. These were often little more than brushwood if there were neither stone nor timber in the locality. Such rafters were covered with mud except for a hole through which the smoke might escape – as in the crofts that MacFarlane visited and which were too primitive to have a chimney. It was necessary to roll the mud roof regularly to keep it flat.[49] This was often done with seg-ments of Hellenic or Roman columns conscripted from ruins because they were ideal in shape and weight.[50] On this elevated 'yard' the harvest could be spread to dry and, more rarely than in Arab countries, the family could escape the sultry *harem* to sleep in the fresh air on summer nights, mosquitoes or none. At any time of day or night, poor light inside the croft drove women to work outside.[51]

Adobe crofts roofed with heavy beams are especially dangerous if there is an earthquake since, should they crash, they kill. Writing of Wallachia and Moldavia, Wilkinson, who knew these provinces well after a long stay at the beginning of the nineteenth century,[52] said that these huts of clay with roofs of straw were useless in very bad weather – the peasants retired to underground cells kept dry and warm with dung and brushwood fires, the basic fires in Ottoman times and dating from pre-history. Dung fires asphyxiated the emperor Jovian in the cold Galatian highlands on the night of 16–17 February 364.[53]

Earl Percy, at the end of the nineteenth century, stated that there was no Moslem city in which hospitality was not cordial and extended by men of every class, race or creed; but he stayed the night in tents because the cabins were airless and reeked of dung and cattle.[54] Beside the croft there would be some kind of lean-to shed for the oxen in winter but sheep and lambs were penned in the open, guarded by two sheepdogs. An explorer rather than a traveller, Percy died before succeeding to the Dukedom of Northumberland.

Occasionally, Chandler[55] found a village with a grand house for him to stay in. These two-storey wooden houses are safe in earthquakes because joists sway and yield just as the shock waves require. Stone stairs led to the upper floor, where a gallery meandered the length of the front in order to shelter the house from the sun; wooden lattices admitted cool air while shutters protected the rooms from winds and rough weather. No *harem* had glass windows, whether in a *konak* (mansion) or at the sultan's palace. Houses were whitewashed, which was a job for women, but colour wash was, and still is, common all over Anatolia and the Balkans. Jackson,[56] one more cleric who travelled at the end of his education at Oxford, wrote in 1797 that Tokat, where the houses were of wood, had a better appearance than any other town in Anatolia. Amasya[57] was akin and both were also alike in being prosperous at that period. Thevenot remarked, more especially of Istanbul, that the trouble with wooden houses was that fires were caused when smoking Turks – of both sexes – fell asleep in bed.[58] With all forms of building, many variations are achieved. There is a taste of Switzerland in the modest houses in the mountain villages of the Black Sea ranges. Built of wood in a forest region, their slat roofs are weighted down with stones because of relentless winds.

Job (4:19) long ago summed up the problem by saying that those who dwell in clay houses, whose foundation is on the dust, are crushed before the moth. In more technical language, dry bricks drain the water from the mortar until it is brittle: this is why the earthquake at Gediz in 1970 destroyed 10,000 houses and killed 1,000 people, whereas Burdur, enduring Force 6 on the Richter scale, lost 15,000 houses but only 60 lives. Worst of all are the houses of eastern Anatolia, which have thick rubble walls and mud mortar supporting poplar beam roofs covered with heavy, flat earth.

Writing at the end of the nineteenth century, Mrs Garnett[59] reported on mud-brick Albanian houses but remarked on horn spoons and a brass lamp among the possessions of one family. One of the problems of all these crofts is the little or no lighting inside them. Lamps would have been luxuries in Anatolia. The fruit, vegetable and tobacco plots were surrounded by high walls with loopholes. Indeed, gardens were the rich part of the women's world and flowers were tended wherever possible. Garnett saw a garden in Mirsis filled with wild roses, jasmine, honeysuckle and clematis. Wilkinson[60] emphasized the importance attached to vegetables in the upland villages of Serbia, where the houses were of stone and wood and the taxes were less onerous than those levied by the Habsburgs.

The addition of a verandah is the first of luxuries and it was called the *hayat* (literally: life). It served as a social centre and was essential for the croft of a successful peasant family. Grandees themselves lived mostly in the towns in Ottoman territories, if only for security, but also because they did not rely only on their rural revenues and tithes. Thus Edmund Chishull,[61] exploring in the eighteenth century, found a richer world when he reached Manisa and was welcomed by an *efendi* whose two-storey wooden mansion had a sofa-room and a pleasure house in the garden besides an open kiosk with a fountain in the middle. But, like a village house, there were no windows on the street side except those well latticed on the second, *harem* floor.

A permanent inhabitant of any village was the sheepdog, which has always been important as a watchdog as well as in defending flocks against wolves. Their own villagers had nothing to fear from the heroic breed, least of all shepherdesses or other women who looked after them. Dogs of all kinds have been allowed to wander in a village among the dunghills and heaps of refuse but that they could be important and cosseted is recorded by Walpole,[62] who came upon a greyhound dressed in warm clothes like a racehorse. The tips of his ears and tail and some spots on his back were adorned with the deep orange dye of *Lawsonia inermis*, or henna.

However, rabies was common and diseases could lay siege to a village and destroy a crop, sheep or the few livestock. The worst plague of all was the mosquito which, well into the nineteenth century, brought malaria especially in the south of Anatolia and wherever there were marshes but these, as we have seen, were gradually drained by the nomads. Nothing could quench the thirst of the *Anopheles* mosquito, which sapped the energy of stricken villages. Flies were the personification of a rural and also urban parasite. As if from the Old Testament, there have been plagues of toads and all kinds of snake especially in the hills. More extraordinary was the archaeologist Mrs Gough's[63] report, while working with her husband in Anatolia after the Second World War, of an invasion of the Painted Lady butterfly in Cilicia while Taşvan on Lake Van is clouded with greenfly at sunset.

The 'wise women' were often experienced and not only as midwives. Their mothers, and through them their forebears, had taught them to detect the type of trouble a local patient might be in and this experience, shared over the centuries, provided a remedy.[64] A child with a high fever in the middle of the night was washed all over in lemon and alcohol and the fever dismissed; and a girl with a temperature almost as bad was soaked in cold water until there could be no more heat in her. A wise woman was not a magician, still less a witch, but an important member of a community to whom everybody turned. A doctor would soon be deserted if he killed too many patients and so would she. Midwifery was rough in the country and the village women were singularly adept at coping with themselves even if the birth pangs came on when the woman was working in the harvest field. Clearly, infant mortality was distressingly high.

The village or small town of Hal in the Elazig region was the subject of two notable reports by Erdentuğ (see pp. 61–2).[65] The place is one example of how appalling life could be for women in one of all too many Ottoman villages where the men took religious beliefs to fanatical extremes. Change came gradually after the Second World War, although male traditions of authority were not completely eradicated. Even as children, the inferior position of girls was established and all had wrapped their heads by the age of 12. (As recently as 1995, Kurds shot two unveiled girls dead in their village.) Even before they were 5, girls were expected to do some sweeping, look after babies and fetch water. By 7, they could guard the vineyard or the lambs and learn the elements of cooking. By 12, they were baking and were weaving socks and underwear.[66] As teenagers, the boys too were at work in the fields, hoeing and reaping, and were expected to prepare the winter food such as *pekmez*, or concentrated grape juice. Strangely, women might no longer hoe after they were betrothed.[67]

The list of the tasks for married women is unending. Apart from looking after the children until there was another one old enough to take on the job, they were responsible for all the domestic tasks such as the preparation and cooking of food. They irrigated the gardens and vineyards, cleaned the crops, collected fodder for the animals in the woods and brought back brushwood for the fires from a distance of 8 or more kilometres, carrying it on their backs. They also carried grain on their backs when they went up to the mill and sometimes again if they and not the men took the flour home. There is something like poetry in the fact that only women could carry water, even after dark, and never a man. Water and women are the springs of life. There was no poetry in their carrying stones for the foundations of buildings which they would plaster and whitewash, but at least men praised them when they carried large stones. On one occasion, the smallest stone weighed about 27 kilograms and was carried the distance of 1 hour to the village.[68]

Saintly women carrying stones is part of Islamic folklore. Thus Martian's Column in Istanbul was renamed the Maiden's Column because a virgin was said to have built it. At Koçhisar there is a stone which is some 5 metres high. This was borne by a girl so pious that she was given the strength to carry it to where a mosque was being built. These stories were symbolic of a girl's sins – which in her case were merely thoughts about the other sex. Suddenly a young man appeared and declared that God was well pleased. The girl died and was buried on the spot. It is not surprising, therefore, to learn that Mount Ida was built by a woman. Christian penitents carried stones (even the Virgin did, it is said) in order to build churches but, after Islam, so did a pregnant jinn at Baalbek. She carried a stone to the temple every day until on hearing that her brother was dead she dropped the stone, sat down and wept. It has been there ever since and is said to weigh 11,000 tons.[69] Female saints have been few in Islam; they include converted Christian princess, but all appear to have been notable intellectuals.

With the village women of Hal there was no reward of sanctity. Almost all the women there were suffering from gynaecological problems[70] due to grossly hard work. This won none of them haloes. In the same village, men carried the corn to the mill if it were outside the town and also ground it. Because it was considered a dangerous and, therefore, manly task they also shook the walnuts from the trees. Presumably, they also helped with hoeing and the harvest itself.

Unusually, spells and magic were practised by men but some intelligent women were allowed to perform. Religion and management were almost exclusively male duties, the former in particular. Women's wishes were ignored and there was no sign of pity when they were exhausted. The saying, 'Let a woman die unless she has fulfilled her tasks' was still in use in Hal in the 1950s. Women were regarded as a field where the seed could be cultivated. Since their heads were nests for devils which must be destroyed, it followed that women had to be beaten so as to drive these fiends away, although only by their husbands and by nobody else. Widows lived easier lives, sifting wheat and cooking grapes, although they could still be shepherdesses. But they had little chance of a second marriage even if they were only 15 years old, while old maids might be able to marry a widower, who needed a wife at once, because they were still virgins.[71]

At the end of her report on Hal, Erdentuğ concluded that, by the 1950s, the women were not frightened of their men. They even tried to fight them and the men were proud of their courage. But she also found that weariness and poverty resulted in a village full of quarrelsome wives while the men were combative and brave.[72]

It is relevant to Ottoman times that recent research in the *gecekondu*, or shanty towns, of Ankara has made clear that women, once they have escaped from their village, have no desire to return. They and their husbands build brick houses twice the size or more of those in the country and install electricity and running water. The hole in the yard is abandoned to its smells. The researchers found a man who was homesick after eighteen years but his wife would have none of it: to return to the village would have meant non-stop work for a woman. In her case there would be wood to chop and carry home, water to fetch and work to do in the fields besides looking after her children and a home which lacked all basic amenities. Nor would there be any hope of an abortion although her family was large enough already.[73] Another wife also refused to renounce comfort and – this is worthy of note by those who are sentimental about the comradely nature of village life – privacy. In the city there was no need to meet with people whom a woman had no wish to see. Moreover, in her own small family she knew what she was eating and whose clothes she was wearing – unlike the squalor of her village.[74]

It is clear that the countryside in Ottoman times had no attraction either in Anatolia or the Balkans. To make matters worse, both suffered from brigandage with the result that absentee landlords were the rule.[75]

However, lack of work in the city could send a peasant home to the country, especially before the First World War and particularly if death in a family created a pressing need for labour in order to save the family lands.

Superstition, Magic and Old Wives' Tales

Superstition in the Ottoman world, as everywhere, was inbred from before history. The myth of Orpheus is an example of the influence of Scythian shamanism travelling into Greece.[76] Iranian migrants to Anatolia influenced the Greeks there and brought with them the Magi, who could control water besides travelling up and down to hell and exploiting the magical powers of plants. In the fifth century BC Empedocles taught this and also about herbs through which he claimed to control the weather besides bringing the dead back from Hades.[77] These pretentious boasts were part of a much older pattern where supposition substitutes for history. That they existed and that they inhabited the forests and hills of Anatolia and the Balkans is unquestionable but the greatest influence on the Ottomans was shamanism.

Shamanism came with the Seljuk Turks from Asia of the steppes, deserts and arctic regions. They inherited such beliefs as that animals had helping spirits and their own secret language.[78] This was associated with the cult of the stag, which was common among dervishes and which manifested itself in the antlers on several major buildings in Tokat and elsewhere. Moreover, shamans were said to turn themselves into birds and fly. The sky, full of holes for the stars, was held up by a 'sky pole' like the tent pole to which, it will be recalled, women were likened as far away as Berber territories. They also believed in the need to purify oneself with water – which has nothing to do with washing for its own sake but is symbolic of the soul and therefore may have influenced the ritual ablutions of Islam. It is because of a shamanist past that the sacred tree or bush beside a solitary tomb of some holy man is still covered with rags, spoons and shreds nailed or tied on by women in search of spiritual or medical help for their families. There is nothing Koranic or scriptural in this appeal to heavenly magic. The rags were torn from the garments of the sufferer and it in no way detracts from shamanism that the belief was shared equally by the Greeks.[79]

Of course, such trees are related to the Tree of Life, most ancient of

Sacred tree and a mother hanging her rag, near Nevşehir (Bob Goodwin)

sacred symbols, which according to the Ottomans had a million leaves.[80] Magical numbers lived on through the Ottoman period with rituals of 40 days, known to Christianity and other faiths, which followed on marriage, childbirth and death. Like 1,001, it could also mean countless. It was a mystical number like 3 and 7. There were feasts of 40 days, like Christian observances, but 40 was also the number of bands of robbers, ogres, jinns and *peris* as well as the Martyrs of Sebaste (Sivas).[81] A superstition in Albania ordained that neither mother nor child could go out after sunset for fear that the Fates might carry them off.[82] One might wonder if the belief had been brought there by Turcoman settlers. In this context it is worth remembering that for nomads there can be no exile until they choose or are forced to settle.

The intensity and nature of superstition in Ottoman lands varied greatly, except for the ubiquitous blue beads or glass in any form with which to ward off the evil eye. This superstitious belief long preceded the coming of the Ottomans and still endures. In the 1920s at Eskişehir, a wise woman was brought to examine a large lump on a mother's neck. The son of the credulous patient was sent to the cemetery to find a fresh bone. After dark, with some embarrassment, the mission was accomplished by an air force officer, Irfan Orga, and a cure effected.[83] A racehorse owner, whose stables were near Bursa, was forced by his head groom to pay for an elaborate and expensive blue bead for an especially valued mount which would have been lame without it. It promptly died and the groom was sent for only to explain that, since the devil had come in the dark, he could not see the charm.[84] No Turkish truck travels without its beads since no chances may be taken. This is what superstition is all about: east, west or anywhere. Once you have seen someone with the 'evil eye', it is difficult to forget it although her glance has done you no harm. Old women in Shiraz get rich on their deformity.[85] Men also appear to achieve the 'evil eye', but not as often. Somehow, this does not arouse the same fears, which is an inverted compliment to women.

Belief in ghosts is not common nor are they always feared. However, in the 1950s when frightened villagers told the *muhtar* of an Anatolian village that voices came from certain graves, he had a watch kept and could respond that no spirits talked there. Ghosts are not jinns, which may account for the general indifference to them. It was nevertheless common to throw stones on the graves of murderers and such in order to keep their ghosts down. The Vlachs in particular had a firm belief in vampires but considered that the friendly village witch could deal with ghosts. Friendly witches or no, Vlachs suppressed such rights as Roman law had offered women and treated them more harshly than even the men of Hal; their reasons appear to have been primitive but without relation to witches or vampires.

If life was too beset with real dangers for ghosts to be frightening, malevolent witchcraft was another matter.[86] In Greece and Romania, Wilkinson reported on the real fear of witches there, unlike Bulgaria, and they were treated with caution rather than animosity elsewhere. Bulgars had less to fear from spirits because they believed the dead to be dead since they set little credence in heaven or hell. There were and are dozens of minor superstitions. In Anatolia such beliefs could be inherited common sense and, perhaps, originally directed at disobedient or thoughtless children. An example is the need to close the windows in winter when, understandably, the demons want to get in out of the cold.[87] This was why children were admonished to keep all windows shut. Related, greater spiritual ties are expressed in the visits of local women to their favourite sacred trees and tombs not only to soothe their worried hearts or minds but also as surrogates for their whole village.[88] With many superstitions, there is no distinction between religions. Moslems and Christians often share in honouring sacred graves in which they put a saint of their choice. In Konya, where the intermingling is particularly frequent, there are the two stones of the Imam Bahlevi whose horses were turned into them. They look vaguely like pack-saddles, and barren women of all sects ride them.[89]

The Albanian fear of nature is surprising in a people so courageous, but superstitions hem them in, including the risk of cleaning out gutters after nightfall, possibly because a hostile spirit might be disturbed. These *vilas* punished the housewife by putting her child up on the roof but always brought it safely down again. Their demons could be good or bad. While some were beautiful, rode horses and were kind, others were bad with hideous faces and serpents for hair – like the Gorgons – and carried other omens of disaster. So did a rainbow over a graveyard elsewhere in the Balkans. As for the evil eye, it could be cured by making a magic circle or sacrificing a black sheep. In all such superstitions lie myths of origin.[90]

In Epirus, in north-west Greece, the beliefs have not died out. One should not wash one's hair on Sunday nor give salt at night. At Vitsa, Pan-like demons terrify the beasts. Asparagus and hellebore are magic plants. Only girls aged between 13 and 14 may uproot hellebore and then only on St John's Day. They wash it, take it to mass, grind it up and pour it into salt for cattle to eat in summer. The villagers also perform mock burials where a boy is covered with lilies and his face with yellow flowers. After a magic incantation, he is told to open his eyes. The youth rises and chases girls with a stick – the one caught is the next corpse. The Vitsians carry a crook all life long and another is given as a funeral gift for a man. On Maundy Thursday, children are bound with osiers, which is a magic twig and their chief talisman.[91]

Medicine offered a whole range of superstitions just as it does today. From the eighth century, if the sick could not take their medicine, then a proxy could. Well-being could be achieved from drinking water in which Koranic texts had been dipped and the next step was to engrave bowls with these. But it was a protective and not a powerful magic although it did soothe gastric complaints – the most common sickness – and difficult labour. It also increased a mother's milk in order to placate a crying baby.[92] It was meritorious for the Ottomans (and other Moslems) to learn incomprehensible words by heart.[93] Mumbo-jumbo or an unintelligible language has always had an affinity with magic.

Superstition led women into hot places. They used the sulphur bath, the Eski Kaplıca at Bursa, in conjunction with a visit to the tomb of the fourteenth-century sultan Murat I.[94] There hung his drum, broken, as was the custom, because it was the celestial bridge to heaven[95] which others might not cross. His bow was deprived of the arrows used to make magical music.[96] The women brought grains of wheat to place on the tomb (and also ate them) because to give the first fruits to the dead ensured a good crop to come. This was a survival of the shamanist cult of the dead and was a half-medicinal, half-religious use of the hot springs.

Also at Bursa is the bath at Kaynarca, which is equally hot. A woman crippled by rheumatism once came to these springs alone at night. She was armed with protection against *peris*. These sometimes fairylike spirits of the streams were rare among the Ottomans and were said to be suckled by sheep. They haunted the bath after dark. After spending the night in the hot room, the woman fell unconscious, not surprisingly, but woke in the dark to feel her limbs being chafed. The shock of a pail of cold water emptied over her head brought her to her feet to struggle to the door, where loyal friends waited for her, and found that she could walk home.[97]

A stranger but more common practice was to grind the bezoar stone to powder which was then used as an antidote for poison. It was sold by perfumers in the bazaar.[98] The stone can be any size but is usually that of an egg. It is opaque and coloured green or brown and is extracted from mountain goats. It can also be extracted from human beings, the older the better for size. Once when a tent blew down in a Mongol encampment, it killed a concubine who appeared to have been selected by fate and her gallstone was removed forthwith.[99] The physician Maurand – who accompanied the great Ottoman Kapudan Paşa (Grand Admiral) Barbaros and his fleet on their return from Toulon to Istanbul in 1544 – recorded the capture of islands and towns the length of the Italian coast. If there were resistance and the town sacked, the older folk were promptly cut open and their gallstones removed without ceremony. After all, they were unlikely to fetch a ransom. Soldiers, like Bulgarian women, had little use for, or belief in, heaven and hell.[100]

A tangled confusion of superstitions is associated with the hare, on which it was believed that one should turn one's back. There were plenty of taboos concerning hares, including those of the Bektaşi dervishes in Albania. In Macedonia, they were not to be eaten on any account. Hares were sacred to the Kızılbaş, who supposed that Ömer, the second caliph (634–644), was changed into a woman and bore two children. When he was changed back into a man, his children were changed into hares. One cannot know when or where the absurd legend of Ömer evolved.

The Village Wedding

Of all the festivals, those to do with marriage were the most costly yet were welcomed even by the troubled father of the bride, although it was likely to be a crippling expense. Also, the household would lose a valuable pair of hands which the father-in-law would gain. The son usually brought the bride back to his home because he was likely to be too poor to farm on his own, and so face all the taxes that freedom entailed and which were paid by the head of a household. Moreover, the boy was probably due to be called up for military service and could not leave his bride alone.[101]

For the bride this abandonment was a serious handicap. She entered her father-in-law's house as a *gelin*,[102] or something akin to an apprentice. And this she could remain for three or even five years unless a younger brother brought home a new *gelin* to take her place. A gentle husband would work upon his parents until they agreed to freeing her earlier to become a proper wife. This, however, had the disadvantage of giving her responsibility and more work. The power of the mother-in-law was such that one might ask whether it were not she that a girl married. Nowhere was this more true than in Bosnia[103] or among the uniquely brutal Liap tribe of Albania where wives were beaten by their husbands frequently and the mothers-in-law offered no defence.[104]

Apart from the inevitable problems between bride and mother-in-law, there were quarrels in any large family and its close relations. Life for children could become intolerable were a stepmother to appear because, as we have seen, the mother was the linchpin of any family for whom the sons retained respect and love throughout her life.[105]

Arranging a marriage was a serious task and was the work of men as well as the two mothers.[106] The village elders would sometimes expect to be consulted, especially if there were a *hoca* or other religious figure among them.[107] In some villages, the *aǧa* or other local notables could also influence choice.[108] Usually, the boys within a family were married in order of age unless the senior was immature: or worse. Cousins or relatives, at least, were preferred and as late as the 1950s half the marriages in the patient sociologist Stirling's Anatolian village were between cousins. The other half were left to villagers only a few hours' walk away.[109] Boys were usually somewhere between 16 and 22 at marriage while girls were between 14 and 18 else it was feared that they might get into trouble. In many villages this meant that the choice of partners was limited and in a very small hamlet there might be no choice at all.

It might be supposed that sentiment did not enter into the contract and, in villages like Hal, this was true.[110] Elsewhere, a humane attitude prevailed and it was possible for a boy to let his mother know whom he would like to marry and for his wish to be met. The girl was less likely to achieve the boy, if any among the few available, she desired.

The bride and groom would have played together as children and then worked side by side in the fields[111] and certainly knew each other well enough to tell an angel from a shrew, a clodhopper from a youth of spirit. In villages where nobody lived more than a short distance apart, it was impossible to prevent gossip about the few boys and girls who were of marriageable age. But if in the fanatical villages gossip was of no account, whereas property or the lack of it was, it must be noted that wealth was not a major factor in the selection of a boy since it did not endow a man with honour, whereas a poor man won respect for his piety and kindness.[112] In Bosnia, on the contrary, a *bey* was a more desirable groom even if he were stupid: and, from his family's point of view, a sharp wife might be able to conserve his property until a son could take over its management.[113]

The officially Christian boyars of Moldavia were very different. The girls were married at 13 or 14 and offers could be made to three or four men which included a large dowry to the detriment of any brothers. Divorce was not only possible but common; the divorced woman kept her fortune and chose her next husband herself.[114] In contrast to Anatolia, marriage was forbidden not only between kin but with godfathers as well.

What is extraordinary is that Koranic law, the *Şariat*, was so flagrantly ignored. This was as true of the *ulema* (members of the judicial class) of Hal as of any village with no religious and legal presence at all. One must conclude that any local *ulema* were only superficially educated else they would not hold so humble an appointment as *hoca* in an obscure locality. The Ottomans were Sunni, the orthodox mainstream of the Faith, and were therefore sustained by one of the four legal schools which formed the pillars that supported it. The rules were strict about not permitting the marriage of kin; this included a prohibition on a marriage between those who had shared the same 'milk mother'. Nor could a second wife be closely related to the first.[115] Theoretically, the Hanifa and Shafi'i schools allowed a bride who was of age to have complete freedom of choice. She had to be of sound mind and choose a suitable match, who was not a social inferior; and, most important of all, *Şariat* law ordained that she should manage her own property. The Maliki school defined suitability as common faith, and the man had to be pious and without physical defects.[116] A woman was of age at 15 and in no circumstances could she be forced into a match against her will.

Wise religions know that while one may lay the marriage table in advance, the pepper and salt of love can only be put there by the bride and groom and also by the assistance of magic. Love potions were sought after everywhere. Among the most interesting were those obtained from the cellars of the demolished castle of Galata which guarded the Golden Horn. Two heroes of the Arab siege of Constantinople were mysteriously buried there, which is why the undercroft became the Underground Mosque. The helpful tomb was that of Sufian. After forty days, a handkerchief laid there turned into an infallible love charm. All too often there was no concern with love in village lore.

In Anatolia, once the match had been decided and the bride and groom had agreed to their union, whether freely or not, their engagement was kept a secret for fear of black magic. Not, one supposes, that the secret was well kept. There was no courtship and were the couple caught making love, both of them might be assaulted. Thus their engagement separated them even more than before and could only be acknowledged by the gifts that the groom sent his bride from time to time. The couple usually awaited the melting of the winter snows so as to marry in the early spring, which was considered the best, but not the only, season. Some four days before the marriage, the groom's house flew a flag revealing the engagement and he gave a party for his friends that included wrestling and dancing. It even included professional entertainers who were men dressed as dancing girls.[117] From how deep a past and with what zoomorphic roots these dances came is of interest because it helps explain the roots of the tradition that these public dances were restricted to the men, unlike those of the Balkans. It is that same fear of wanton behaviour that forbade a woman displaying herself. (This fear extended to judicial executions, where it was considered essential to preserve a woman's modesty by killing her concealed in a sack.) Thus it was that a bride continued to be fiercely guarded in her room. Her virginity mattered more than she did.

In the Ottoman period, then, marriage linked families and not individuals. Thus, when the groom gave presents to his bride he had also to give them to her family. They might consist of money or even land, cattle and horses, tools or a plough if his family were wealthy. The bride's brothers might receive a horse or a pistol, the latter only after the laws forbidding the arming of villagers had weakened in the seventeenth century. Both the maternal and paternal uncles of the bride were also favoured. The gifts were carried on trays preceded by drums and pipes for all the village to admire or scorn. Traditions were strict in order to prevent inexcusable extravagance due to rivalry between families. Even the cost of the girl's gold ornaments was agreed between the families in advance.

The gifts to the bride's family were returned on the appointed day in the form of watches or pistols to the groom while the bride would give shirts and socks or handkerchiefs made by herself to the family of the groom as a part of her dowry. From an early age, she and her family would have spent the evenings knitting or weaving her trousseau which would proceed in a cheerfully painted box to her new home. But all these gifts and trousseaux were subordinate to the bride-price, which could be economically crippling for the father of the groom even if he had tried to save up for the marriage. A daughter was lost to the family, although maternal love would wish her on her way to future happiness. At least if she married a man in her own village, the girl would not be cut off completely. Nonetheless, there would be tears when the bride mounted her horse to ride to her new home – she would be a loss to her family which needed her hands in easing the burden of toil.

If the parents were lucky, the problem could be solved by simply swapping brides and grooms: the girl of one family married the boy of another and vice versa. For the very poor no such collaboration was possible: the cost of the wedding feast might be enough to plunge the father into debt and if a loan from the *aǧa* were his only recourse then it might burden him for life. What no one could escape was the marriage tax. The rich paid 60 aspers and lesser merchants and tradesmen, 40. Peasants paid 30 aspers and widows between 15 and 20.[118] This money was shared between the local military leaseholder, who was a *sipahi* (cavalry officer), and the provincial governor although the *sipahi* hoped to keep all of it for himself: the government saw none of it. This tax was always incorporated into the bride-price. Because of that and because of the loss of the daughter as a worker, the bride-price had to be paid all at one time for fear that the balance would never materialize.

Three days before the wedding, the bride was immured in her home, which was filled with women relations and her friends so that she was never alone. The groom's womenfolk set to work to prepare the feast, splendid and ruinous, which could only take place in the open since a village had no hall.[119] There were thudding drums all day on the eve of the wedding and the groom would leave tumblers of nosegays and herbs at the houses of the guests. There would be more dancing at his home that evening. Meanwhile, if the couple were from an island, groom and bandsmen sailed round to land where they could to play and collect coins and paper money for the bride, to hang round her or pin to her dress. Sporadic rifle fire went on until the wedding was over.

The great morning came on a Thursday or a Saturday. The red bridal sheet hid the bride's face from her future husband but his parents would have visited her and been given fruit and nuts. She did not take part in the feast or stir outside while the men danced. Meanwhile the grandees from town rode in to their own shrill music. They were followed by their *harems* riding astride like men. Domestic slaves and retainers were also mounted. All wore their finest garments, rich turbans and flowing robes. The horses were caparisoned with embroidered bridles, head-pieces, rich housings and the inevitable large blue beads round their necks. Their long tails were bound with bright-coloured ribbons. The band at the rear was also mounted and included kettledrums, pipes and cymbals. Extraordinarily, there were mounted dancing girls, venal and debauched – although too gross to be voluptuous. All these guests participated in the celebration of the marriage of a sweet virgin with, possibly, an equally virtuous young man.

The cooks would not eat before the men were finished. The drummers never stopped, but there were two drummers and only one drum or exhaustion would have set in. The celebrations died away and the groom went home to await his bride. If he had a horse, or had been able to borrow one, he sent it for his wife who had reached the moment of sad farewells.

The bridal party with its escort of young men was led by a *hoca*, if the village had one. He sang prayers by way of blessing but often the religious celebration was postponed since there was no such person at hand. The ride of the bride was escorted by young men and could last for hours if the husband's house was in another village. She sent two presents ahead of her: one was a mirror to ensure the couple's happiness;[120] the other (if possible, wrapped in silk) was a Koran. It goes without saying that the youth who delivered it had to be rewarded. The mother of the groom raised the Koran above her daughter-in-law when she entered the house.

Not until they were alone would the husband see the face of his bride. According to folklore, a stilted conversation then ensued in which he would call her 'beautiful one' to which she would exclaim, 'Sir!' To this his reply was, 'Look here!' To which she demurely answered, 'It cannot be done.' But he simply asked, 'When?' and she replied, 'Tonight'. Whatever happened after that, she must prove to be a virgin. There had to be blood to show or she would be in physical danger from the watchers. In the morning, the married couple returned to the bride's home to kiss the hands of her parents but then they spent fifteen days apart before the 'Invitation of the Fortnight', when they stayed three days and nights at the bride's home again and the groom received his gifts. The girl was likely to be the only wife – unless she proved to be sterile, when she herself might find a second wife who would, after all, be her companion as well as sharing the work. If her husband was brutal and beat her too hard, then she had the help of her mother and, more immediately, her neighbours. These and relatives were quick to reconcile the pair if they quarrelled. As already mentioned, the Liaps of Albania were exceptional in the cruelty of their dominance of women. In the main, however, women were not and could not be deprived of their power to wheedle, remind and scold.

The Virtuous and the Not So Virtuous

The nomads were not the only men who were prepared to capture a bride: as many as 5 per cent of marriages were achieved that way and duly registered. Captured brides were usually accepted in the end. Inside the village the consequences were stormy – elopement certainly cut the costs but it also meant that the bride had no dower and was economically defenceless. The families had to act as if furious and frequently were. The man could not take the girl to his house but went instead to that of a relative who eventually reconciled the humiliated parents to the match. Her family might ignore a woman for years while the man could be in danger of being shot by one of the men in it. In any event, he might be forced to go away until the storm died down.[121]

There were cases of enduring hatred but this was much more likely if the man, abetted by a posse of his friends, had taken the girl from another village. Her menfolk were likely to mount their own posse and attempt to snatch her back. This could result in a bitter feud stoked by loss of face and money which could fester for generations and continue to shed blood. However, some abductions were arranged simply in order to save money on the dower and the bride tax.[122] In Bosnia, bride theft was common among Slavs if less so with Moslems. There were plenty of heroic and epic poems to justify the deed and the girls were usually willing. Local *aǧas* and *beys* stole pretty Christian girls and even raided Austria and Slovenia as late as 1885.[123] But honour creates fanatics. In the late nineteenth century, when a man made a crude joke about an Albanian girl, she later shot herself on the church steps and her brothers shot the man.[124] Today this is unlikely: in 1950, when a boy from a new settlement of Bulgarian refugees eloped with a girl from a Turkish village, the tumult did not last longer than honour demanded and the couple were welcomed back.[125] Under Ottoman law, severe penalties would have been exacted.

Such problems still continue. There is a reformatory near Ankara holding 250 boys aged from 12 to 16, half of whom have committed murder in blood feuds which are still common among Kurds. Others have abducted girls either with their consent or by force. Since any association with a girl outside marriage is impossible if the pair are to survive, peasant boys and men risk long years of imprisonment if they use force, calling on friends to help if a girl is likely to resist. Willing girls can be abducted for a tenth of their bride-price. But if the girl's courage fails her and she seeks help from her father, then the boy goes to prison and she must fetch what price she can. This is one reason why the educated village youths today are anxious to go to university, even if they never attend classes, and so escape immense parental pressures and segregation although the rules are now weakening.

The Armenians believed in the indissolubility of marriage and in the divine right of paternal power. The father housed the sons and their descendants even to the fourth generation when the girls married as early as 12 years old. As in many Moslem families, brides were the humblest subjects of their father-in-law and had to ask permission to speak. When the patriarch died, his widow retained her authority but went veiled in the street. The women of the house made the furniture as well as the clothes and were usually rich enough to employ Greeks as maids, a job that the Armenian girls hated.[126]

As for the gypsies, they had no use for marriage at all; from time immemorial couples considered themselves tied by nature rather than by God's or man's law. Writing at the turn of the eighteenth century, Wilkinson stated that in Moldavia at least the women never refused their favours and were allowed to stroll about the country. At 15, they had to pay tribute but had few means of earning a living. Both men and women made common iron tools and baskets in order to earn their absolute essentials. They also stole trifles but never to enrich themselves. Ten to 15 families camped near a town or a highway and were well placed for finding clients. Wilkinson reported that there were 150,000 or more in slavery. They were strong but lazy, lived in filth and dressed in verminous rags, except for the children who were naked at all seasons. They might either be owned by the government or privately bought or sold. Privately, they were employed in the kitchens of the landowners, which were filthy. If their vice and laziness became intolerable, they were punished by a fellow gypsy. Yet they brought up the boyars' children and acted as wet nurses. They were treated as if brutes by the population and supplied public executioners who often had neither experience nor skill.[127]

∽   ∽   ∽

With Moslems, there was little known record of extramarital sex and no one possessed a common-law wife. A man travelling on a long journey would be met at the larger *kervansarays* and the *hans* of towns with the offer of a 'temporary wife' who would look after him. She might well be Jewish or Christian. This survival of an old Arab custom of *mut'a* was recognized by the Shia Moslems but not the Sunni. The Sunni traveller avoided this prohibition by not stating which school of Islam he belonged to. The contract stated the length of the relationship and the gift of as little as a handful of dates was all that was required. If there were any children, they were in effect the responsibility of the woman's family although the law makes clear that they belonged to the father. There can be no doubt of the Prophet's hostility to a custom which was prevalent among armies on campaign.[128] The result of this system was that, as with all the world, there were women of ill repute (since they were prostitutes in all but name) in the *kervansarays* and also in the *funduqs* (market areas or shops) of European merchants.

Adultery was harshly punished and, according to the *Şariat*, the woman ought to have been stoned to death but there is only one case ever recorded in an Ottoman court.[129] This was in 1680 and it is likely that other issues were also involved. In 1553 the Imperial ambassador Busbecq recorded seeing an adulterous woman at Amasya who was led through the streets on an ass for which she had to pay, and she also had to reward the public executioner for each of the 100 strokes she had endured. She had even to kiss his hand and thank him. Several dogwood sticks were broken on her. There is no mention of the man.[130] In Seljuk times both partners would have been stoned to death.

The greatest of the Seljuk mystics of Anatolia, Celalettin Rumi, married twice. When his first wife, Kira Hatun – a woman of renowned sanctity and the mother of Rumi's son and spiritual heir, Veled – died, her funeral proceeded through the town gate of Konya when suddenly, and inexplicably, nobody could take a step further. Veled, after half an hour, began a holy dance and the journey to the grave continued after Kira Hatun had explained to Veled that a man and a woman had been stoned for adultery the day before so she had to intercede for their souls which were now in paradise.

Into the twentieth century men were, in fact, punished but more mildly than the woman because supposedly more easily cleansed of sin. The penalty for adultery was imprisonment, banishment or divorce. Theoretically, the woman might even be killed in revenge but more often her head was shaved and she was sat backwards on a donkey to be driven away.[131] Not even wives who had been left alone for years by

migrant husbands were forgiven. Everything was not quite what it
seemed, however, and in his novel, *Undying Green*, Yaşar Kemal has
given an account of Batty Behir's wife who was well known in her village
because she made a point of going to bed with every adolescent in the
place.[132] Educationally speaking, she earned her keep. If the lads of the
village were not living too far from a town where there were recognized
whores, then temptation lay waiting for them. Prostitution was toler-
ated. Rumi was reproached for his humanity towards such women but
silenced his critics by claiming that they protected respectable women
from the lust of men. In the fourteenth century, Ibn Battuta reported
that Greek slave girls worked as prostitutes for masters who included a
number of the *ulema* at Ladik. The girls even went into the men's
hamam without anyone stopping them. Young men were allowed to
misbehave for a while but, when this attitude went too far, the
neighbours and elders would wait on the father and tell him that the
time had come for his son to settle down.

Divorce

The *Şariat* was clear on the subject of *talak*, or divorce. If a husband
repudiated his wife then he lost all rights over her. It was Mohammed
who introduced a waiting period, the *idda*, of three months without
menstruation in case the woman were pregnant – if so, the husband
must maintain her until the child was born. He was allowed to take the
woman back during that period, even against her will. *Talak* was simply
achieved by the man's renouncing his wife three times before witnesses.
If he pronounced the phrase twice only then he might keep his wife
provided that he treated her kindly. But the third time was final and he
could not maltreat her in order to make the woman pay to be allowed to
go. A wife could not ask her husband to repudiate her but she could
have recourse to the Ottoman courts and a surprising number of women
did so. God would punish her if she sought divorce without reason. Men
and women were beseeched not to forget generosity to one another and
two arbiters were required to negotiate between them.

Apart from morality, what was at stake was the wife's dower over
which she had complete control down to the last goat, sheep or newborn
lamb. She might own much of the land but it was not likely that she
owned the house and so the husband had to give her time to find a
home. But, if a child were born, it belonged to him. If the wife had

nothing to live on, the husband was required, in most cases, to support her. There could be no further cohabitation unless the woman married a second husband and divorced him. She was then allowed to remarry her first husband.[133] Obviously, all this concerned people of property and not villagers. Indeed, the complexity of the legal position would require a chapter to itself. In the west, too, divorce was chiefly concerned with property.

For villagers, divorce was effectively impossible but a man could get rid of a wife who he thought was not carrying out her duties, especially if she had the village against her. A restraint even for an *ağa* was the expense of the bride-price. Madness was an accepted reason for divorce but the lunatic became the responsibility of the community. A madman had no rights whatsoever but no obligations either and could not be treated as a pariah or a scapegoat; but any charity was personal and not laid down by law.[134]

The dervish attitude to divorce was summed up in a nineteenth-century Albanian convent pamphlet:

> As the man so is the woman, one in kind and not to be separated. It is a very great misfortune if a man divorce and he will have great need of a second wife. Never have a wife living far from her family so that she may easily return. There is no veil save the veil of modesty.[135]

It might be added that dervishes themselves married. They then spent two nights of each week at the *tekke* and the rest at home with their families.

The Childless and Those Deprived

'A house with children is a bazaar: without them it is a cemetery,' declares an old Ottoman saying. There was nothing more important for a woman than to bear a son[136] although mothers loved their daughters for with them they remained intimate. Were a wife to die, the bereft husband would usually marry again at once. The Albanians could not have too many boys and the worst curse on any woman was, 'May you be childless!'[137] Another common curse, 'May you blow up!', might be seen as related. There were more men than women in the Balkans, which could have been due to the preferential treatment enjoyed by boys over girls.[138] In Bosnia, a barren woman might be abandoned even if the couple had been in love.[139] Miscarriages were dreaded and frequent and were the terror of the childless. To miscarriages must be added high infant mortality rates and the failures of a plethora of wise women.

Nor did magic appear to help although there were all manner of protective spells. Long before the Ottoman conquest of 1453, a pagan custom grew up and later became attached to the mosque of Şehzade in Istanbul. Just before noon on a Friday, however dreary the weather, barren wives still come to stick pebbles on the cistern in the outer courtyard. The women race to touch the north-east minaret when the first note of the call to prayer is heard. The symbolism is obvious enough. Fortunate women, whose prayers have been answered, offer crumbling cake to their supplicant sisters in the hope that their wombs be seeded.[140]

The Christian parent in the Balkans, from the mid-fifteenth century until the seventeenth, had one other affliction which increased the number of spinsters in a village and was to spread to the Anatolian provinces at the beginning of the sixteenth century. This was the Christian levy. The system varied but each village had to supply a quota of boys at about puberty for the janissary corps. The list was drawn up by the priest from the baptismal roll and there was no court of appeal. This meant that every five or seven years or so the 'drover', as the recruiting officer was aptly named, went the rounds of a province enrolling these boys. The mothers were left to their grief and the fathers were deprived of labourers. Maternal sadness was mitigated in the days of the levy because an only son could not be taken nor the son of a widow.[141] A boy of spirit would not be so sad as his mother – he, at least, was being rescued from the poverty of village life and given the chance to excel and rise to the highest ranks in society. Some of the recruits kept in contact with their families and one Grand Vezir – Sokollu Mehmet Pasha, at the time of Süleyman – was to be assassinated because he filled too many posts with distant relations.

Those Who are Left

The loneliness of widowhood could be relieved by family and female friends even if a woman had no children. It remained improper, however, for men to visit her or for her to visit men. She was helped to earn a living but nothing else was done for her even though she might be only 15. Her only hope was that for fear of losing family property, a brother of her late husband would decide to marry her. Similarly, a widower might marry the sister of his deceased wife. Otherwise, a widower might take a widow because he was desperate for a house-keeper. Orphans had no rights to their father's land but were dependent on the charity of their uncles. The girls usually went to the towns to become servants.

There was a strange conflict between the concepts of womanhood and maternity. To the husband, a wife was something to be loved at night and so a man returning from a long absence would be welcomed back by the neighbours and not see his spouse until dark – she was only a women even if she had borne him children. His mother, on the other hand, was gentle in essence and words and more precious than life.

A common saying was, 'Others may have a flock but I wander after a single soul.' No wonder Majnun went mad and no longer knew who Leyla was (from that tragic Sufi story of the boy who fled into the desert and found God and so cut himself off from his grief-stricken beloved). Leyla was tragic since she met with widowhood although she had never been married to the only boy whom she loved. Most girls, fortunately, are not Leylas nor boys Majnuns. There were a number of popular sayings suggesting that love was possible, from the equivocal suggestion that love does not obey the law, to the answer of the nineteenth-century Persian ambassador who, when asked if he believed in talismans, gallantly replied that the ladies were the only talismans he knew.

Other popular advice included the following. Parents should marry a daughter as soon as possible because, if they do not hurry, she will marry a trumpet-player. Parents are warned to reject a boy about whom his mother boasts. Another saying points out that there is no need to marry a son in a hurry as there is with a daughter. The groom's parents should never buy cloth without inspecting a sample; and, before choosing a bride, they should study her mother. Ottoman poetry is full of love poems but originally they were the verses of Sufi dervishes who directed their love towards the Almighty even if disguised as a rose.

Food

Ibn Battuta was an invaluable observer and had a fine palate. It is clear that, of all the countries in the Islamic world in which he had travelled, Anatolia pleased him the most. His praise of the delicious viands given to him is not informative but the fact that the women only baked once a week is, as is the fact that they baked exceptionally for him so that he praised the delicious warm bread. Elsewhere, he ate crumbled bread, loved by the Prophet, served with seasoning and topped with lentils soaked in butter and sugar.[142] In the hinterland, nomads served him with pounded rice and curdled or mares' milk, horsemeat and some mutton. In Antalya, he praised the delicate fruit and the apricots in particular, with their almond hearts. He made a reference to malted Biza, which could have been *boza*: still made from fermented millet as a nightcap in winter, it can be potent.

Women ruled the kitchen and it was unthinkable for a man to prepare food. If a woman left him, some men could not even boil an egg. In a woman's slender armoury, cooking was the sharpest of swords.

Some of the food still eaten in Turkey has Byzantine and doubtless far older roots. Bulgur, or ground wheat kernels, was clearly a staple, quick to cook but slow to prepare, since it had to be searched for grit as late as the 1950s and the wheat cracked. Byzantine porridge consisted of a bulgur dough with goats' milk and yoghurt. This was dried in the sun for several days until it turned to powder, which then could be made into small balls or rolls and stored for use as soup. The nomads made a similar provision for the summer *yaylas*. This was bulgur rolled in the hands to make dumplings with cream (the thick *kaymak* of the buffalo) or yoghurt. The dumplings were very solid and had a sour nutty taste.[143] *Tarhana* – a dish made of dried curds and flour – was prepared as food for shepherds.[144] In the Black Sea mountains the nomads' staple diet was the bulb of the autumn crocus.

Walpole[145] was correct when he said that finding good food in Anatolia could be luck and localized. In a poor village, Bornabaşı in north-east Anatolia, the olives were only outdone by the caviare. The rivers of the Black Sea were still rich with sturgeon at the end of the eighteenth century.[146] Breakfast of bulgur and milk was the rule in Kurdish regions[147] and eaten with the almost universal wooden spoon. In Hal, the speciality was to roll out dough and cover it with mincemeat and cooked onion; this was then covered with a second layer of dough and grilled on top of a brazier.[148] Mrs Scott-Stevenson at Killis found the most primitive bread oven: a hole in the ground, fired with vine tendrils, to heat a sheet of iron on which were laid flatcakes as thin as blotting paper which cooked in a few seconds.[149] Near Yalova the opposite practice occurred. Hot stones covered with dough were buried overnight to produce warm loaves by morning. In Antep, however, the bread was made of flabby, rolled-up strips which were, according to Scott-Stevenson, as unpalatable as they sound.

Meat was rarely eaten except for chicken, and then not in many villages. *Pastırma* was the name given to any meat preserved with garlic and spices in the sun. Lamb as young as possible with its skin roasted to crackling was the most desirable meat. But more usually a goat was stewed. Busbecq[150] recorded baby lamb boiled to a jelly with honey. In towns there would be kebabs, pigeons and chicken. The seas and rivers were rich with fish for men to catch, including the forests of the Black Sea coast and their trout, only matched by the flying trout of Erzerum. There were wild raspberries: and also mutton stew. There was fine honey – usually a woman's province – all along the coast. The hives were hollowed-out tree trunks like those of the Turcoman but the honey of the Pontic Alps had the distinction of being so intoxicating that, according to Evliya Çelebi, this was the nectar that drove the troops of Xenophon mad.

Fruit was the solace of the poor even when rough and ready and half wild rather than from the many orchards and gardens. The apples of Nevşehir were considered the best by Scott-Stevenson,[151] who also noted that bunches of grapes were hung in the dark to keep. Pomegranates were not only eaten but grown for their dye for use with Morocco leather and were gathered by women in search of a little money.[152] They were representative of women all over the country who scoured fields and hillsides for the local herbs.

Items recorded by the tax official at Bursa market between 17 and 26 June 1502 give some idea of the abundance of fruit and vegetables available in a town which was the centre of a rich agricultural region. The fruit included several varieties of apples, peaches, grenadines and grapes, as well as no fewer than twelve sorts of plums. Then there were apricots, cherries, Maltese plums (the harbingers of spring), oranges, melons, water-melons, dried fruit, pistachios and almonds besides cucumber, courgettes and aubergines, carrots, cabbage and beans. Honey, butter, sesame oil and *pekmez* (the juice of unfermented grapes) were also recorded.

Such abundance came from a woman's world, as did the produce of the fields, but it was men who did the market shopping. In the province of Erzerum in 1848 the crops were sown as soon as the snows melted in April because the season was short. Lentils, peas, beans and millet were followed by wheat, barley, rye, lucerne, linseed and vetches to be ground for the cattle. Both linseed and hemp were compressed for oil.

When the marshes froze, there were cropped reeds and coarse grass. This formed fodder for animals in winter and was used to make mats, and for roofing and heating. Gardeners came down from the mountains and the valleys near Tortum to grow lettuce, cabbage, tarragon, Jerusalem artichokes, spinach, mustard and potatoes. The locals sowed the fields with turnips, beans, peas, chickpeas, carrots, onions and cucumbers. If the frost came early there was no fruit – which must have been true of the seventeenth century. The crop was buried deep in winter frost and dug out when required. Between times the peasants loaded oxen with rock salt, wood and soda to market at the nearest town. Charcoal was made from birch and dwarf oak from the Kars region in order to warm the house but was rarely used for cooking, which peasants did over an open fire.[153]

In about 1250 hashish entered Anatolia from the Near East where it had long been frowned on as a habit-forming drug. The poppy was held by dervishes to secrete *kaif*, or the quintessence of the soul. The Bektaşi order was said by the nineteenth-century authority Brown to make naked novices, under its influence, take secret vows.[154] If they did take such vows, they were those of perpetual celibacy and their nakedness would have been symbolic of the purity of their intentions. There does not appear to be any written material about this in any archive of the Bektaşi order. Certainly, a great number of the rich became addicts and chose a path which, in most cases, led to the asylum. The women cut off the poppy heads, which gave the leaves a fortnight in which to ripen; these were then harvested and beaten to dust, which made the best-quality hashish (*sigirma*). The rest were ground (*honanda*). In Egypt and Syria this powder was mixed with butter but in Istanbul it was made into pastilles with syrup and smoked in a *naghile*. Mixed with costly spices it became *baharab* and took one to paradise. Hashish was, of course, prehistoric and known to the Neoplatonists.

Women in the Country

Considering that he was a Moslem in the days of the implacably conservative Almohads, the renowned twelfth-century scholar Ibn Rushd (Averroes) was remarkably critical of orthodoxy. He accepted Plato's ideas about the equality of women in respect of civic duties.[155] The Roman laws had forbidden a woman to hold public office and when she was not the chattel of her father then she was that of her husband. In

Greece, women were confined to a gynaecium – the parent of the *harem* – and in Persia they were little else than slaves. Even Zoroaster extolled women who were rich in goodness because they were obedient to their husbands. The Koran attributes the blame for the expulsion from Eden to Adam rather than Eve.[156]

All the Islamic economic fiats placed women in an inferior position to men and, in general, this applied to moral edicts as well. Yet one third of the dealers in property in eighteenth-century Aleppo were women.[157] Polygamy is still seen to cut down on prostitution but is, of course, the privilege of men. If it were not for civil law, a woman could only escape from her husband if he were palpably brutal, impotent or insane.[158] Apart from her neighbours and parents, public opinion in a small community was a protection except in the most bigoted villages like Hal or among the exceptional Liap clan in Albania. Other Albanians, like the Tosks, treated women with consideration. Divorce was common, however, and valid grounds included a husband's excessive corpulence or long absence, in addition to the reasons stipulated in the Koran. But then Albanian women were remarkable. They took part in vendettas. In the latter half of the nineteenth century, a quarrel between two men on a village green became an affray in which a 17-year-old girl was the most ferocious fighter. Albanian women even aided their men in war and would carry the mutilated bodies of their kin onto the battlefield in order to excite the warriors to revenge their loved ones. They closed their doors on their menfolk if they could use a gun and had been less than courageous. Because of the respect in which men held them, they were frequently chosen to negotiate with the enemy. Not surprisingly, men would never fight women. The fact remains that, although they were near equals at the council, they were not completely so.[159]

∾   ∾   ∾

In Ottoman times, women were not likely to be beheaded, imprisoned or even molested; consequently, when there was a grievance it was the women who were sent to protest. In Izmir in the nineteenth century, the women – their faces covered except for large and angry eyes – went to clamour before the gates of the governor's house to demand that he repeal an unpopular measure. They waved their hands in the air and screamed with shrill voices before retiring unmolested. In 1828, when a woman attacked the old *aǧa* she left him dying a painful, lingering death. In June of the same year, a new tax at Menemen led to serious excesses, men protested and the peace of the district was endangered for some time until the government ordered troops to intervene.[160]

Brigandage

When Bosnia and Bulgaria were conquered by the Ottomans in the fourteenth century, the choice was between Turkdom and serfdom. The landowners became Moslems as fast as possible and, with the fall of Herzegovina, the conversions were complete.[161] The serfs retreated into the mountains and, with their raids on villages in the valley, became petty bandits. They stole crops since a peasant's possessions were too few to matter. A profitable trade was carried on by pirates[162] in collusion with the Circassians who stole and sold girls and boys, especially from the steppes. They would plunder indiscriminately in their hurry and then select the prettiest girls and most handsome boys. Abbesses in the Balkans were prepared to act as dealers. There had been fairs and markets in the large villages of the Balkans where the Serbians sold timber to Venice, for example, but brigandage put a stop to any fairs outside town walls.[163]

In Anatolia in the sixteenth century, young sparks among the peasantry robbed the religious colleges in order to escape to the Balkans while the *celalıs* spread to Macedonia and Bulgaria. In 1791 disbanded soldiers, who were Bulgarian and Serbian peasants, roamed the country intent on pillage and that old sport: rapine. Many Moslem smallholders were allowed to keep their weapons for use against bandits. The mountain folk, who had nothing to fear from them, helped the brigands and even acted as spies. They would watch out for the *zaptiye*, or police, who were themselves known to be in league with the brigands – as were the landowners. It is a situation like that with which the Mafia plague Sicily.

Brigands were of all races and some were women, including the Greek women of Macedonia; but women usually retired and returned home after a few years in the mountains. In the late nineteenth century, Spano Vanghelis actually had her own gang. She wore a calico skirt and a swarthy vest and her chain of office included a silver miniature of St George and the Dragon. When she was finally defeated by Mehmet Pasha and submitted, she was allowed to return home on the principle of live and let live.[164]

The notorious Ali Pasha of Yanina would have none of this and created a police force of ex-bandits, who included many brothers or cousins. Alarmed, the villagers recruited large bands of robbers who burnt the pasha's districts. He had no difficulty in burning, hanging, beheading or impaling anyone who could possibly be involved and so reduced outlawry that he could open up the country to merchants. He controlled 1,000 estates until, in 1822, he was in turn put down by the central government and his and his sons' heads were sent to the capital.[165]

At the very end of the Ottoman period, there was a note of the Robin Hood in brigandage which is epitomized by the landowner in Aydın who, while living in the town, built a stockaded summer house with its first two floors windowless, in the middle of his farmlands. The brigands were deterred until a born leader gathered as many of the discontented as he could and led a siege that reached a climax when his men broke through the stockade. Short of ammunition, the *ağa* was afraid that hand-to-hand fighting might ensue and a truce was agreed. The brigands promised to leave his property in peace in return for a great feast once a year. Many years later, the feast was forgotten by all but the elderly *ağa*, who liked to recount the drama sitting on the balcony with his gun across his knees. The last time was when he saw something move in the shrubs and instinctively fired, as he had of old, but this time shot his grandchild dead.

Mysticism and The Law

Throughout Islamic centuries, some remarkable women had emerged, including several female mystics ever since Rabia al-Adawia in the time of the Prophet. Umm al-Khair of Basra in the eighth century was known as the Queen of the Mystics and as the womb of the germ of Sufi thinking. From her, some would allege, came the Sufi request that when a person was dead, their good deeds should be hidden like their sins. Women had always been close to the dervishes and in the ninth century there were women's convents in Aleppo. Some orders accepted women provided that they had been well educated, while others admitted women to the order as associates.[166]

The *şeyh*, or master, of a dervish convent could and did marry, and there were rooms in the *tekke* for his wife and children.[167] At other times, the *şeyh* and his family lived in a separate house and deputed the daily running of the foundation. Mrs Garnett met the Mevlevi *şeyh* of the *tekke* at Manisa, the second most important house of the most intellectual of all the orders, living in his own house. His first wife was dark-haired, handsome and haughty with an ill-tempered expression. The second was a Circassian girl who clearly lived in awe of her. To quote verses by Yunus Emre, the father of Ottoman poetry (d. 1321):

> *Clearer than any moon each face,*
> *Their every word a perfumed thing,*
> *The blessed maids of Paradise*
> *Stroll, the name of God repeating.*[168]

In both Arabic and German the sun is feminine and the moon masculine. Thus one might imagine that the mosque was the moon where the men gathered and the tomb of a *şeyh* or saint was the sun where the women held their own meetings. This separation is of importance in understanding the relationships between the sexes in Islam. It does not alter the barbarity of wife-beating if a wife is disobedient. In the eighteenth century it was recorded by Blackstone (the greatest of English legal minds and whose handbook was the guide to police action even after the Second World War) and continued into the nineteenth century in the west.

Marriage had always been a civil contract and the law under the Ottomans did not begin to change until after the upheavals at the beginning of the nineteenth century and the reforms of the Tanzimat period in the middle of the century. In many ways, they were more tolerant than laws in the west. Without question, until the married women's property acts of the 1870s in Britain, the law was far fairer to women in Islamic countries even if only half as fair as it was to men. A woman's property was unquestionably her own nor could she be deprived of it by divorce. The contract was subject to immediate change with the adoption of the Swiss civil code after the flight of Mehmet VI (1918–1922), the last sultan. At a stroke the retrograde punishments were cut down but in the past the cruelty of Koranic laws had been mitigated by the Ottomans and, indeed, by the *kadıs'* (judges) reluctance to apply them.

Some of these laws were ordained precisely to protect women. Thus those who accused an unmarried woman of fornication and other misdeeds had to produce four witnesses – a far from easy task – or be sentenced to eighty lashes.[169] If the fornicating woman was married then she was the responsibility of her husband who had to bind her to the house until she mended her ways.[170] In Ottoman times, the whipping of women appears to have been mainly restricted to any guilty of sodomy and this was accompanied by a heavy fine. But all fines paid by women, or by their husbands for them, were half those paid by a man and the family income was taken into account. If women came to blows and tore each other's hair or beat each other, and they were not veiled ladies, the *kadı* had to see that they were severely chastised. The fine was 1 *akçe*, which was less than a day's wage. But if the lady were veiled, then the husband was ordered to pay 20 *akçe*. The modest nature of the fines would imply that these fracas were common happenings. Procuresses were severely fined while harlots were paraded round the district sitting on a donkey facing the tail. The woman's face would be blackened and smeared with filth or entrails. A crier went before proclaiming the offence in order to incite the crowd to pelt her with more filth. In some cases harlots were banished to places like Cyprus, which were unpopular; along with them might be lazy watchmen, gypsies, lepers and their families who went with them.

For men, there were fines for abducting a boy or a girl but there could also be 200 lashes, the maximum that could be applied without the probability of death ensuing. Arson was a crime of the first degree and the culprit was seated on an old horse daubed with pitch which was set on fire and the rider, mercifully, strangled. The horse had the worst of the punishment. Death was stipulated for murder, apostasy and highway robbery. Abduction and other serious crimes might result in 5 or 10 years' service in the galleys. A high proportion of the oarsmen at the battle of Lepanto in 1571 were common criminals rather than prisoners of war like Cervantes. There were various forms of ignominy for false witness and this was also a part of the punishment of defaulting members of the *ulema* class itself. Their crimes included agreeing to marry a man to the girl whom he had abducted. As punishment, the *ulema*'s proud and often long and distinguished beards were shaved off. Finally, an orphan's guardians were heavily fined if they appropriated any of their charge's property. One example is that of an Istanbul woman in the seventeenth century who was accused of misappropriating 1,000 skins while she was the trustee of the children of one Hacı Himmet.

Legal punishment in Istanbul was not as harsh as it was in Iran, but elsewhere in the Syrian and Arab territories the laws were cruel and local custom allowed to have its way. Torture of an accused or a witness was possible in the capital but was rare, principally because a very high percentage of all crimes were admitted on the excuse that the accused had 'yielded to the devil'. Since torture was ordered implacably for perjury there was a real incentive to avoid it by partially admitting one's guilt. These restricted confessions, if discovered to have withheld evidence, meant a sentence to the galleys. However, women were not sent to the galleys; nor were they allowed to be shopkeepers, who might be nailed to the door of their shop by the ear because of false measure or adulterated goods. It was clearly folly to take a woman away from her home and children in a society where adoption was forbidden, even if this law was sometimes broken. Thieving was not a misdemeanour of which Ottoman women appear to have been culpable unless they were members of a clan of beggars.

They could be victims of political violence, however, though only rarely. In one case, the wife and children of a hated Grand Vezir were stripped naked and paraded through the streets. On 15 November 1808 Bayraktar Mustafa Pasha, the Grand Vezir of Selim III, was thrown from power and perished when he deliberately blew up the powder magazine at the Sublime Porte (his official residence); his wife saved his *harem* by hiding them in the ice house in the grounds where no mobster ventured and no fires took hold. But, by and large, the streets were safe as were the homes of ordinary people in Istanbul. The rampaging and frequent fires were savage enemies enough. The fortunate few who had the time could carry their valuable possessions to a major mosque or its court-yard where the distance from other buildings and the stone walls might help defy the conflagration. The mosques and the *medreses* (religious colleges) were places of refuge, particularly for women and children in times of unrest. They should in no way be seen as sanctuaries either for wretched miscreants or for politicians.

Blood and Protection in Village Life

When considering village life, one has to come to terms with violence and its causes because of hot blood and also because of the mores of peasant society. It is useful to consider the problem in terms of actual individuals involved. Fortunately, there is a recent account of the lives of two villagers (both born before the First World War), in their own words, which is particularly illuminating. They reveal, for example, that sexual problems between neighbours did not necessarily end in fighting. One man who surprised his wife in bed with another man, for instance, was content to divorce her. She disclaimed her lover and went to Istanbul where she married someone else. There was no outward display of anger. But our couple's story from the final years of the sultanate is very different.[171]

It begins as a touching romance. The girl could see her lover at a distance just as he could see her. When the boy was 18 (his loved one was five years younger), he was determined to marry her as soon as possible. She was not unwilling to overcome her fear of vigilant eyes and meet him in a barn, and this entirely virtuous encounter was repeated on another occasion in spite of the strict tradition – made all the more oppressive in a village that had both a mosque and a *hoca* to run it – that adolescents might not touch each other or even hold a conversation. This particular match had to overcome family anger because of the lack of money partly due to the death of the girl's father. However, the persistent groom finally achieved the marriage but without a religious ceremony or the *hoca*'s blessing. Since the girl was only 13, it was necessary to approach the *muhtar*, who was a relation, so that the records might be shown to be wrong and her age altered to 15. The bride was certainly not 15 when she watched her husband undress in front of her since she had no idea what his embraces and caresses would do to her. Her education was completed rapidly for she appears to have become pregnant almost immediately.

The groom was a strange youth who had not known his father. In his modest croft there had only been room for him to sleep with his mother. Now that he had a one-roomed home of his own, he had his mother brought to live there and divided the room with a curtain, which was a common enough practice. However, he would sleep with his mother until midnight and then cross over to his wife's bed. One is not surprised that the stepfather was hostile to the groom and, although the young man rode out the scandal when rumours about his behaviour spread round the village, he soon escaped with his wife to Ankara where his mother was to join them. The stepfather had spat on the path and threatened the youth with his own son: as soon as he came out of prison for killing a man. Unperturbed, our hero reminded him that he was a great friend of the murderer and had no reason to fear him.

Some years later, her family summoned the wife home from Ankara, where life had proved a bitter struggle, and in a moment of docility (such moments were becoming increasingly rare), she went. She brought her first child, a daughter, back with her and was pregnant again. This was the cause of bitter jealousy because her elder brother-in-law had importuned her before her marriage and made himself obnoxious by never leaving her alone. He had no children by his first wife, who had died, nor by his second. There had been bitter wrangling over the clothes left by his first wife because the man was now hostile to his young sister-in-law and denied her any right to them.

The man's hatred for her was finally too much for him and he gave way to rage and jealousy that she should have a child when he had none. While the mother was hard at work with the harvest, the man took a pointed cattle goad, grabbed the little girl who had strayed from her mother and impaled her from her anus to her mouth. The miserable mother did not need to call for justice; her enraged brother took a knife and pursued the murderer but he escaped and no more was heard of him.

This is a first-hand account of life in a village that has no match in the tattered records of earlier times. It is accepted that village life did not, and could not, change over the centuries. Individuals escaped for this reason or that as did the heroine of the account above. Until old age, her relationship with her roving husband grew steadily worse.

The Harem of the Çakır Ağa Konak, Birgi (author)

CHAPTER 4

Trade and Wealth

The Town

There was a higher percentage of townsfolk in Anatolia and the Balkans
in the fifteenth and sixteenth centuries than there was in Europe: 1
town-dweller for every 2 peasants. Town households were smaller than
those of villages. Except for Istanbul, the towns were not large apart
from Bursa, which had a population of over 80,000. Edirne, the second
capital, had some 20,000 but Ankara had only 12,000 and was followed
by Tokat, Konya, Sivas and Sarajevo with only 5,000. Salonika, with its
population of over 25,000 in the late sixteenth century, was exceptional
because, just as Izmir was to become later, it was an important trading
port. This was due to the influx of Sephardic Jews from Catholic Spain
who made up more than half the population. The other half was divided
between Moslems and Christians. It was the silk trade that accounted
for the rapid development of a green Bursa which only wilted at the
beginning of the seventeenth century.[1] Although relatively small, the
towns welcomed many travelling merchants who therefore had large
hans, or hostels, in which they could stay, but had to bring their own
mattresses, quilts and cooking pots. The towns also employed seasonal
peasant labour which was invisible on the tax rolls. Most of these
peasant hirelings returned to their villages but others remained and
recreated their hamlets within the sheltering walls of the town: cousin

attracted cousin and, in a strange environment, comradeship was essential for survival.

The walls of a town were all-important during the *celalı* period of trouble in the seventeenth century when the villagers found life too dangerous in the country where harvests were looted. Walls were not only important as a defence against brigandry but also because, when the gates were shut at nightfall, no one could escape without inspection. Later, the walls were to be quarried for building materials.

Within a town like Konya or Kayseri, there were strict districts for commerce and for homes. The latter were also divided by religion and, to a lesser degree, race. This was the one remaining element from the early days when the non-Moslem *mahalles,* or quarters, were walled and order was kept by the chief rabbis or the bishops in charge of their flocks. They were self-contained and the necessities of life could be found within them. The virtue of the system was that the rich lived among their fellow creatures. In time, the restraints dwindled and they tended to live near each other rather than be centres of charity within their own districts. Each residential neighbourhood had its own shops, such as a baker or grocer, but any serious trading took place in the bazaars of the commercial district including the central, but open, fruit and vegetable market. Merchants in their *hans* congregated together. Out of this developed the covered bazaar where gates could be locked and guarded by night and where, also, the display of goods was not restricted by bad weather. It was a totally different way of life from that of the village, where there might be no shop at all and where markets and fairs had been closed due to the lawless state of the provinces.

There were crimes in the towns, partly because the peasants brought their family feuds and enmities with them.[2] Bachelors, who were often jobless young villagers with no resources, had to live in their own ward and were firmly locked in at nightfall so that they should not trouble respectable households. There was a very deep division between the established citizens and the newcomers, who appeared to be barbarians but who quickly assimilated some of the ways of the town although continuing to follow their village mores. The effects of infant mortality were felt throughout society. If this is not taken into account, prior to the nineteenth century the average life expectancy was 27 years, but if the number of children who died before the age of 5 is subtracted then an adult could hope to live until nearly 50.

By the eighteenth century, the Christian population in central Anatolia had increased in size and wealth by some 5 per cent and they were buying better homes. By then, the Armenian population for the most part spoke only Turkish.[3] Town life was so different from that of the country that rites of passage, such as birth and marriage, have to be looked at afresh since the disposal of property was more important than an impoverished peasant could imagine. Women, if determined, could follow trades privately and there were rich money-lenders among them. Often, a widow was provided with a house before her husband's death and a modest share of his estate in trust. More elaborate wills left her the income until the sons grew up, when the elder would usually be responsible for looking after her. Polygamy was more frequent in the towns: this reflected the wealth of the men rather than a different moral attitude. In provincial towns, the number of men with two wives was as nothing when compared with the wealthy elite in Istanbul. There in the eighteenth century, the Şeyhülislam (Grand Mufti) Feyzullah Efendi – as notorious for his greed as he was for the ill advice that he gave his sovereign, Ahmet III (1703–1730) – fathered countless children by many wives, although never more than the legal four at one time. Like the sultan, the *ulema* believed in large families with plenty of daughters to marry off because of the importance of the extended family: through it they could protect their own interests after their death and within it good posts could be obtained for their sons.[4] Since Feyzullah's misdemeanours resulted in his dying a terrible death in 1730 at the hands of an infuriated populace in Edirne, whence he had fled from Istanbul, his marital network had much to do once he was safely buried and his chests of treasure dug up.

A Middle Class

In a provincial town such extravagances did not arise. The life of the place depended on its handsome, middle-class homes and its rich merchants' *konaks*.[5] Every house had its own courtyard, if not a garden, overhung by mulberry, plane or acacia trees. The better homes were surrounded on three sides by both a garden and a courtyard but presented a windowless front to the street at ground level in order to maintain privacy.[6] At the upper level, latticed windows flourished and a great gallery overlooked the garden and kitchen courts. Building plots were often irregular in shape and so the first-floor rooms projected over the street in order to gain space but also to create rectangular rooms. If the house had three storeys, there could be further poetic projections for the top floor and a further increase in domestic space.[7] The survival of Safranbolu, situated between Ankara and the Black Sea, enables one to see how visually satisfying such a town could be. Where there was timber, as there was at Tokat, for example, the houses were wooden and would eventually be tiled. In Kayseri, where wood was costly, houses of importance were built of stone by the end of the eighteenth century since it was plentiful and labour was cheap. Amasya beside its green river (Yeşil Irmak) used both materials.

Externally, the lath and plaster infill between the wooden beams and struts was often painted red but, curiously, the frames of the windows and their lattices were left unpainted. What was integral to them all was the inward family life which looked down into the courtyard so that the cooking could be supervised from a verandah. This reflected a love of the open air which reached its apogee in Ottoman society, when it was often difficult to know if one were indoors or out. But from the latticed windows onto the street, it was pleasurable to keep account of the goings-on of the neighbours without being seen although they were well aware that they were being watched. It also gave a feeling of security since there was always a neighbour to report untoward events.

The gardens were meant for shade and so trees took precedence. Nonetheless, flowers were lovingly tended and they included roses, jasmine and carnations, according to the climate, side by side with cabbages and green vegetables. Indeed, garlic was planted round rose-bushes as a defence against greenfly. There were fireplaces in the winter room, or rooms. These were *ocaks*, or hearths, with projecting hoods. The *divans*, or fitted sofas, were ranged along three sides of the room against the walls, with shelves and niches above them for knick-knacks, and flowers and pots for display. There is a clear impression that life in winter was spent waiting for the spring as if only the summer mattered. In these *konaks* there could also be summer and winter salons or a whole floor devoted to the *harem* for family life and another devoted to the *selamlık* and the guests. It was the intermediate spaces that showed some relaxation of the absolute rules of segregation. The *divans* were covered with mattresses – which yielded but were not soft – and parades of cushions. The door, sometimes on a diagonal, opened onto a narrow fore-hall. Along its wall was a series of cupboards which stored bedding and also a private washroom with water jug and sink and even running water. The room itself was raised up one or two steps, making a clear social differentiation between it and the little open lobby where the household waited.[8]

To the servant girls from a village, there can have seemed very little relationship to the life of their own homes. The mistress of the house had no work to do except run an orderly establishment: the more the servants, the more exacting this could be. She would certainly occupy herself with the young children and unquestionably she would spoil her sons – although by the time that they were 7 they were supposed by the *Şariat* to have been taken over by their father in order to mix with boys and men. But even after circumcision, perhaps the most significant rite of passage for a boy, there seems to have been little waning of covert maternal power. A woman's sons would rise to their feet for her and would treat her with respect even when, with age, her mind was on a darkening journey of its own. There was still time to be bored although neighbours came to gossip and the embroidering of clothes, kerchiefs and napkins was practised as assiduously as it was by equally bored rich women in the west – who, at least, by the nineteenth century had the novels of Sterne and Scott to read and not just the Koran. Women of any standing learnt the rudiments of music and could sometimes sing better than their servants, some of whom may have been trained before they were sold in the market.

The market was the centre of trade and therefore the main source of the wealth of the town. But there women of good family allegedly never strayed. Instead, women pedlars came to the door and cheered up housewives who were confined for so much of the day. In every street, men peddled goods ranging from water to cooked foods as well as bits and pieces of ribbon, thread or even clothing: old clothing at that. This was very different from the rare visits of pedlars in the villages. If some of the culture of the town was assimilated by mothers and daughters of the well-to-do, more was gained by the wives and children of artisans who could themselves follow a trade although never become the member of a guild nor work in public.

The diversity of these trades was a measure of the civilization of the town. They were deeply affected by boosts in exports of woven goods to Europe because weaving was mainly a woman's skill. Towns like Salonika, Edirne, Ankara, Bursa, Tokat and Dıyarbekir (the latter chiefly a Kurdish city) prospered because of this market.[9] Almost every other form of the sixty-eight crafts registered in Ankara was the province of the male and this was true elsewhere. There were cobblers, carpenters, candle-makers, goldsmiths, grinders and barbers. Only the spinning of silk and Angora goats' hair and the weaving of carpets were left for the women and young girls, who were employed at low wages. When they worked for themselves, however, women sold their work in a corner of a back street, earning them no reproach and achieving a modest income. There were also the laundries but in Istanbul, at least, only women of the easiest virtue worked in them since no one would suppose them to be other than libertines: no other trade exposed women and girls in public in order to sell their services. This did not mean that prostitution was not important, especially in the *hans*. There were three types: the woman who had her own room, the woman who went to the room of her client, and those who consorted in the open because woman and client were both too poor to rent rooms. These included youths from villages who had saved up in order to walk many kilometres to the town for no other reason than sex.

Perils on the Roads

Women travelled even where the roads were bad. Some even rode horses as if they were Mongols, but the commonest transport was a cart if the road were good enough. Otherwise, women travelled in panniers hung either side of a horse. Many of the townsfolk were landowners who had no intention of living on their estates if they could avoid it, but they or their family would visit their farms in due season and the house was usually sufficiently furnished for them and their party to stay briefly. They, their relations and many hangers-on would set about bottling fruit, collecting honey in jars, making pasta and creating a caravan of provisions for the winter larder. They picnicked and enjoyed themselves in the fresh air and made the most of their break from the restrictions of home life.

Journeys could often be dangerous because bridges were not in good repair and the fords were unmarked or at best badly signposted: as Mrs Scott-Stevenson discovered when her groom attempted to carry her on his shoulders across a broad river. He was soon wobbling under his burden and finally fell and she was left to struggle her own way to the farther bank. Her husband and his friends, once they had recovered from their fright, found her soaking to be exceedingly funny.[10] Centuries before, Ibn Battuta had witnessed a more serious disaster. He had set out for Gebze with his slave girl and two slave boys in the company of a Turkish woman on horseback accompanied by her manservant. At the ford at Sakariya, she was thrown from her horse. The servant tried desperately to rescue her but both of them were carried away. Men on the opposite bank dived in and saved her but the servant was lost. He had mistaken the site of the unmarked ford. Later, Ibn Battuta's own girl fell off the back of his mount while crossing yet another ford but was quickly rescued and admonished for her carelessness.[11]

Apart from beggars, among whom were the Kalandar dervishes with women amongst them, only great ladies travelled far except for the few who undertook the *hajj*, or pilgrimage to Mecca. It was necessary to travel in company and properly protected at the pace of the camels, which were the most important baggage animals. These were carefully tended and were not expected to exceed their limited mileage each day, which depended on their breed and the weight they were carrying. It was nothing to encounter a train of 1,000 of them burdened with lumber from the forest round Karamursel on the Gulf of Izmit or a load of wild liquorice root on the road to Aydın.

Such a journey was long and without joy since the *kervansarays* and *hans*, though plentiful and grand in some cases, were without comfort: but the traveller was safely locked in at night. Nor would a Wife of Bath have been permitted to enliven the journey although it must never be forgotten that rules were quietly broken in Ottoman times: and since. A few remarkable women who did travel in the provinces have left no record of their escapades before the nineteenth century. There can be no doubt of the provincial nostalgia for Istanbul. In the nineteenth century, itinerant painters, whose frescoes are gifted with humble charm, travelled from place to place painting scenes on the walls of the main rooms of *konaks* or even mosques. Again and again, the subject would be the great mosque of Süleyman or a paddle-steamer on the Bosporus, as if each house were lived in by Chekhov's 'Three Sisters' with their refrain of 'Oh, to go to Moscow!' – anywhere rather than Berdichev or Malatya.

The Great City

At first glance, Istanbul was overwhelmingly large compared with a provincial town. Including its suburbs, there were 600,000 inhabitants towards the end of the eighteenth century[12] and possibly 5,000 domestic slaves as distinct from those of royal households and the elite. When one considers the number of migrants from the Balkans and Anatolia, it only seems surprising that there were not more since the continual decrees forbidding peasants to settle were ignored. The hordes had never ceased coming. But it was a city of catastrophes where death was the richest harvester. Until the second half of the twentieth century, the city was unable to maintain its population by natural increase. In the sixteenth century the population of the Balkans fell from 8 to 3 million. Romania's population of 1 million in 1700 was halved a mere 50 years later. Only the population of Salonika rose steadily. All these regions were also subject to one disaster or another.

The greatest enemy was the plague, which at its peak in 1467 achieved a climax of 600 deaths in a day in Istanbul. Each year the foretaste of an epidemic came in late March or early April and finally blossomed in August to die away by October. This coincided with the campaigning season although there was no recorded connection. It was the right moment for the sultan and his troops to be away from the capital. The disease also struck in the Balkans. The population of northern Bulgaria, Bosnia and Belgrade suffered badly in the eighteenth century. In Istanbul 100,000 people died in 1719 and 1770; in 1786, allegedly, no less than half of the city's population perished. This is hard to believe even with mass graves. There was no question of cremation. The caravan from Iran[13] was the source of infection as were merchant ships in Izmir. Ports in general were the worst affected places.

A devastating earthquake struck Istanbul in 1508, and in 1688 Izmir was completely destroyed by another. Successful trading towns were rapidly rebuilt but those that were struggling were finally ruined.[14] Early in the morning of 22 May 1766 there was the worst earthquake recorded in Istanbul since Byzantine times and the terrible weather of the sixth century. Much of the city was damaged, including the domes of major mosques. But because most of the houses were built with wooden frames, they were shaken but survived.

Great fires were frequent and devastating, particularly in the eighteenth-century city when area after area was burnt to leave them full of the giant bird-cages described by the merchant Roger North in the seventeenth century. These wooden ribs survived to make rebuilding easier in a few cases but whole neighbourhoods were left derelict for decades. The fire of 1787 attacked the suburbs in Thrace and killed 40,000 people. On 11 September 1687[15] – exactly a century before – fire had broken out in the palace of Topkapı and reached the Harem. Not only could it have been prevented and put down, had fire-fighters been allowed into the Harem, but the women could have escaped if the eunuchs had not barred the doors to prevent them exposing themselves in their own garden: a thought more horrifying than the flames. The governor of the city ordered the gates to be opened but his command was resisted until new orders came from the sultan himself and the terrified prisoners fled the flames although one great lady died of fright next day.

Successive governments made it a first principle that Istanbul should never be without bread, another tenet learned from the Romans. Each time that there was a shortage, there was a moment of crisis.[16] There were certainly periods when grain was dangerously short. On one occasion, the Grand Vezir lost his nerve and it was the sultan himself who rode out to confront an organized phalanx of women who were protesting in force. He persuaded them to go in peace and bread arrived rapidly. It was in short enough supply to rise in price, which meant that the poorest suffered, but the situation never reached famine conditions[17] although malnutrition contributed to the spread of epidemics and the lack of resistance to disease. Although the approach of famine saw shops looted[18] and attacks on churches and foreigners, there was little looting of property as such. Until 1860 the city's water was good,[19] due to reservoirs in the Belgrade Forest and pipes from the hills and mountains of Bulgaria, and it had been the best imaginable until 1732. Yearly, some 530 million litres were collected. But water stored in cisterns had not been used for drinking since before Byzantine times.

The poverty-stricken and the homeless leave few records, but they existed in numbers and among them were criminal elements given to violence.[20] The unruly students, hotheaded and arrogant, were as bad; leaving aside the overbearing bullies who had once been the victorious janissaries. Dalloway attributed most of the robberies and murders to the soldiery and to clan feuds.[21]

The beggars were banded in a guild of their own and their master was exceedingly rich. Many belonged to a dervish order and many of these knew nothing about Sufism but were charlatans. The Kalandar order believed that courtesy was a concession to worldliness when one's duty was only to please God. The women attached to the order performed the same ritual as the men[22] and, by way of thanks for a gift, would therefore stroke their chins as if possessed of luxuriant beards – as did the children. They wore scanty rags in all seasons and the children followed in their steps. There is no doubt that they were miserably poor and to be found all over the empire. Passers-by were embarrassed and hounded by one group after another while they danced and shouted during the mosque prayers until silenced by gifts.[23]

The worst slum in Istanbul was at Yedikule, the Castle of the Seven Towers, where the stench of the tanneries outside the wall and the grime of the inhabitants alike put honest women to flight. The tanners and their families out-gypsied the gypsies while rootless bachelors pursued such women as there were or robbed the men to the extent that the captain-general of the janissaries had to inspect the neighbourhood every evening. One is left with the claim made by Anderson (whose research was financed by Robert College, now the University of the Bosporus) that there were 1,000 whores in Istanbul, a figure invented by himself and certainly an underestimate were one to include Pera or Üsküdar. A police survey of 1921 shows there to have been between 4,000 and 4,500 such women of whom half were unregistered. There were Greeks, Armenians and Jews but very few Turkish girls among them[24] except at Üsküdar.

Social Services

After the conquest of Constantinople in 1453, Fatih Sultan Mehmet founded his hospital with 70 rooms and a staff of 200. There were musicians and singers to cheer the insane, who made up by far the greatest number of inmates. The wilder sufferers were chained and, at the corresponding hospital founded by Süleyman the Magnificent in the sixteenth century, were kept in an entresol where they could be neither seen nor heard except by morbid sightseers. The care of the sick was the duty of the family, which meant the women, until the illness became too grave or, with the mad, the patient became unmanageable. There were areas for both sexes with appropriate nurses but men occupied the larger part of any hospital.

At Avratpazarı, there was one hospital devoted entirely to women which had been founded by Hasseki Hürrem, the wife of Süleyman. It was in an area where women could trade in goods and where at one time there was a market for women slaves. The entrance was not through a grand central gate but a door at the side. This opened into a vestibule where the visitor had to turn sharp right as a protection against a man glimpsing a woman patient. The staff were all women and nursing lore was handed down from generation to generation. There were no women doctors. A male doctor was only permitted to take the pulse of a veiled woman so that he had to diagnose her condition from her wrist, her own diagnosis and any moan that she emitted. There grew up a tradition of loud moans and groans in order to attract attention to the particular source of pain. Some women were believed to be in close contact with the spirit world.[25] Their skills must have worked from time to time or the psychic ladies would have been put out of business. The odds were even. But magic was always seen to be evil, even when it could lure the supernatural powers to fulfil their duty of healing. All objects in nature were still believed to be alive and to inhabit the spirit world.

The heart of the welfare policies of the Ottoman administration was the *Vakuf* (the Arabic *Waqf*). Put simply, a wealthy man endowed a charitable foundation in order to do good with his wealth as a form of after-life insurance. His donation also served to mitigate death duties, which could not be levied on such an endowment. Moreover, the directorship of such an establishment was as well paid an office as was possible since it would remain the exclusive right of members of the family. There were no municipal services and the *Vakuf* was, therefore, a keystone of the social order.

All was not quite as liberal as it appeared, however. Most princesses founded and endowed charities, a task delegated to them by the sultan. An example of this was the grand refuge and soup kitchen founded in Jerusalem by Hasseki Hürrem. The sultan agreed to her using state assets on the project, which was a corrupt way of displaying personal benevolence for the good of the princess's soul. The transaction casts a shadow over the light of royal charities. The foundation had a mosque, numerous rooms for pilgrims and the large kitchen which supplied bread and soup to the poor twice a day. It supported 182 old or helpless men, but also women and children. Later, the tax revenues from 25 villages had to be added. Chicanery and corruption set in during the eighteenth century but appear to have been eradicated with some severity.[26]

The Streets

Life in Istanbul was not very different from life in other cities and the streets were thronged with working-class women as well as men. Apart from pedlars of everything from water to blue beads, there were singing women[27] who amused the passers-by. Naturally, the fountain became the rallying-point for women and gossip and was the centre of the life of a neighbourhood. But until the nineteenth century, no woman of any status walked in the streets unless protected by a man.

Woman on her way to the hamam, *followed by her slave* (F. Taeschner, *Alt-Stambuler . . .*, Hanover 1925)

Most women had no status to worry about and were to be seen everywhere. Social taboos faded and by the late nineteenth century women frequented the bazaars, which then deliberately catered for them, while the space given to armour and weapons ceased to dominate the immense Covered Bazaar in Istanbul with its two magnificent *bedestens,* or halls, for the sale of valuable goods and, for a time, the auction of slaves. The city was always remarkably free from ruffianly behaviour towards people whom the men did not know. It might be said that the person most likely to be hit on the nose was a male cousin. Only in the twentieth century are there references to boorish behaviour. Raw recruits pushed unveiled women off the pavements but this appears to have expressed the arrogance of ignorant youth and irritation at seeing a plum which they could not pluck rather than expressing a religious or political view of changing times.

Slavery

Ottoman slavery belonged very much to its times, which it overran in the nineteenth century just as did the United States, in the view of newly sensitive British statesmen of the era. Both societies were concerned with obtaining rough labour cheaply and this was hard on both men and women. In the Ottoman empire both could hope to be reprieved and to work for themselves. The women were only educated in domestic work or decorous idleness and most were illiterate like many of the men. This generalization ignores some successful, able and gifted women who were determined to liberate and sustain themselves.

Forms of slavery in Islam were inherited from far and near and had a long history. They produced a large and powerful military caste and a number of mothers of sultans who were remarkable for their skilled use of power.[28] Since many Ottoman slaves were manumitted, a freed man had a special relationship with his former master and could be adopted into the family. The Abbasid dynasty was so voracious that the family had 33,000 kin. Patronage was merged with procreation so that a slave could say, 'You are my people. It was you who trained me.' A slave was not just a financial investment but an emotional one as well.[29] Manumission was contractual if a woman bore her master a child and slaves often converted to Islam so that they could not be resold after the death of their master.[30] The *Şariat* ordained that no Moslem could be a slave. Manumission was an act of piety.[31] It was traditional to praise a master who educated his slave girl, then freed her and married her.[32] Some Ottoman women were well enough educated to meet scholars on equal terms but they never became teachers as women did in tenth-century Spain. There was also an adage that women were not taught to write but only to know the Koranic chapter on Light by heart. In the great days of the empire, there were far greater numbers of imported slaves and this was reflected in the considerable number of manumissions.

In Cyprus in the seventeenth century, to give only two examples, a son inherited and immediately freed his late father's slave and a widow freed one inherited from her husband. One statistic on Cyprus shows that two-thirds of the white slaves sold were male whereas only half the black slaves were male. Slaves came from Russia, Caucasia and Hungary besides one Greek, Georgian and Croatian each, all male.[33]

Bursa records reflect much the same situation, with the freeing of 280 men and 221 women between 1492 and 1493, and 363 men and 335 women between 1501 and 1503. These records show that, although many different races were involved, between 1511 and 1513 there were two principal sources of slaves: Russia supplied 125 men and 111 women and Bosnia 46 men and 47 women. There were also 32 Albanians, 30 Circassians, 19 Poles, 18 Indians, 9 Croatians, 8 Franks and only 3 blacks. There were only 2 Tatars, Wallachians and Serbs, and a solitary Georgian.[34]

Success was possible for freed slaves. On gaining her freedom in the sixteenth century, a trained silk weaver at Bursa procured a loom and became prosperous by selling brocade.[35] Brocade was made by slaves because it was such heavy labour; for the same reason, Venetian and Genoese traders bought Levant slaves for the Italian market.

Since manumission[36] meant that there was a perpetually diminishing slave force, lively markets were created in Istanbul and Bursa, which proved an incentive for frontier forces to raid for merchandise. By the end of the sixteenth century, Tatars were the chief suppliers and slavery was the main support of the Crimean economy. In 1578, 17,000 slaves were imported. There was also a trade between Antalya and Alexandria in black slaves who were rounded up by Arab traders, sometimes by purchase from the tribal chieftain. The boys were deprived of their manhood in Coptic monasteries (such mutilation was abhorrent to a Moslem), where a high proportion of them died. Black women were bought to be domestics while men went to labour in the farms of the elite. There were even slaves who had their own property but it was centuries before they lost their servile status although some mingled with the free peasantry. In Bursa, a slave could work independently after a period of time specified in his contract; but it offered no guild rights, just as all domestic servants were unprotected. More than one Bursa woman was a textile dealer; others were rich enough to be able to cover their losses in a bad year and were even able to procure large loans.[37]

When White visited the Istanbul market in the mid-nineteenth century, he described it as lower down from the Column of Constantine than the Byzantine slave market had been.[38] Although the slave market was beginning to decline, it was still open from 8 a.m. to noon on every day except Friday. One end was in ruins and was no better than a rubbish dump. In the middle of the modest open *meydan* (square), there was a small *mescit* (mosque) which has now been rebuilt. The railed platforms where the merchants sipped their coffee can still be imagined but they have been built over, as have the rooms with latticed windows where the women were held in privacy. The two sexes were kept strictly separate and the women were dressed. In front of the mosque were the men from Africa and behind them were the white. On the east side were newly imported black women whose ignorance meant that they fetched a low price. They increased in value when they were trained since it was skill as servants that mattered. White women declined in value if they were 'second-hand'. In February 1843 a fine black who was recommended as a cook and seamstress had already been sold thirteen times over because of her ungovernable temper. An old *molla* (doctor of Islamic law) got her cheaply at £17. An unhappy girl who refused to walk was hit on the mouth and her nose bled. This was the only cruelty that White saw.

The gallery for 'second-hand' men, who were in chains if they misbehaved, was filled with thieves, arsonists and several others who were guilty of indecency. They were almost naked and sat sadly on the benches while women were inspected in private.[39] In 1831 the traveller George Keppel, later Earl of Albemarle, described the market as having the men in the middle and the women round the outside.[40] He noted that on the day of his visit most slaves were children who were well dressed. They were sold by auction as well as by contract. In the 1820s the Rev. Walsh noted that the inmates were cheerful and that there was none of the horror, grief and weeping that he had expected.[41] Cheerful and gay, the slaves used every means to attract attention and invite purchase.

By the middle of the nineteenth century, the Circassian dealers had moved to Tophane on the slopes below Pera, the European quarter, and by White's time the number of Circassian girls was declining. There were other white women along with them who had been bought to be educated and then resold. In three or four years a speculative purchase could fetch six times the original price. It was here that young and wealthy libertines came to select concubines. In the mid-nineteenth century a black slave intended for domestic work cost between 1,500 and 2,500 piastres, or 5,000 piastres for someone exceptional. But however beautiful she might be, that was the limit. A white girl without a defect could fetch 10–15,000 piastres and even 45,000 if she was exceptionally beautiful and well educated. Such a girl was likely to become the wife of some grandee. If Egyptian women were poorly regarded, Abyssinians were much prized.

The average number of slaves for sale on one day was about 300, a third of whom were not 'new'. There was a higher tax on white slaves than black. In the sixteenth century the slave market in Istanbul was in Jewish hands;[42] the white women were Circassians, Russians or Poles in the main, and they were taught music. Until the end of the seventeenth century, no Christian could purchase a slave unless a Moslem friend acted as an intermediary. In the sixteenth century, Sanderson, a leading English merchant in Istanbul, had found that the auction of Christian slaves of both sexes took place in two market halls – presumably the two *bedestens* in the Covered Bazaar – and not in the open as was the case later. One may conclude that a market approach was more successful than sale by auction.

When purchased, the slave was entitled to have a contract drawn up. This would specify, first, that she could neither be hired out nor leased and, in theory, she could not be resold without her consent. In practice, slaves were sold and they could be married to whomsoever a master chose. The men could prepare for manumission and buy property; they could even set up in business but each was responsible for his own debts. If the slave died childless, the master took everything that he had left. Some slaves were bought to perform particular tasks which, when discharged, meant that they were set free. Few women were able to follow such routes to freedom and manumission, after about a dozen years. For them, freedom was not necessarily a blessing any longer. However, the owner had to provide for them and not just thrust them out onto the street. Many preferred to stay rather than face a life which was the equivalent to that of a widow without children since the demands of *harem* life, even for a servant, were rarely arduous.

Concubines were in a class apart, promoted by their beauty of face and person. Ideal beauty was established by the Uyghurs as an oval face with an Augustine nose surmounted by black brows that met. For a concubine there was the possibility of marriage with her master even if she were to be the fourth wife. Only the wealthiest men could afford such a luxury since nothing could be taken from the first wife, yet all four had to be treated equally by Koranic law reinforced by custom. The size of their rooms, the richness of their dresses and the elegance of their furnishings had to be the same for each.

After signing her contract, the slave was taken to the tax master and her dues paid. There followed a period of probation in case there were undeclared defects to discover. At their new home, black women would be proudly displayed but white women were secluded in the *harem* or its garden. Slaves, however, were slaves. They could be killed wantonly with impunity for any offence although the household were likely to restrain violence (and even if there was violence, the punishment was a modest fine). Ironically, property laws stipulated that the theft of a child who was a minor was a crime if she were a slave because she had the value of her purchase price – whereas the theft of a free child was not a crime because she had no recorded worth.

One other class of slave deserves mention because of his great influence on all the children of a family. This was the emasculated boy from Africa who acted as *lala*, or nurse and tutor, whatever the sex of the children until governesses came to replace him. The relationship often achieved a deep and lasting friendship into old age and the slave rarely left the household. The daughters, in particular, were unlikely to neglect him. The boys could remain good-looking even in old age when many eunuchs' faces shrivel felinely. Indeed, for obvious reasons, these were esteemed for their ugliness. There were voluntary slaves in the palaces of grandees who would advance their own preferment, but these had nothing to do with the market.[43]

In Cairo in the eleventh century Ibn Butlan, a Christian physician and theologian, wrote a guide to the purchase of slaves. It began forthrightly by stating that a lecher should never buy a slave because he would decide at first glance, which it was foolish to do. One should not buy at fairs or carnivals: at such sales, a boy could be transformed into a painted maiden. (This had its own ambiguities at a period when women's roles were everywhere performed by males.) It was just as possible to colour the eyes, dye the hair and fatten the cheeks of women.

Moreover, unguents and paints could cover sores, even those of lepers. It was essential to be sure that a female slave was not pregnant and thus it was necessary to feel breasts and stomach and also to be certain that she had no desire for salty food, which indicated a craving due to pregnancy. One should also beware of lesbian girls and of merchants who encouraged girls to flirt outrageously with passing young men.

Ibn Butlan gave a list of the virtues and vices of various races which would certainly be considered scandalous today. Turkish girls were prized but, in theory, no Moslem might ever be sold in the market in Istanbul. Elsewhere, they were esteemed for their beauty, their white skin and sweet eyes, and for having golden depths for generation. When they bore children, they treasured them. They were also refined and clean and did not have bad breath. But they could be sullen and had no sense of loyalty. Greek girls were rivals. These blondes were well-meaning, trustworthy, obedient and adaptable. Their serious blemish was their meanness. On the other hand, Armenian girls may have been beautiful but they had ugly feet and were coarse and dirty, thieves and useless for pleasure. However, they were well built, strong, energetic and hard workers.

Of the black slaves, the Zaghawa were considered the worst by Ibn Butlan. They were vicious and ill-natured grumblers, useless for pleasure, and did terrible things. From the country between Nubia and Ethiopia, the Bujja, however, were golden, beautiful, smooth, tender and brave: but they also stole. Ranked above all of them (even the Indians, who were prone to catch diseases) were the Nubians. They were tender and possessed delicacy, were pure but firm and religious and combined chastity with submissiveness.

In the mid-nineteenth century, the Ottoman government was actively suppressing the slave trade. The slave market in Istanbul was abolished in 1847. The Red Sea trade continued but with help from the British navy was more or less eliminated by the end of the century.[44]

Birth and the Nuptials of the Grand

The rites of passage of the rich were great occasions for lavish entertainment in the case of birth, circumcision and marriage. The more of these events the better for the *harem* because it drew the complex interrelationships of the clans together, including those directly related and those only distantly connected by marriage. It

Midwife wearing a hotoz *headdress and carrying her staff, early nineteenth century* (A.E.M.)

meant a break in the monotony of daily life even if that was not always as boring as it was reported. For some, attending the celebration of the birth of a child was like going to the opera in Paris or London. There was the rigid etiquette, dressing up in the finest clothes and jewels and, also, the bringing of symbolic gifts according to one's purse.[45]

When the mother was six months into her pregnancy, the midwife made her first formal visit. The profession was held in such respect that she was entitled to a staff of office with which to mark the dignity of her walk. The position was hereditary in many cases which gave it an extra gloss. The midwife was a woman of a certain age and much experience and had probably acted for the family before or at least for a kinswoman or else she was popular with the families in the neighbourhood. When the mother's time was near, the walnut birth chair was brought to her room. Walnut was considered benevolent and the chair was extremely practical, with a solid rim as a seat and strong arms for the mother to grip when the child was actually born. It was believed to be the most comfortable and safest way of giving birth so long as there were willing hands to receive the baby. Of those there were many: not that the midwife would let anyone else interfere.

Customs varied slightly at the cutting of the umbilical cord. The common practice was for the midwife to cry, 'God is Great' three times and then give the baby its original name: for a girl, Eve (Havva), and for a boy, the names of heroes: Mehmet, Süleyman, Iskender . . . In Islam, it will be recalled, Eve is no more to blame for the expulsion from paradise than Adam – indeed, one gets the impression from the Koran that he was the more responsible for the catastrophe. Above all, Eve was the first woman's name and it was given to her by God. The father, who was sometimes present throughout the birth, then made the call to prayer three times unless an *imam* were present. The father then gave the child its real name – since every woman in the world could not be called Eve. Sometimes it was the father who pronounced the child's name as the cord was cut.[46] The baby was then bound, swaddled and dressed. As a precaution against the evil eye, a Koran, a blue bead and a clove of garlic were hung over the bed under a silk canopy which the newborn would later treasure for luck. Only then could the father escape back to work.

On the next day, mother and child were removed to a sumptuous bed in the reception room, which was covered in rich quilts embroidered with gems. All was now ready for her to receive the long train of guests who came with gold coins. They were served with coffee, tea, or a special sherbet made with red-dyed sugar and cloves. Sipping one of these, the guests would call on God to bless the mother's milk. They made a din and puffed out clouds of smoke from their *naghiles* so as to drive evil spirits away. Astrologers then determined whether the bringing out of the cradle should be on the third or the seventh day.

On the day chosen, for the first time since the birth, the mother got up for prayers and the lavishly decorated cradle was brought out. There were fresh and dried fruit and nuts to eat and gypsies danced. Then the midwife led the way for the women who had come to see the baby placed alone in its cradle. Life could return to normal; the ceremony was completed; the baby had been separated from its mother and had survived the period of greatest danger. If it cried, it was given a marzipan in a stocking to suck and if that failed it had a dose of poppy-seed oil.

Forty days passed and then the mother took the baby to the cool room of the *hamam*, which would become very much a part of the infant's life. This purification ceremony had very ancient roots from long before the Virgin Mary's celebration of the occasion. There was nothing now to look forward to until the emergence of the first tooth when there would be more gifts and renewed songs and dancing. Wheat that had been softened by boiling was sprinkled on the baby's head and thirty-two grains were threaded into a necklace.

This was a lavish version of what greeted a child in a village just as the marriage ceremony was also much grander. It was not simply that the celebrations were more elaborate and costly but that issues of property and wealth were so much more important.[47] From the time that a girl first wore the veil at the age of 12, her mother was actively concerned with finding her a husband. She also had the *harem* hard at work preparing a trousseau which would include embroidered cloths, furnishings and rugs. The child would be taught to sew and also to cook. But she was not necessarily taught to read until late in the eighteenth century. Like letter-writing, many regarded it as a waste of time. The Mongols had overcome the problem of a girl wanting to marry an unsuitable fellow by marrying her before puberty. In some primitive Asian tribes, children could even be engaged in the womb if great political inheritances were involved. Among the Ottomans, infant marriages were almost taboo outside the sultan's family.

Elopement was rare in wealthy families although it did occur. At the very end of the dynasty, the son of the Great Chamberlain was to escape over the palace wall and carry his bride off to what proved to be a very successful marriage. This was exceptional and not at all like the village boy whose parents were too poor to raise the bride-price: he had to carry off his girl if he were ever to marry at all and he knew that probably he would be quickly forgiven.[48] A reverse of this story is contained in a miniature showing a mother who was determined to put a stop to her son's philandering and made him marry an old woman hidden under the bridal cloth. This woman was said to be very wealthy; she had also agreed to play her part in the deception and she let the boy divorce her there and then. The hero was so horrified that he agreed to marry a more suitable bride as quickly as possible. As with the poor so with the rich, and there does seem to have been some latitude in the choice – but not before the professional matchmakers had earned their fee.

One problem was that while the prospective mother-in-law could admire the bride-to-be at the *hamam*, the groom was not available for inspection. Sometimes the final concessions over property meant that the matchmaker would introduce strangers to each other who were new to the parents as well. In most cases there had been contact between the two mothers even if they were not connected by marriage. The negotiation of bride-price, dowry and the gifts that the groom would give the bride could be lengthy. Once concluded, the bride and groom were told of the maternal choice and they were immediately under pressure to let their marriage go ahead. The groom sent his future fiancée gifts of jewels, fine clothes, perfumes and mirrors as the first of the presents which would continue to flow at intervals just as with a peasant boy's engagement. After three days, the agreed contract was drawn up and the *imam* went to see the groom and read the contract out. At this point, agreement was assured and, after pledging himself three times, the groom signed the document. The *imam* then hastened to the bride's house and spoke to her from behind the *harem* door. Once she had assented, the document was taken back to the groom and, in theory, bride and groom were immediately cut off from each other.

Eventually the week of the wedding arrived. On the Tuesday the bride was formally bathed at the *hamam*, which would be crowded with gossips. On the Wednesday she was given a piece of gold and she put on her henna which was a symbol of happiness. Thursday was her wedding day, when the bride was established in splendour. The women brought her gifts with which to hedge her hair. For a brief moment, the groom was admitted to admire his invisible bride under her heavy red veil. He then rejoined his friends and the male members of his family in order to enjoy the wedding banquet. Just like the village boy, he then proceeded to his new home, or that of his parents if he were too young to have one of his own, in time for evening prayer. The bride was brought to her new home and at last the couple could be alone.

Writing on Bosnia, the historian Lopasic quoted an adage by way of consolation for a disappointed bride – it is better to be with a boy even if he is stupid.[49] (Such a marriage could occur because the groom's parents wanted a capable woman to manage his affairs.) Once again, on the Friday, bride and groom attended festivals separately, each with their own sex. Then on the Monday there was a final celebration for the older members of the family.[50] The girl now had her own room and servant but would rarely see her husband by day. The boredom of the long days was broken by visiting traders who dealt in expensive stuffs, by music if the girl or her servant could play an instrument and, presumably, by sighs. One rich Bosnian's wife was numerate and she was busy some of the time on the household accounts. This must have been true of women all over the empire since intellect was not confined to the Balkans. There were many visits within the families and visits to the rites of passage of a plethora of young relations.

The Last Rite

Death was not a festival but in Islam it was the most important day of anyone's life. This is why it was celebrated by those who remain behind: and not a birthday. When death came and the family filled the room, the last breath was a signal for wailing to which paid mourners added professional cries. Thus demons were kept at a distance and the soul was safe. If death were slow in coming to a Yakut, a mug of water was placed beside the bed so that the soul could wash itself in the moments before departure: the Yakuts were not worried by death because they believed that Hades was simply dark and boring.

After death, Ottoman women were washed by their own sex with gentle hands because the body was still conscious of pain. Seven balls of cotton wool were covered in calico and soaked in warm water, to be inserted in the seven orifices of the body. Cotton wool was placed between the fingers and the toes and also in the armpits. The body was completely clad in a sleeveless white shroud which was of particular sanctity if the owner had brought it back from the *hajj*. Pepper, spices and rose-water were put in other crevices – the work was completed swiftly because, according to the *Şariat*, the corpse had to be interred on the following day. Rich shawls were laid on top and three straps pulled under the body.[51] In theory it was time to go, but in practice this was not always true. In Central Asia caravans of the dead on their way to a sacred place could horrify travellers across the desert. And when Süleyman the Magnificent died on campaign, he was said to be ill and his corpse was carried for several days concealed from all but the Grand Vezir, Sokollu Mehmet Pasha, so that his son, Selim II, could meet the army and claim the throne: which he did. The corpse of Cem took months before it at last reached Bursa from Italy.

The women stayed behind because their cries might disturb the dignity of death. Christians and foreigners were also excluded. One other strict rule was that a corpse could never be cut open even if a crime had been committed. Only a mother who was with child was exempt. Four men carried the body to the cemetery on a stretcher and they were changed after the magic number of forty paces. It was considered an act of respect to touch the bier, just as it was in Greece. The grave should be as deep as a man's belly and a woman's shoulders.[52] Six mourners took hold of the bands to lift the corpse off the stretcher and since she came from the earth, to the earth was the woman returned, lying on her side facing Mecca. Celalettin Rumi, the great Sufi mystical poet who effectively founded the aristocratic Mevlevi order, was very clear about the rites of burial. The Mother can nurse her child better than a coffin. This should never come between them because the dead should be committed to the earth and no intermediary should intervene between the child and the long affectionate Parent.[53] If the deceased were poor, she might share her grave but only if there were a wall of earth dividing it into two.

The *imam* called on a dead woman by her name and that of her mother. If it were unknown, once again as at birth, a woman was called Eve. After walking three times round the grave the mourners left, but the *imam* remained to perform his most important task because of the mysterious connection between soul and body. He waited for two angels to appear and was there to guide the deceased with her answers to their questions.

After either seven or forty days the ceremonies of commemoration were held. The Ottomans sometimes waited fifty-two days, which was unique in Islam. Strictly speaking, the ceremonies were not religious. Women's gravestones were carved with flowers and verses of hope and if a headstone fell it was considered unlucky to set it up again. In the sixteenth century, cypress trees were still planted and at the end of each year were measured to see if they had outgrown other trees planted at the same time. If so, that soul was nearer to heaven.

The peace of a cemetery, its shade and the recognition that in the end is the beginning made them favourite places in which the Ottomans could walk or sit. Moreover, if possible, there was a beautiful view to admire and from which to draw comfort. This was quite apart from a family's affection and loyalties, which were renewed beside a loved one's grave.[54] Many couples used to wander among unknown graves and sit, hand in hand, upon some lettered stone to exchange their vows and to lay plans for the future on the very threshold of the past – provided, that is, that no ill-omened rainbow bridged the graves. One must suppose that the young did manage to escape home taboos in the early nineteenth century and find somewhere to be alone together, and not only among corpses. In 1810 Hobhouse – a friend of Byron and a future British cabinet minister, and on a special military mission to Turkey at the time – saw groups of ladies walking or sitting on tombstones or within coloured tents pitched in the nearest open area.[55] Movable stalls selling sherbet, ices and fruit were surrounded by children and their attendants, who watched local wrestling since the sport had religious as well as ancestral connotations.

The Home and the Escape from It

The richer women enjoyed a somewhat pointless life of family celebrations, visits and picnics. Within the tight world of the *harem* their relationships with their husbands might prosper. If the wife's looks faded and he took a girl for pleasure, nobody was surprised. Their affection for each other and their children could make life tolerable if not idyllic. Women could succeed in having their own way and the ablest participated in decisions outside the home. Isolated in their comfort, they suffered little from the rubbish heaps and the packs of dogs that plagued the poor. One traveller noted Jewish women sitting on rubbish in Balat admiring the view but added that it was the only place from which they could see the Golden Horn – there was no question of their escaping to the meadows of the Bosporus. The rich had one other escape that was denied the poor and that was the *hajj*, for which their closeted life ill prepared them.

The *hajj* was an obligation laid on all Moslems except the poor, who could be represented by someone from their neighbourhood. The well-off could also substitute a scroll of miniatures depicting the stations on the road and, finally, the Great Mosque at Mecca. These were important since it was not the duty of a husband to pay for his wife's journey: it was she who had to give him her own money. There were occasions when a husband paid, not out of the goodness of his heart, but because the couple were childless and they made the pilgrimage together in the hope of finding God's beneficence.

Usually, only a small percentage of a caravan was made up of women. Some wealthy princess might travel with a garden carried on the backs of camels and with skins of water which were constantly replenished. Her tents were silk salons and she brought her own guards.[56] She was not likely to be an Ottoman. Only four royal Ottomans, and no sultan, ever made the *hajj*: they included the wives of Ahmet II (1691–95) and Mahmut I (1730–54). Even for a rich man, the tent would be humble and his camels carrying provender be few. The expenses were higher because for each camel loaded with his belongings there had to be a second carrying food for the beasts.

There were reports of women being abandoned at some poor town or miserable desert village en route to Mecca because they were too weary to proceed or were ill. Although they had paid in full, they had become a burden. Tricked and robbed in every way by many scoundrels on the route, most nevertheless survived to see their homes again. Even the wealthy who earned money by taking goods for sale as they journeyed could be reduced to poverty and beggary. Every possible disaster lay ahead, especially when the main caravans had united at Damascus and had paid their considerable dues to the *beylerbey* (viceroy or 'lord of lords'), who was enriched by the pilgrimage every year – that is, if he were lucky enough to hold his lucrative office for more than twelve months.

The journey was from water source to water source along well-established routes. Caravans could be very large indeed and shortages of water were inevitable at one point or the other. Then there was the terror of murderous bedouin raiders who attacked stragglers and even the flanks of the caravan. Moreover, it was the duty of the troops to defend the heart of the caravan where the sultan's gifts[57] were carried, including the great embroidered cloth that enveloped the hall of the Kâbe (Ka'aba) stone and which was renewed each year. It took precedence above all else: for the black stone of Abraham was the eye of the needle of the Moslem compass. In 1580 there were 40,000 pilgrims and 64,000 animals carrying supplies. In 1807 soldiers and officials alone needed 600 camels and the pilgrims numbered 80,000 men, 2,000 women and even 1,000 children. It was, however, local women who were accused of misusing the mosque courtyard by bringing their children to play while they chatted in the sanctuary.

View over the Harem at Topkapsaray, with the tower of the Divan and the chimneys of the kitchen behind

CHAPTER 5

Bedfellows

'It Is Not Enough to Sleep with Women'[*]

As we have seen, the institution of the *harem* is a reflection of the Byzantine gynaecium and those of many older civilizations as well. Its concept is that of the privilege of privacy and the protection of women, whether in a modest home or the palace of the sultan. Prior to the nineteenth century, most is known about the wives and daughters of the ruler and even with them there are gaps in their histories. With some of them nothing is known except the dates of their death. In the early days Christian princesses or daughters of local lords were married by the *beys* (rather than sultans) of the Ottoman dynasty. Such marriages were political just as they were in Europe. Even Murat II (1421–44; 1446–51) preferred marriage alliances rather than actually conquering a kingdom. Protection was less costly than war and the tribute was collected for him.

As with Nilüfer, the powerful wife of Orhan, these women could be strong-willed and well able to rule the capital when the sultan was away on the frontier. The policy resulted in the royal children being half-Christian in origin; and many of their mothers were covertly, but with

---

[*]Turgut Uyar, poet, 1927–1985.

the consent of their husbands, still Orthodox in their beliefs. When there were several dynastic marriages, the women were subordinate to the first wife to bear a son – it was he who would become heir to the sultanate although the succession was not always in the direct line, particularly if the boy were too young to rule. Curiously, it was succession by uncles that eventually did the most harm to the dynasty because it brought intellectually or emotionally impoverished men to power.

In the fourteenth century Murat I married several Greek princesses, including a daughter of the powerful Byzantine family of the Cantacuzenus. His senior wife was a Greek like his mother and assumed the pretty name of Rosebird or Bluebird (Gülçiçek or Gökçiçek) after the marriage. She was to bear him Bayezit I (1389–1402), known as Yıldırım, or the Thunderbolt, who was a swift-moving commander reliant on his prestigious cavalry. It did not save him when Timur came and he was defeated at Ankara in 1402 in spite of the loyalty of his Christian troops. Deeply influenced by his mother, Bayezit married Christian wives who included a daughter of the emperor John V Palaeologus. But the wife who mattered the most to him was Despina, a daughter of Lazar I, king of Hungary. She was accused of wielding too much power but she was not the mother of his eventual successor, Mehmet I (1413–21), after an interregnum devoted to civil war between the four royal brothers.[1] She was famed for being captured with the sultan after his defeat at Ankara and was probably made to wait at Timur's victory feast. Three months later, the sultan died of humiliation and despair and her own tragic history after this is lost. Had she been the mother of a sultan she would have been better remembered, but it is not clear if Mehmet was her son.

∿ ∿ ∿

At the beginning of the sixteenth century, Selim I conquered Syria and Egypt after first routing the Shah of Iran. He himself was conquered by cancer and left a widow who was the mother of Süleyman Kanuni, or the Law-giver (1520–66), known in the west as the Magnificent. It is clear that Hafise Sultan was a formidable disciplinarian and could keep her son's Harem under her control although the inevitable rivalry between Gülbahar Sultan and Hasseki Hürrem was fierce, since the two mothers were fighting for the lives of their sons. Gülbahar had borne Süleyman his heir, Mustafa (following on the tragic death in 1543 of Mehmet, who would have made a brilliant sultan), before Hürrem had entered the palace. The problem was simple. In order to prevent a War of the Roses or the fratricidal strife that followed after the death of Yıldırım Bayezit in 1402, Mehmet II had decreed that every brother of a new sultan should be strangled by a silken cord (it was deemed blasphemy to shed royal blood). Were Mustafa to become sultan then the sons of Hürrem would be doomed and their sons as well.

After the death of Hafise Sultan, Gülbahar had to fight hard and long to protect Mustafa: that he lived until 1553 and the age of 38 is a tribute to the tenacity of her hold on Süleyman and also to his humanity within the law. But the sultan was not young in 1553 (he was approaching 60), and Mustafa had unwisely let his popularity with the army grow until the Grand Vezir Rüstem Pasha, who was Hürrem's man and married to her daughter, could warn the sultan that his son was a threat to his life. Inevitably, Mustafa was executed in the royal camp at Amasya.[2]

That Gülbahar survived her son's death and was not exiled to the Old Saray is evidence that Süleyman continued to be fond of her. She had come to him at Manisa where he was governor, perhaps due to his mother. She must have been chosen by her, if the sultan's mother did choose, because of her vivacity and her looks. It was surely this zest for life that carried her into old age with but one married granddaughter to console her – the other had predeceased her – with shared memories of Mustafa.

When Gülbahar died at the age of 80 in 1581, she was buried beside Mustafa in his *türbe*, or tomb, at Bursa which was large. It has outstandingly fine panels of Iznik tiles. The Grand Vezir had to resign and Süleyman's reign was now troubled by Hürrem's rival sons, Selim and Bayezit, who were fighting for their own lives. Bayezit lost, although he was probably Hürrem's favourite: but this was after her own death.

Of their mother we know more than usual and, at the same time, very little. Most of what is known is gossip fed to Europeans who had never even stepped inside the *saray* and whose informants told them what they wanted to hear but not what they really knew, which was mostly nothing. Alexandra (as Hürrem was originally called), the daughter of an Orthodox priest, was said to have been born in Ruthenia. She herself laid claim to being a Pole. She was carried off by Tatar raiders who knew at once that she was valuable goods. She was sold to the then Grand Vezir Ibrahim Pasha, the lifelong and most intimate friend of the young sultan, and probably fetched a high price. There can have been no question but she was a virgin for Ibrahim, against whom she was to bear a grudge for having been briefly her master, thought her fit only for the sultan to whom he presented her.

She was the most secretive and hidden of women by inclination and we are told by witnesses who never saw her that she was small but well-proportioned. Probably she was and, whatever her face may have been like, it must have been transformed by intelligence and wit. Since she was a Slav, she is likely to have been fair but the only certainty is that no portrait among the thousands of her was either drawn, painted or engraved from life. The fashion for hanging versions of them in the salons of Venice, where she was known as Roxelana, had the one virtue that whatever she looked like she did not look like them. She was born intelligent and was to live among highly intelligent people including exceptional, if disagreeable, Grand Vezirs like Rüstem or Sokollu Mehmet Pasha, whom she did not like. She could not but be hostile to the latter since he was a supporter of Gülbahar's son, Mustafa.

Hürrem, who ousted Gülbahar from Süleyman's passions, she certainly hated. Gülbahar is said to have called Hürrem 'sold meat' while the others called her 'Bosfor Sultan', meaning Sewer Princess; while there is no proof of this, the gossip probably reflected the natural hatred of one for the other. It was what the 'witness' would have said herself or himself in such circumstances. It should be borne in mind that the inmates of the Harem itself would not be in a position to report anything unless they were eunuchs. Moreover, Mustafa, when he was governor of a province, took his mother with him. Added to this, the women in the Harem may have fought for the throne for their sons, but they also fought for nothing at all out of sheer boredom. It is difficult to believe that Gülbahar would call Hürrem derogatory names which could be applied to any woman who was or, in her case, had been a slave. The thwarted mother could have thought of subtler insults, and probably did, but the lamb does not insult the veal in a butcher's shop by calling it 'sold meat'.

That Hasseki Hürrem captivated Süleyman from the first day to the last is true. When she predeceased him on 18 April 1558 he wrote one of his indifferent poems, but which never lacked passionate sincerity, in which he called her the springtime of his life. Movingly, since she was in her 50s and he in his 60s. And, movingly, it was in the springtime when she died. It cannot have been simply that she could read his mind – and there were gossips in the streets who spoke of witchcraft. The charge was so well enhanced in European households that it is difficult to eradicate from the history books. For thirty-eight years, Süleyman was in love with Hürrem with all his initial ardour. When she was gone, he had the great royal architect, Sinan, build her a tomb which was decorated with those dazzling spring flowers which only the potters of Iznik could achieve. He gave up pleasure. Gold was abandoned for earthenware and he was soberly dressed when once he had been arrayed in splendour. Her only real rival had been Ibrahim,[3] who had been Süleyman's boon companion from their youth. He was a quite exceptional statesman but was corrupted by power and lost his panache and modesty. With Hafise dead in March 1534, Ibrahim was exposed to Hürrem's enmity: in 1536 he was assassinated in his room in the *selamlık* at Topkapısaray which opened out of the sultan's apartment. No one was arrested and all the court was against him so that the charge has always been laid at Süleyman's and Hürrem's door.

In January 1541 there was a fire at the Old Saray (Eski Saray) in the centre of the city. For a time this was the home of the sultans as opposed to Topkapısaray which was the centre of government. It meant that the sultan was kept apart from his family all day and had the inconvenience of riding home through the crowd in the evening. The story was that Hasseki Hürrem seized her chance and succeeded in having the Harem moved to Topkapısaray, leaving the old palace to the women of dead sultans, except for the almighty Valide, and for the Harem hospital where royal confinements took place. She could now see her husband every day at almost any time. However, there are records that the then royal architect, Allaüddin, had supervised the building of a Harem at Topkapısaray between 1526 and 1528.[4] This was long before the Hürrem legend and, indeed, Kritovoulos wrote of 150 girls at Topkapısaray and 250 at the Old Saray as early after the conquest as 1475 – since the Greek was Mehmet II's secretary and accompanied him everywhere, his account may be accepted. One may speculate that the Harem was enlarged in the 1540s, which required the building of formidable vaults. At that period Süleyman was planning the building of his great complex on the Third Hill, the grandest possible site for a great mosque in the city. It meant the destruction of half the old Harem garden with its kiosks and waterworks, copses and singing birds.

Whatever the cause of the fire, which in any case was not sweeping, Hasseki Hürrem was now installed as a married woman in the Harem with grander apartments than before. She was endowed with an income of 5,000 ducats a year. Every girl in the Harem was entitled to *paşmakluk*, or slipper money, but the queenly income awarded Hürrem was in the form of a legal dowry and in no way a salary. Splendid festivities celebrated the wedding about which, sadly, no detailed account has yet been published.[5] It was an achievement that this was all but impossible even when royal alliances had been abandoned.

There was only one tragedy for Süleyman that could rank with Hürrem's death and that was the death from cholera of their son Mehmet on 6 November 1543. It was for Mehmet that his mourning father had built the first of Sinan's great mosques, and a tomb more brilliant than any that had gone before. The Şehzade mosque in Istanbul is a measure of Süleyman's misery. This Hürrem was able to assuage and, except when he was away on campaign, she could not bear to let him out of her sight. They spent their last long winter together at Edirne in the sprawling palace of pavilions in the woods and gardens on an island in the Tunca river. It was from there that she was carried to the Old Saray and its hospital to die. She was never to be the Valide and rule the palace for her son.

Selim II (1566–74) preferred wine and poetry to government which, ironically, he left to his mother's old enemy, Sokollu Mehmet Pasha. By now Sokollu was, like all Grand Vezirs, married to a princess which meant that he had to relinquish his first wife. There is a pretty, contemporary account of Hürrem and her daughter Mihrimah paying a visit to Selim II at Manisa where he was governor and his wife Nurbanu was pregnant. They were installed in the *yayla* above the palace and it must indeed have been a holiday from the formalities of court life. Both sultans and their wives did pay visits to their families. There is a sad miniature of Süleyman with Mustafa in Anatolia, for example. They also visited the royal tombs at Bursa. Like Gülbahar, mothers went with their young sons to their provincial governorships to supervise them: but not Hürrem whom Süleyman could not spare, or only for brief visits.

Selim II's sister, Mihrimah, accumulated vast wealth with the help of her rapacious husband although both spent enormous sums on charitable foundations partly, no doubt, to protect their children against death duties since all the privileges of royalty were denied them in almost all cases. It was better than being strangled. Mihrimah was said to have been the richest woman in the world: this was the cause of her fame in the nineteenth century, not her splendid mosques, and explains why there were so many grand hotels called after her along the Riviera.

Mihrimah's husband, Rüstem Pasha, was said to be a coarse Croat or

Albanian or Bosnian, almost what you please, all the more so because the intermingling of races in the Ottoman empire made such classifications dubious. He was also said to be brutal and rude, yet one ambassador found him courteous if serious; the rest appear to have relied on yet more gossip. One has no doubt of the loathing created by his economic policies, including a precipitous rise in taxes and the utterly venal sale of offices. His determination to combat inflation and the economic decline of the empire, partly due to the malevolent effect in Europe of the import of American silver, made him an invaluable minister and not 'the Louse', the title he earned from the populace, among others. The pinnacle of hatred was achieved when he put a purchase tax on flowers, which were particularly cherished by Ottoman society: but not on vegetables. Yet he must have been agreeable to his wife and he had the courtesy to die before Süleyman else Mihrimah might have found it difficult to run the Harem for Selim II.

Within the Harem

Astonishing numbers of women have been said to inhabit the Harem at Topkapısaray, so many that they would have had to live standing up. Even the sober Alderson suggested that there were 2,000 girls at one time. This is hard to believe even assuming that the figure included the servants probably bedding down in their dormitories in the vaults. In the time of Mehmet II who built the palace, his secretary, Kritovoulos, wrote that there were 3 or 4 beds to a room. In 1499 Bayezit II had 10 girls at Topkapısaray and 80 at the Old Saray, and this is a credible number. One reason why the girls were not forced to sleep in one another's arms was because they were weeded out. Another is that those *kadıns* who were mothers of the sultan's children, and the Valide, had serving girls who were members of the Harem. Hürrem had 100 maids of honour and a plethora of servants who did not sleep in the Harem itself. When married to Hürrem, Süleyman had no use for other women and the girls in the Harem were not concubines, although still chosen for their beauty. Its only function then was as a finishing school to educate elite girls to be the wives of the pages of the Palace School (Enderun Kolej, or College Within) when they graduated and received their first appointments.

Selim II's wife, Nurbanu, had a modest number of girls in her Harem: a total of some 150 students although there were allegedly 1,500 at the Old Saray.[6] This is an improbable number although there were large buildings there. Originally called Cecilia, Nurbanu was the illegitimate daughter of the distinguished Venetian house of Vernier-Baffo.[7] In September 1557 on his way from Corfu to Istanbul, Hayrettin Barbaros Pasha captured 1,500 youths and 1,000 girls, including Nurbanu who was then 12 years old. The admiral promptly gave this luminous and laughing beauty, from a canvas of Titian or Veronese, to the sultan.[8] Her Turkish name means the Princess of Light. Süleyman gave her to his son Selim, probably upon his appointment as governor of Karaman, when he was 18, in 1542. She was a year younger and well trained.[9] On 4 July 1546, which was the day of Barbaros' death, her son was born in the *yayla* above Manisa. Selim loved her as much for her great intelligence as for her beauty. She retained her loyalties to the Venetian Republic and wrote letters to the Doge. Since Selim avoided his official duties as best he could, Nurbanu's influence was considerable, especially when it came to the peace treaty signed on 7 March 1573 between the Ottomans and Venice and which was made possible by her *kira*, or agent.

Kiras brought trifles and luxuries to the Harem and executed all sorts of commissions. Those who were intelligent had great power for good or bad: such was the case with the *kira* of Safiye, Nurbanu's future daughter-in-law. But Esther Mandali was wisely chosen as *kira*: she was the daughter of a saintly father and herself renowned for her charity. It was she who handled Nurbanu's affairs with the Bailo (Venetian resident ambassador), Nicolo Barbarigo, and who wrote her letters for her.[10] One of these thanked the Doge for a bale of silk and the next for twenty-one damask robes in two colours and nineteen of cloth of gold. The third letter was concerned with a Moslem captive. In 1580 Nurbanu again thanked the Doge for gifts of gold and silk cloth. More significantly, Esther added that she was sure that her mistress retained many recollections of her homeland. Yet another letter complained about Nurbanu's own missive being lost at sea and she wrote brusquely about a gift of lapdogs because they were big and long-haired – they should have been white and small. When she was ill with cancer, her final letter was a request for cushions. She died on 7 December 1583 and the cushions probably arrived too late.

Selim II liked to sleep in the Harem and his son, Murat III (1574–95), made his home there. His beloved Safiye's failure to produce an heir after twenty years was to force Nurbanu, the first mother of a sultan to be called Valide Sultan, to ply Murat with concubines in order that he should achieve a son. She succeeded all too well since the surplus twenty or so had to be strangled after his death – so immediately, that one boy was not allowed to finish his cherries.[11]

Girls admitted to the Harem by gift rather than purchase had a clearly established curriculum.[12] They were a dazzlingly beautiful assembly since pashas vied with each other in search of girls who were worthy of their sultan in the hope of his favour. Thomas Dallam (who was sent to Murat with the gift of a water-organ combined with a clock from Queen Elizabeth I of England)[13] reported that he had stolen a brief glimpse of a few of them playing ball in their garden and, for once, his report is likely to be true because he was one of a very few foreigners to see the Fourth Court. Their plaited hair hung down their backs with tassels of small pearls woven onto the end and the worthy Lancastrian organ-builder declared the girls to be very pretty indeed. A little cap of gold perched on their heads and they wore pearl necklaces, a brooch and earrings. Their white breeches were fine as lawn so that the atmosphere was nearer to a monastery than a bordello. The rule of silence was strictly kept but they had fun knocking off eunuchs' turbans and pushing the stately gentlemen into the outdoor basin.[14]

The Pyramid

The Harem may be seen as a pyramid at the apex of which the Valide sat in far from lonely state, since all important business passed through her hands, not least discipline without which life would have been impossible. The women could be punished and beaten if they were insolent. Should they continue to be disobedient, they were sent to the Old Saray, stripped of their savings and so left without hope of marriage or any other future. Any girl suspected of witchcraft was threatened with being flung in a sack in the Bosporus; at least, according to Ottaviano Bon, the Venetian representative in Istanbul from 1604 to 1607. Until 1582 the Harem was under the same administration of the white eunuchs which controlled the Palace School where the elite boys were trained for the chief offices of the empire. The structure of training was the same too, but not the subjects. Both had affinities with the guild system. For example, the young girls were admitted to the Harem as *acemi*, which was the same term as that used for the boys and meant cadet rather than recruit. Like the pages, they were *kul*, or members of the larger family of the sultan, rather than slaves who could be bought or sold. The white eunuchs could propose which graduates

The Social Structure of the Ottoman Harem at Topkapısaray

Valide Sultan (queen mother). Mother of sultan. Ruled the Harem and was secluded on the death of her son

Hasseki Sultan (chief royal lady: princess). Mother of son(s); secluded if her only son died

Hasseki Kadın (mother of daughter/s). Four lady favourites ranking as wives. Could remarry on death of sultan

FREEDOM

ikbal or *hassodalik*
('fortunate girl': sultan's favourite).
If she had a child, she became a *kadın*

gözde or gedik
(girl 'in the eye' of the sultan)

privileged graduates of the Harem school

cariye or, Persian, *şahgird* (pupil; novice in training). Had lessons in music, singing, dancing and the arts of poetry and love; also in Turkish, Persian and religion. A few graduated: the rest were likely to marry officers or officials graduating from the Palace School (Enderun Kolej)

eunuchs and women servants

None of these women were Turks since no Moslem could be made a slave.

from either school might be married to each other.

The novices were registered and their training began at once. They were admitted to a dormitory with *divans* along the walls and there were old women in charge of groups of ten of them. Lights were left burning all night to expose lesbian advances.[15] To prevent beastliness, long radishes, cucumbers and such were sent from the kitchens ready cut: so extreme was the need to prevent wanton behaviour since young, lusty and lascivious girls without men could only have unchaste thoughts.[16] They were taught religion, and to sing and to play a musical instrument, along with dancing, poetry and the complex arts of love. If they graduated from their apprenticeship, they went on to learn to read and write and the skill of telling stories. Stories were important everywhere in the empire and nowhere more so than in a *harem*. Every night one of the *One Thousand and One Nights* was read, or so it was said. The *Nights* include heroes and heroines and some noble souls but, since such characters are often dull, the stories are more often about vagabonds, promiscuous women, sorceresses, criminals and unscrupulous judges, mountebanks and lying holy men. It is the world upside down, which does not mean that it was an exact mirror of the daily life of Baghdad or Istanbul.

Even at this level, failures still occurred but they could hope to be sent out into the world with some recompense, including their possible marriage to a failed student of the Palace School. The next promotion was to *gedik*, or the 'privileged', who had been seen by the sultan and who may even have had contact with him. They were not only beautiful but also intelligent and amusing besides being skilled at making love although they were still virgins. If a meteor like Hürrem entered the Harem, and the sultan was a Süleyman, the whole system broke down and the girl graduated immediately. *Gediks* were girls chosen by the sultan. At various periods these girls ranked as *gözde*, or 'girls in the sultan's eye'. He might select them more and more often so that they joined the elite *ikbals* or *hassodaliks* who were in sight of the top of the pyramid, since to reach it they had only to become pregnant and safely deliver a child, preferably a son. These ranks varied over the years and were not always used.

Girls who had slept with the sultan graduated to their own rooms with their own slaves and kitchen maids and their own eunuch. If a female child was born, they moved to a larger apartment and became a Hasseki Kadın, or mother of daughters. They had the right to remarry upon the death of their sultan. They were the favourites who enjoyed a handsome income compared with the pocket money that they had received before. With motherhood they had crossed the frontier and were free. If they bore a son, their ambitions were indeed achieved. At very least they were the Hasseki Sultans, or mothers of younger sons, but these royal ladies were secluded and, if the boy should die, they could not marry again.

The Baş Hasseki was the mother of the eldest son and she more than anyone had to be secluded were the prince to die before her. She was the chief royal lady for so long as she lived and on her son's accession became Valide and ruled the Harem. In theory, his death meant her seclusion and the loss of all her powers. Thus the Valide Mosque of Safiye Sultan could not be completed by her when Mehmet III died in 1603 and it was left decaying for sixty years. She was well looked after in the Old Saray but had no access to any funds except her own. There was one Valide whose personality was such that she overruled custom: Kösem (see pp. 138ff). Troubles began when a girl became an *ikbal* because she could not help but be seen as a rival to those of the same rank and therefore be involved in the factional politics which were the zest of Harem life.

In the sixteenth century and afterwards, when the sultan selected his girl for the night, he usually came to see her or wrote to her in the morning so that she could prepare herself down to the last eyelash and the last drop of balm besides assuming clothes the like of which she could only have dreamed of wearing. The consummation of her mission took place in a special room within the Harem: never in the bedchamber of the *selamlık*, where pages and old women were on guard with candles all night. There was no question of the sultan conquering the *ikbals*; it was they who had to conquer the sultan. Humility at the entrance to the bedchamber was something different, once between the sheets, for a woman of spirit like Hasseki Hürrem when she turned one night into thirty-eight years of love. It is untrue that girls crawled in at the foot of the bed, as if a slave deserved humiliation: this is merely western gossip. But there was humility and obedience unless teasing pleased the monarch more.

When the Sultan Dies, the Valide is Born

When the sultan died there was no turmoil except for the cold-blooded execution of the younger brothers. Even that was done quietly by the mutes – until, that is, December 1603 when Ahmet I became sultan at the age of 13 and under the influence of his mother spared his 12-year-old brother Mustafa's life, perhaps due to the public disgust and the unrest that had followed on the stranglings that accompanied Mehmet III's accession. Safiye Valide left immediately for the Old Saray like an ex-prime minister and Handan Valide took her place. She was to die a violent death: one among the few Valides who suffered this misfortune. She was disliked by her son who was, probably unfairly, accused of being responsible for her death by poison eighteen months later. It is more likely that she was poisoned due to Harem intrigue rather than her son Ahmet I's dislike for her at the age of 16. In the manner of the Renaissance, there were dwarfs at the *saray*. Handan built them a village and their own ship because she had an affection for them.

Within a fortnight of the sultan's death, at the latest, a new Valide proceeded in state to the palace with the extraordinary privilege of riding in a litter, and later an open carriage, without wearing a veil. She was, therefore, the one woman in the royal entourage whom the populace knew by sight. The procession was very grand indeed. The French explorer and reliable witness Tavernier described that of the Valide of Süleyman II (1687–91) which did not take place until seven months after his accession for reasons which are unclear.[17] He succeeded in November but Saliha Valide did not move until the following July, when the old lady had only 18 months to live.

At 6 a.m. a disorderly band of janissaries and horsemen proceeded to the *saray*, including kitchen officers. Then came the city's governor, who was well mounted and clad, along with his officers in coats of mail and helmets over their white turbans. The cavalry arrived in their heron plumes but a new batch of janissaries was as disorderly as the first. Tavernier had a poor opinion of the equipment of the masters of the ceremonies because their uniforms were garnished with small bells. There followed yet more officers and 600 royal gardeners who were also the royal guard. Then came 200 judges in Spanish leather buskins and white turbans, followed by 60 descendants of the Prophet's family in huge green turbans and also representatives of the Şeyhülislam, who never appeared in person on such occasions. Now came the gorgeously dressed chief pages with 50 grooms, well mounted and magnificently clad, only to be followed by a shambling troop of black eunuchs. These were followed by the coach of the Valide herself with her daughters. Then came 12 coaches filled with female slaves and, lastly, 4 great wagons full of snow for use in the Harem. It would be interesting to know why snow was included since it must have been supplied regularly. The Valide was received at the Gate of Felicity (Bab-ul-Sa'adet) by the sultan himself, who took care to honour his mother as did all his male subjects.

This is but one more example of how the Ottomans had always had a respect for their mothers which was far deeper than required by the Koran. Even the Mongols had no difficulty in accepting the Queen Mother as regent.[18] The Mongol ruler Yesü Möngke, who was never sober enough to give a falcon to a falconer since he drank alcohol as an antidote to cholera, let his wife perform his duties. Mehmet III visited his mother every morning: only afterwards did she send for the Chief Black Eunuch and proceed to conduct the business of the Harem.

The Valide began her reign by sending a jewel-bedecked dagger to the Grand Vezir and also a sable coat both to him and to the Şeyhül-islam.[19] Now that the Harem had a mistress, the new sultan paid a formal visit to the girls: they were lined up on each side of the Golden Road, which is the backbone rather than the artery of the establishment. They might not look at their master, who scattered gold coins amongst them. No girl could see the Valide without seeking an appointment; she would then present herself in her *entari*, or state robe, and remain with head bowed and hands clasped throughout the interview.

Although the women were kept apart in order to protect their modesty, there were ceremonial occasions within the Harem apart from that ordained by the strictest observance of etiquette. Ceremonial, and the state occasions of a court where the mystery and uniqueness of the sovereign had to be preserved at all costs, were inherited from the Byzantine past. Yet the girls were granted permission to go out, presumably properly escorted and for exceptional reasons. If the Valide died before her son, he escorted her body to the Gate of Felicity and it was then carried on to the place of her burial under the ward of the Grand Vezir. After the forty days of mourning were over, the ministers paid their last official visit to her tomb and the women of her entourage retreated to the Old Saray. They were usually wealthy from the many gifts that they had received and stored in their personal boxes and therefore had hopes of procuring a husband. Some did not want to marry but remained pensioners, content with old friends, and could sometimes go on a visit to Topkapısaray.

Living in the Harem must at times have seemed like living in the waiting-room of a provincial station. Just enough people came and went to make relationships lopsided. It was not that one had lost one's ticket but that one wondered if one would ever need one. The girls were able to play ball games in their garden with its large pool. There was a second pool under the chamber of Murat III which was heated by an enormous boiler in winter. Twice a week they were allowed to walk in the palace gardens under escort and after a crier had warned everyone to leave on pain of death. From time to time, they went out in closed wagons to picnic in a carefully chosen beauty spot guarded by eunuchs. Later there was the summer Harem built amid gardens on the shore of the Sea of Marmara where it looked out onto the Bosporus. It appears to have been capacious enough to take the whole of the Harem but far fewer girls went to the summer palace at Edirne while many or most remained behind for one lucky visitor, Thomas Dallam, to peep at. The Valide and her women also had access to a large chamber built on top of the Gate of Majesty (Bab-ül-Hümayün), which was the great entry to the *saray*.[20] From its parade of windows onto the public street below, they could watch state processions and throw gold coins to the crowd.

The Chief Black Eunuch held the keys to the Harem and was as powerful as a minister. His room overlooked the door and nobody could enter without his permission. Late in the seventeenth century, Sarı Mehmet Pasha reported that the Grand Vezir had to bribe the Harem women, the eunuchs and the retainers if he were to gain entrance. Often, when money was short, it required all the guile that the minister could muster. The women were in the clutches of agents of people outside the *saray* who used them in order to influence the sultan. In the same way that traders visited the private houses of lesser subjects so were the agents essential to the life of the Harem at either *saray*. As for the *kiras*, they were to go much farther down the road of corruption than had been the case under Nurbanu; their power over the women, and through them the sultan, brought them incredible riches. It began with acquiring luxuries for the great ladies at considerable profit and also privileges for themselves. Their purchases included clocks for which the women had a passion. Some were gifts like the one that came with Dallam's organ. This lost its works when the organ was broken down by Mehmet III but the case can still be seen as the finial of the throne of Ahmet I. At one period in the eighteenth century, Chishull regularly spent a day maintaining the clocks in the Harem, when all the women were out of the way. La Motraye claimed that his own account of the Harem was based on his visit, real or imaginary, when he was disguised as Chishull's assistant.

The origin of these traders lay in the expulsion of the Sephardic Jews

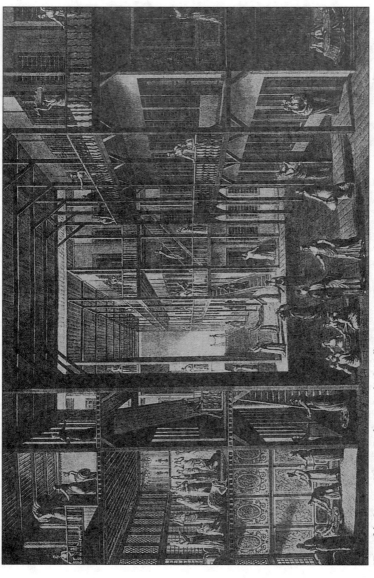

View of the Summer Harem, Topkapısaray (A. I. Melling, Voyage Pittoresque de Constantinople et des Rives du Bosphore, Paris, 1819)

from Spain in 1492. They came mostly with no money but bills of exchange on the related banking houses elsewhere in Europe. The foremost of these exiles was the head and matriarch of the Marreno banking house of Mendés. Donna García Mendés settled in Istanbul in 1552 under the protection of Süleyman the Magnificent. She was deeply involved in the European trade and had a network of agencies which specialized in spices, drugs, raw silk and precious stones. She even extended credit to kings. The power and splendour of Istanbul in the sixteenth century were unparalleled. Esther Kira,[21] or more correctly Esperanza Melci, was a Jewess of Italian origin whom Sanderson rudely called a short fat trubkin. Her popularity and unlimited influence at the *saray* were due to her obtaining everything that was wanted. This enabled her to win contracts for herself and her sons and also to be awarded important tax-farms. The women and the eunuchs were more devoted to each other than most people but Esperanza was an exception because they were in her pay. It was due to them that Mehmet III (1595–1603) awarded her the sheep tax and the tax on Christians, farms which would delight the most rapacious. She invested her fortune in trade and following the mutiny of 1600 and her death, she was found to have 400,000 ducats in ready money besides vast investments in goods in transit. She also owned 42 estates in various localities.[22]

The squalid sultan, Mehmet III, had even granted the revenues of the *sipahi* cavalry to the commercial genius and a mutiny was inevitable. It is impossible to understand why this was not foreseen even by ministers like those of Mehmet. When the mutiny finally broke in 1600, the terrified sultan and Valide turned Esperanza out of the *saray* as fast as they could. She fled by boat towards the Black Sea but the mutineers caught up with her and she was dragged ashore. They set her on an evil-smelling horse on a frame for firewood. On 1 April the *sipahis* gathered in order to drive her to the *saray* of the Grand Vezir, Ciğalazade Sinan Pasha, who waved to them that they should do what they liked. (Ciğalazade was an aristocratic Genoese convert, which explains why, when he was defeated in 1602, he committed suicide, a crime that is very rare among Moslems.) Pulled to the ground, Esperanza was stabbed and trampled to death along with her eldest son who had turned Turk. The second son had fled just in time. The two corpses were dragged through the streets to the Hippodrome and left for the dogs to eat – except for Esperanza's right hand, which was cut off and nailed to the door of the second most senior judge, the Anadolu Kadıasker, for he had often kissed it and fawned for her favours. The Grand Vezir was deposed but his successor was even more corrupt.

The Valide was that Safiye who, it will be remembered, had failed to complete her mosque. She was born in about 1550 and Murat III was devoted to her from when she was 13 and first became his concubine. Her greed is revealed in her three letters written to Queen Elizabeth I, or which Esperanza wrote for her. The first merely acknowledged a letter from the queen but the next thanked her for the arrival of a state coach. Safiye was most pleased with this splendid coach. It had travelled by sea and she and the sultan went out in his golden caique to greet it. With it came Dallam and his famous organ. Safiye reciprocated by sending Elizabeth a crown studded with pearls and rubies, three towels, a robe with a girdle and two gold-embroidered handkerchiefs. She then asked for fine cloth, dresses, cosmetics, distilled water for her face and odoriferous oils for her hands. The dresses were sent separately from their sleeves. In the west it was the custom to keep them in pieces and the maid sewed and pinned her mistress into them. The Venetian Bailo Morosini, who appears to have known Safiye, said that she was witty and quick-tongued but haughty and possessed all the bad characteristics of the native Albanian which she may or may not have been. Twelve years later, he found that she had become prudent, patient and wise.[23] She was intelligent enough to be regent in Istanbul when Murat III was away on campaign.

If ever there were a Valide who wielded paramount power she was Kösem Mahpaykar, the Greek[24] mother of Murat IV and Ibrahim and grandmother of Mehmet IV. Originally christened Anastasia,[25] she was said to have been called Kösem in reference to her fair and hairless skin but the word could also mean 'leader', and leader she was going to become. Certainly, she was both beautiful and intelligent. When her husband Ahmet I died in 1617, she succeeded in having his brother Mustafa succeed him.[26] This was partly due to her lavish bribery of officers and officials.[27] Otherwise, the throne would have gone to Osman, the son of her bitter rival, and her own sons would have been in danger since the law of fratricide might well be reintroduced. Hadım Hasan Pasha himself fuelled the rumour that he had paid the Valide for the Grand Vezirate. The court was vibrant with scandals.[28] Kösem dominated Mustafa but such was the power of the Chief Eunuch that his assertions that Mustafa was insane were believed and the sultan was deposed. Thus Osman II (1618–22) came to the throne after all and Kösem and her entourage were banished to the Old Saray: but at least her sons were not strangled. Osman was deposed in turn and then killed by a corrupt Grand Vezir and the janissaries.

Kösem returned to the *saray*. Her son Murat IV, who was born in 1609, succeeded to the sultanate at the age of 14 in 1623. Either his mother did not wish to – or, more likely, could not – control her teenage son's licentious and male-orientated excesses and those of his brotherhood of friends. For five years, he left power in her hands during a period of worsening unrest which led to a very real threat to the throne. But after these five years, when he was 19, Murat took control of his empire and within a few years had achieved despotic power. He had evidence of the corruption of the *kadı* of Iznik and hanged him as an example. The *kadı* was a high-ranking member of the *ulema* class and the Şeyhülislam expressed disapproval only to be summoned back from Bursa to Istanbul where he was hanged in his turn. He was one of the only three holders of the office ever to be executed.

If Murat was unbalanced, as he was later to become without a doubt, he was also intelligent as well as brutal. He won the loyalty of his un-disciplined army by sharing hardships with them and using his saddle as a pillow and the ground for his bed. Nor was he a commander who led from the rear. His respect for his mother never wavered and he appointed her regent when he was away on campaign. One night his bedchamber was struck by lightning, which resulted in a brief break-down, but it is likely that his mind was already disturbed. The heavenly attack was enough to stop him drinking for a time, which for some might indicate a return to sanity. But he fell ill and became increasingly and frighteningly fierce although he had enough wits to perceive that the Ottoman house was rotten to the core.

Perhaps because he had faith in the Han of the Crimea, who was the heir designate were the Ottoman family to vanish, Murat decreed the extermination of all male members of his family including his own four sons. Only Murat's brother Ibrahim and his children were left alive and the man was probably the most degenerate Ottoman of them all. Murat was clearly dying when he remembered them but Kösem persuaded him that they had already been executed. Much as he still honoured his mother, the paranoid sultan demanded, not without reason, to see the body of this man who was no less unhinged than himself. Kösem suc-ceeded in delaying the display of a living corpse until Murat's death rattle assured her that he was safe. Murat departed for eternity and his mother had no time for grief as one unhinged son was exchanged for another.

She ruled in place of Ibrahim whose devotion to his concubines might well have filled the Harem with exhausted girls in their hundreds. Kösem was known as the saviour of the Ottoman house and this increased her prestige even when the new sultan's gross extravagance, which included cladding rooms from floor to ceiling in sables, and a prodigious sexual appetite made his downfall inevitable: even before he kidnapped the daughter of the Şeyhülislam from the *hamam*, or so it was said by gossips, because her father refused him her hand. But he did endow and marry her and, with a weird twist of etiquette, her father stood in for the groom by virtue of his office.[29] To make matters worse, Ibrahim soon sent his bride home. If true, it must have been in a hurry because she died on 25 April 1647. The deposition of Ibrahim had already been effected on 8 August 1648. He was strangled by the mutes ten days later,[30] after that fatal knock on his door which he had anticipated throughout his brother's reign.

Ibrahim was succeeded by Kösem's 6-year-old grandson, Mehmet. The Valide now faced the crisis of her reign since her daughter-in-law should have succeeded her. Turhan Hadice was only 21, however, and was in no position to withstand a woman so dominant. The reigning Valide promoted herself to the non-existent rank of Büyük Valide, or Great Valide, and remained at the *saray*. But Turhan soon set to work building a party of her own both inside the Harem and out. Kösem eventually took fright and decided to replace Mehmet with his younger brother Süleyman because his mother was docile. But a Harem is crocheted with spies and Turhan acted before it was too late. There were clear political issues other than monomania. For one, Kösem was allied with the janissaries and so was unpopular with such government as there was. Yet it was a janissary officer within the palace who had her lured out of the Harem into the Eunuchs' Court and then strangled her with her own braids in front of their mosque.[31]

Kösem left wealth and estates even after a life devoted to charity and the building and endowing of religious foundations. The city was so distressed at her death that, without any official order, mosques and bazaars were closed for three days and public mourning continued for a fortnight.[32] Kösem's wits had sustained her in power since no Valide had any legal right to her continuing authority. There was nothing in Ottoman law that made her regent in the western sense of the word. She was astute at marrying her daughters off to *vezirs* almost before they had abandoned their wet nurses. She was known as the Mother of the World but was, it would seem, a very bad mother of her own children whose happiness could never have been her first concern. She was buried beside her husband, Ahmet I, and could claim to be the last of the great Valides.

Turhan Valide faced prodigious problems which led to the visible approach of political disintegration when she performed her last, and possibly only, great service to the empire. The little-known Albanian recruit to the janissaries, Mehmet Köprülü, had suffered a career full of reversals. As a page at the Palace School, he gained little preferment and at the advanced age of 47 was merely ranked as a cook in the palace kitchens, where his quarrels and disobedience led to his expulsion. His intellect and integrity, and his loathing of laziness, created enemies all around. A few men of rank perceived his ability and he was promoted under their patronage until they fell from office. Moreover, such a career as he had was ludicrously ill-fated. As a local governor, he was captured by the rebels whom he had been sent to quell. He was relegated to minor posts and was deeply in debt when he was forced to retire upon the death of Kösem.[33]

Gradually, throughout these dreary times, Köprülü had built up a circle of close friends who held political debates and considered various schemes of government. There had been nothing like it before. The worthlessness of the men available to take the seals of office of Grand Vezir had Turhan in despair by September 1656. It was then that the two office-holders and most powerful personalities in Köprülü's circle requested an audience of Turhan, who was told that there was only one man of the hour. On the 14th, she sent for him in order to hand over the seal of office and was without more ado presented with a written list of demands which included the end of intrigue by palace favourites, absolute obedience to the Grand Vezir and her own personal abstention from interference in affairs of state. Having tried in vain to find someone else prepared to take office, she signed the decree the next day. At 78, Köprülü was Grand Vezir and ruled ruthlessly and with courage – including riding out to overawe a mob – for five years until his death in 1661, having founded a dynasty of Grand Vezirs. Turhan lived twenty-one years more and died five years before her son, Mehmet IV, was forced to abdicate in 1687.

There is a reference to the Valide in an important letter from the merchant Jacob van Crayesteyn of Smyrna to Jacob David, a fellow merchant of London, written in May 1677. In it, he reported receiving a letter:

from a friend saying that the great sultan [the very far from great Mehmet IV] had publicaly [sic] entered Constantinople in unusual pomp together with his mother [Turhan Valide] and the Grand Vizier. And as the great man is now trying to keep his head he has demanded the head of his brother [the future Süleyman II], but since his mother is very protective of him no one knows how it will turn out. Two days after the said great lord entered Constantinople he forbade any woman to be seen on the streets any more and one afternoon, sitting in his Seraglio by the sea-side he saw sailing by some vessels with women, which ran aground. He had the poor women drowned. If things go on like this one wonders what is coming next . . .[34]

Grooms for Princesses

Princesses were married to Grand Vezirs almost automatically, otherwise they were married and remarried to senior officers of state. Dalloway claimed that a sultan told his daughter that he gave her a man for her pleasure and a dagger for her revenge. The husband had to repudiate any previous wives and any infidelity meant that he was stripped of wealth and strangled. This may have been more symbolic than real – a daughter of Selim III on a visit to the Morea gave her husband twenty-five beautiful maidens: they had no children. Another older example of leniency, at least,[35] was that of Süleyman's Grand Vezir, Lütfi Pasha, whose stringent and essential reforms made him many enemies. In 1542 he allegedly ordered the mutilation of a Moslem woman taken in debauchery. His wife, Şah Sultan, sister of Süleyman, heard of the sentence and was revolted.[36] She bitterly reproached him and Lütfi Pasha was furious. He set about the princess as if she were a commoner but her screams alerted her eunuchs and they and the guards restrained him. The angry sultan did not execute Lütfi but ordered his divorce and sent him into exile on his estate at Dimetoka in disgrace. There is evidence[37] that the princess was interfering in politics and intriguing with Lütfi's opponents, including the Kapudan Paşa, Hayrettin Barbaros. Lütfi Pasha's fall clearly marks the beginning of Ottoman economic decline. In exile, he wrote his remarkable history of the Ottoman sultans which is still a valuable source of information. Şah Sultan did not marry again. There was good reason to execute a man who had assaulted royalty yet there was no dagger and no confiscation of his estates. Perhaps the mutilated woman was an invention.

There were some princesses whose affection for their husbands saved their lives as when Fatma Sultan pleaded with her brother, Murat III, for the life of Siyavuş Pasha and was successful. He was to outlive her by twenty-one years. Due to Evliya Çelebi,[38] more is known about Kaya Sultan and her husband, Melek Ahmet Pasha. In 1633 Evliya himself fired a rocket from a boat on the Bosporus to celebrate Kaya's birth. In 1644 she was married to the Grand Vezir, Melek Ahmet Pasha, only to die during a terrible miscarriage fifteen years later.[39] It is clear that she and her much older husband were very happy together and shared each other's dreams. She was rich and munificent and her loyalty was such that there is a vivid account of her driving to the *saray* of Siyavuş Pasha and complaining to the Grand Vezir's wife about a great injustice. The minister was immediately summoned and made his excuses. Kaya raged at him, calling him a tyrant, and then went in a fury to see the Valide. It is interesting that she had no difficulty in gaining admittance to the highest officer and lady in the state. It is hardly surprising that she was to die since the midwives had their arms into her up to their elbows in pursuit of the dead child. Melek Ahmet Pasha was heartbroken to the extent that the Grand Vezir Köprülü Mehmet Pasha rebuked him: 'You ought to be ashamed of yourself. She was only a woman.' All the *sultanas*, or princesses, came to visit her tomb.

Melek Ahmet then had to marry a harridan of a princess, Fatma Sultan, becoming her fourth husband. From their nuptial night she importuned him for money, brought with her a brigade of indoor and outdoor servants and was as shameless and immodest as she was extravagant. When he complained to the sultan he merely replied, 'You have quarrelled with your wife? These things happen.' When the pasha died, Fatma tried to seal the rooms of his vast palace but the steward sent a message to the Grand Vezir who ordered all seals to be broken immediately. The princess fled in disguise, abandoning her coach.

On inspecting Fatma's life, it is not surprising that she was an outrageously spoilt child and adult egotist. She was Kösem's daughter and born in 1605. At 19 she was married to the Kapudan Paşa, whom she divorced in order to marry Kara Mustafa Pasha – he was executed in 1628 warm, so to speak, from the nuptial bed. She then married another admiral, who was also executed three years later. It was only after twenty-four years that she was ordered to marry Melek Ahmet Pasha because she was all that was available. After his death she was hastily married to yet another pasha who was dead within three years, thus setting her free to marry her last pasha at the age of 62 – he may have outlived her since he did not die until 1678. Any man who married into the sultan's family was awarded the title of Damat, or son-in-law, a high honour that does not seem to have done many of them much good.

Fatma's sister, Ayşe, was also born in 1605 and at the age of 7 was married to her first Grand Vezir who was executed when she reached the age of 9 – it is not clear if they ever saw each other. She was then engaged to a hero who died when she was 16. In 1627 she married yet another Grand Vezir when she was 22. After he was assassinated, she married a pasha who was dead by 1636. She then had three years' peace until she was married to another pasha, who lasted four years. Finally in 1645 she married another hero, Voynuk Ahmet Pasha, who died when she was 39. She was then left a widow, and presumably a very wealthy one, until she herself died in 1656. That she cared for any of these six men is not clear; nor, with her or any other princess, can one trace any evidence of there having been a love, to relieve the monotonous parade of mature and busy husbands. To add irony to the story, her first husband was the widower of her younger sister who had died when she was 6. Ayşe herself had one child who died in the cradle. So much for dynastic marriages.[40]

Bon unkindly summed up Ottoman women by saying that although they might not be conversant with any other men than their husbands, fathers and brothers, and although they lived in lodgings apart, by themselves, out of the sight of men, and always went abroad with their faces covered, virtue was its own reward. Assisted by the anonymity of the veil, many women:

> being extraordinarily wanton, are very dishonest and lascivious, who taking the opportunity of their husbands absence, at the wars, or in some long journey, under colour of going to the *Bagnos*, and being covered withall, go whither, and to whom they lust, knowing that the worst of it is to be put away, if so be it [that they] should at any time be discovered.[41]

It is hard to believe that the marriage of a princess was ever other than politically motivated since even an older girl was unlikely to have seen a possible husband, let alone to have spoken to one. If she were only a child, the husband could be responsible for her upbringing. The wedding decided on, the sultan would usually present the princess with a palace into which the couple would move and for which the husband would be responsible. Marriage into the sultan's family may have been designed to create goodwill but, since all the expenses of the household would be paid out of the husband's treasury, marriage could be a form of masked supertax that undermined the large store of wealth that ministers had acquired by one means or the other.

Many girls were married before puberty and almost all to men much older than themselves: this was not always a disaster. A later Fatma Sultan, a daughter of Ahmet III, was married to his Grand Vezir, the remarkable Nevşehirli Ibrahim Pasha, when she was 13 and he was 51. He was executed to save him from the mob when he was 63 and she was 24 and devoted to him. At the age of 5 she had been married to her first Grand Vezir, who died when she was 9. After Ibrahim Pasha she did not marry again and died at the age of 29. There was also a child of Mustafa III (1757–74) who was engaged at 4, but her fiancé was executed the next year. She was then married to the Grand Vezir when 7, and was a widow at 8. She was spared until she was 17, when she was married for twenty-five years to a pasha who outlived her by ten years.

None of this made a marriage unimportant and the festivities were considerable.[42] First there was the procession of the trousseau from Topkapısaray to the house of the groom. It was led by the captain-general of the janissaries in ceremonial dress which included a *batterie de cuisine* that shone and also clattered – the ranks in the janissary corps were related to the kitchen by tradition. The soldiers were followed by the reciters of the Koran, the chief of police, the Chief White Eunuch, stewards, the chief architect and so on. Then came the festal palms of gold and silver (*nahil*), glowing with fruit and sweets and flowers symbolic of the hoped-for fertility of the bride. Next there were two large gardens made of spun sugar and carried on the shoulders of four men. Finally came the gifts, duly guarded, including jewellery, mosquito nets and hundreds of bejewelled cushions. Then the officers of state followed in order of rank, with the Grand Vezir and the Şeyhül-islam walking together. Finally, the military band heralded the mules loaded with furniture and so on. Everyone had a reward.

Preferably on a Thursday, a grander procession, which took an hour to pass by, escorted the bride to her new home. In it was everyone of rank or importance, including the Sherif of Mecca and the Chief Black Eunuch. The bride rode in a silver coach followed by the great ladies of the Harem in less spectacular carriages and then came the girls. The horses were splendidly caparisoned, the band played and the festal palms appeared once more. Palm shapes had long given way to fir formations but the origins go back to Hittite times in Anatolia or even earlier. They also appeared at circumcision festivities and were the responsibility of a special guild. Evliya Çelebi claimed that some were so big that they were made of iron and had to be carried by hundreds of galley slaves. Some were so huge that the projecting upper storeys of houses had to be pulled down and then rebuilt. In 1646, to celebrate the wedding of a 4-year-old princess (whose husband was executed two years later), two palms were as high as minarets and numerous houses were defaced in order to make room: to be repaired, allegedly at government expense.[43] The palms were sometimes of silver and real jewellery was used to represent birds. Marriage festivities could last two weeks or more and the whole city, including the women, would seem to have taken part.

The day before her wedding, just as with ordinary people, the bride went to the *hamam* but a princess was attended in one of the baths inside the *saray*. The customs were the same. She was conducted by her mother and a grave-faced relative and was presented to some 200 ladies who came with gifts. On the occasion that Lady Mary Wortley Montagu (the famous author of an exceptional account of life in Edirne and Istanbul) witnessed in the early eighteenth century,[44] the 17-year-old girl was attended by others as naked as she, because they were dressed only in their long tresses, revealing the whiteness of their skin and the beauty of their large eyes. There was dancing and singing but nothing but dignity. Lady Mary had previously remarked upon the decorum of the bath and, although she was oddly dressed in Turkish eyes, she suffered from none of the disdain and whispers that she would have endured at home. Everyone was modest although naked while their maids were busy dressing their hair. Some gently tried to persuade their English visitor to undress but when she came to her stays they assumed that her husband had locked her in.

As the wife of an ambassador, Lady Mary was well received and in Edirne she paid a formal visit to the wife of the Grand Vezir of the moment. The Chief Eunuch handed her down from her carriage and after passing through several rooms, with girls lined up on both sides to honour her, she reached the great lady who was dressed in sables and rose to greet her. Neither she nor her husband lived ostentatiously since both were of an age to think only of God. But when her guest proceeded to the palace of another minister, the young wife was living in splendour. Her beautiful Harem girls were dressed in embroidered

Women in a hamam, 1793. Note the attendants, children, high pattens and silver washing bowls (I.Ü.K.)

brocade gowns and this time two eunuchs conducted Lady Mary to a flowering pavilion where she hardly knew whether she were in a garden or a kiosk. She was received by a flawless beauty dressed in a gold brocade kaftan and embroidered white slippers. There were twenty lovely maidens in the room, four of whom were playing instruments and the others dancing by turns. When the guest left, she was presented with a silver basket filled with embroidered handkerchiefs.

Later, in Istanbul, she was entertained by Hafise Sultan, Mustafa II's widow, who was only 34 years old. Her palace[45] was striking and very grand. Lady Mary lamented the exquisitely embroidered tablecloth, napkins and towels which she grieved to use. The hafts of the gold knives were set with diamonds and round about were the perfumes of Arabia. One of the ordeals of these intimate but grand receptions was that the fifty dishes were served one by one. The princess laughed at the idea that a sultan would throw down a handkerchief in front of a pretty maiden in the Harem. She explained that he would never choose from any but the senior students, so to speak, and always requested their attendance that evening by letter and with a gift. Nobody anywhere crawled in by the bottom of the bed.

The many rooms in Hafise Sultan's house were large and sumptuous. The winter apartments were furnished with figured velvets and the summer rooms had Indian quilting embroidered with gold. But the princess herself outshone the setting: she was dressed in exquisite materials heavy with pearls and other gems and with no fewer than three necklaces reaching to her feet, weighed down by a great emerald or contrasting jewel which mocked a rope of mere pearls or rubies.

Common Folk

There were many Ottoman women who could claim characters as strong as those of any Valide. Among them was the legendary old peasant woman who braved the sultan's camp to complain that his soldiers had stolen her hens. 'If you can't keep your army in order,' she told Süleyman the Magnificent and Law-giver, 'then you've no right to be sultan.' There is a miniature to support this story but it would be more convincing were it not that the story had attached itself to other monarchs too. There is, however, a much better and totally authentic story which has been researched by the late Dr Susan Skilliter.[46] It is all the more interesting because it reveals that Süleyman in the days of his glory was human and humane besides being remarkably restrained as became a good Moslem ruler. It tells us more about the character of Ottoman women than do most other events.

Two Turkish girls on a pilgrimage to Mecca by sea were captured by the Grand Prior of the Knights of Malta, who was then recalled to take command of the French fleet. Because he knew that Catherine de Medici already had and liked a Turkish girl in her entourage, he brought his girls to be a present for her. She welcomed them and within a year they were converted to Christianity and in 1558 christened Catherine and Marguerite. But an Ottoman spy in the employ of the French court wrote to their mother, Huma, declaring that they had been converted by force. The mother's fight for their freedom began.

Meanwhile, the girls had married into the French nobility and they were clearly enjoying their new life away from their formidable mother. Huma was at work importuning the *Divan*, or council of state, and had to be driven away by the Grand Vezir on several occasions. However, Mihrimah and Esma Han, the wife of the then second *vezir*, Sokollu Mehmet Pasha, rallied to her side and Huma had the whip hand. It was an international issue which involved good and bad faith over the exchange of prisoners. This was what neither the sultan nor his minister desired. In 1565 envoys were sent both to and from each government without success. Süleyman was almost driven to break his alliance with France because he could no longer appear in public without Huma importuning him. The French ambassador was badgered daily and could not get his work done. The daughters were implored to write to their mother to say that they had no desire to return home and it is not clear whether letters did arrive. By now Selim II was sultan and the capitulations with France were agreed. Huma importuned more than ever and then seems to have reached a point of exhaustion because she accepted a modest pension. She had also been confronted by eyewitnesses who insisted that her daughters were not slaves but well and happy.

The event illuminates the justice available to a simple subject under Ottoman rule. A tiresome mother with what to her was a real, but in fact imaginary, grievance was able to present written petitions to her sultan when he rode past and it is clear that these were read if only by a *vezir*. She could repeatedly confront ministers in the *Divan*. French ministers were harassed and the alliance between the two countries placed in jeopardy by the determination of a mother. While her daughters were enjoying life at the French court and were happily married to rich courtiers, couriers were travelling to and fro. Ambassadors toiled. Great expenses were incurred. The only character who emerges with less than honour is the Grand Prior, who should never have attacked an Ottoman ship in time of peace. God dealt with this brilliant and handsome offshoot of the house of Guise. He died of pneumonia in the splendour of his youth in 1563.

Seventeenth-century carriage of the Valide Sultan (F. Taeschner, *Alt-Stambuler . . .*, Hanover, 1925)

A surviving araba *at Küçüksu on the Bosporus and its eighteenth-century fountain* (author)

CHAPTER 6

The Chrysalis Cracks

Byzantine Pomp and Circumstance

The Ottoman sultans took over aspects of Byzantine rule because they were conscious of becoming the emperors of New Rome, in all but name. For many years, their real aim was not the conquest of Vienna but the old Rome and the recreation of a greater empire. The thought certainly inspired Mehmet II, and his successors were left with a residual but declining hope: fostered by the allegiance of such an oddity as the Lord of Osimo, who explained that the name of the modest Italian town was derived from 'Osman'. No such thoughts had occurred to Seljuk sultans but then they had never conquered Constantinople. The uniform of the royal guard, the *peyks*, was copied, plumes and all, from their Byzantine predecessors' wardrobe and a *harem* was a reflection of the gynaecium. The gallery of Hagia Sophia remained the place for women.

Common to the late Middle Ages was an obsession with ideal types rather than with particular individuals and, although individuals mattered at both courts, the Ottoman and the Byzantine, this did not alter a view of the world and human life which was inculcated into the masses.[1] Real people were replaced by symbols, making it easier to rule ruthlessly if needs be. And needs be, it often was. As for the victims of a system which all too often destroyed grandees without warning – due to rivalry, tyranny or their own blind ambitions – a good Byzantine did not pray for the world but the strength to endure it.

Innovation was seen as a heresy by both the Orthodox Church and Islam, and this could not but be a cause of pessimism among women in particular.[2] What is childbirth but innovation? Women were allowed to take their problems to the Ecclesiastical Court but, among the founders of the Church, the supposedly liberal St John Chrysostum was adamant that women should be seen and not heard. This was very much the attitude of the sultanate to the women of the Harem though there were exceptions such as Süleyman the Magnificent and Selim III. There had been Byzantine priests like St Athanasios who, as late as 1300, took to his heels if he saw a woman. Men such as he, hermits and monks, may merely have been aware of the fragility of their own virtue as opposed to the impregnable self-control of St Anthony the Dogheaded, as chaste as he was beautiful. He was pursued by maidens until, one night, he prayed to God to put him out of his misery. He awoke in the morning with his own brain and powers of speech: but with the head of a dog. Another saint was saved from such advances from the moment he was born: a barren woman prayed for a son until she was driven to promise that he would become a monk or, if by mischance the baby were a girl, a nun. St Stylianos of Afragonia was delivered complete with beard and tonsure.

Veiling women, in theory, moderated ardour under both Byzantine and Ottoman rule. No account was taken of the enticement of the unknown. Powerful women – and the empress Theodora was one among many – emerged at the Byzantine court just as they were to do at the Ottoman. At the latter, however, it was impossible for a woman to succeed to the throne, as did the empress Zoe who not only was young at 50 but had outworn three husbands. Some women were sufficiently admired to provoke the greatest compliment that a Byzantine male could offer a woman – which was to say that she had many manly virtues. These included snobbery; hence the rule that no true Byzantine could marry a foreigner.

In Byzantine men's eyes, and those of women by default, the sole purpose of marriage was procreation (just as it was with the Ottomans and in much of the rest of the world at this time). This view applied in particular to monarchs, even if homosexual, because they were in need of direct heirs. If there were uncles or brothers, by 1600, the succession did not, in theory, need to pass to the eldest son or a brother.

The not so crazed yearning of the dying Murat IV to put an end to his decadent family, it will be recalled, was frustrated by his own death else the sultanate would have passed to the Han of the Crimea. Under Murat, and at other periods, the Giray Hans were already ex-officio members of the *Divan* because there was a very real chance that the Ottoman dynasty might end. It is pleasant to know that there are descendants of these Hans living in Turkey today. By way of contrast, at the end of the ninth century, the emperor Leo VI the Wise had reached the end of his tether when a third wife died childless. Three marriages were the most that the Orthodox Church permitted. Leo was nevertheless determined to marry his mistress, who had already borne him a brilliant boy. In the end, the Patriarch gave in but the marriage was considered scandalous. It is probable that it is Leo who is begging Christ for forgiveness of his sins in the mosaic above the royal door between the inner narthex and the basilica of Haghia Sophia. The legitimized son grew up to be one of the most distinguished and civilized of emperors, Constantine VII Porphyrogenitus, or 'born to the purple', meaning born in the royal bedchamber, which was columned and revetted in porphyry, the imperial purple marble. The latter title was somewhat misleading, unless taken literally, because he was not born in this chamber although he wore the imperial purple in the end. Among the many similarities between Ottoman and Byzantine rule, the most notable was that, despite the household being patriarchal, the mother ruled.

Tell Me Where is Freedom Bred, in the Heart or in the Head?

The problem of marriage for the Turks was that none of them, not even the sultan, in theory, could make a slave of a Turkish woman because one and all of them were Moslems. After the early years of the Ottoman empire – which were awash with dynastic marriages with the daughters of Christian rulers for the simplest territorial and political reasons – in all but a few exceptional cases, sultans lived with slaves on whom they bestowed no dowry because that would betoken legal marriage. Nonetheless, when a new sultan acceded, his mother became the first woman in the land. The family origins of such women were of little interest even to historians, if not to the gossips of the diplomatic corps and their governments. Since the nineteenth century, this accounts for western chroniclers battling to find the native provenance of a Valide even if they only had hearsay for an archive. The result has been the perpetuating of several bits of a tattered imagination being hung, even recently, to the masthead of veracity.

The situation has not been improved by Turkish chroniclers who, in making the mother of Mehmet II into a Turk, did not appear to notice that, were this a fact, his noble father, Murat II, mystic and passionate believer though he might be, was accused of a wanton disregard for the ordnances of his faith. One historian[3] was convinced that Süleyman's mother was Turkish in obedience to a Turkish source. This even gives her father as Abdülmennan, a name that was conventionally given to slaves, or the fathers of slaves, and not to freeborn Turks. We even have the mother of the conquering Selim I, the Grim, called a Montenegran,[4] although there is no evidence where Ayşe originated. Even Kösem Valide, who was generally believed to be a Greek, was said to be a Russian by the Bailo of the time, Pietro Foscarino. He also called her *Zam*, meaning the Spirit, and described her at 50 as not yet worn by time; a claim which recalls that of the empress Zoe.[5]

Of the mothers of later sultans, we can only be sure of the provenance of seven out of eighteen. Of these, one was Russian-born, one was Cretan, two were Georgian and three Circassian. There is evidence that some of the others were Armenian in origin. The one thing that is clear is that if Selim II could claim to be half-Turkish, the last of the Ottoman dynasty, the caliph Abdülmecit II (1922–24), could claim to have one fifty-fourth part Turkish blood. But since Selim could not, the claim is spurious.

∾   ∾   ∾

The story of the women of the Harem at Topkapısaray went on for centuries without radical changes, if not without drama. A maid set the palace on fire and another allegedly stole the cradle of Ahmet I, if not for long. It is difficult to imagine where she could have hidden it. The existence of a prison in the vaults under the later Harem buildings is revealed by her scrawl of innocence on the wall of a cul-de-sac together with others by maids as unlucky as herself. One wonders whether these handwomen could write and, if not, who wrote the messages of despair for them. With such a large establishment, a prison was obviously necessary – Harem women could hardly be sent to the galleys. Women could be beheaded for grave crimes but whereas men were exposed with their heads under their arms, women were put in sacks for the sake of decency. They were not then automatically flung into the sea.

The change in Harem life began with the sensitive and unusually intelligent sultan, Selim III, who was murdered in 1807. Part of his zeal for reform came from his mother, Mihrişah Valide, to whom he was devoted. A Georgian, she was said by Dr Neale (the pre-eminent physician of his day who made a tour of Germany, Poland and Ottoman territory at the beginning of the nineteenth century) to have had more influence on her son than any other Valide had done before.[6] It was certainly she who introduced baroque to Topkapısaray, and to her own gorgeous apartments in particular, rooms where one feels that one should only eat Soufflé Rothschild and drink pink champagne: were it not for the evocative landscapes from a dream country frescoed where there is space in a carbuchon-encrusted, gilded decor. Her influence was all the greater because of the intellectual power of Yusuf Ağa over both the mother and the son. Yusuf was a highly intelligent favourite who had been born in Candia and, if a true Ottoman, also had some premonition of the future in the nineteenth century. Selim III married eight wives in the desperate hope of having a son but without success. One wife, Refet Sultan, survived him by sixty-two years to die in 1870. As for his own mother, she had the fortune to predecease him and escape witnessing his tragic murder in his mother's music room at Topkapısaray by reactionary janissaries and others who detested his reforms of the army.

Neale was a doctor of sufficient repute for Selim to invite him to visit his mother when she was terminally ill in the hope that he might offer a remedy more efficacious than that of the court doctors. To this we owe a genuine insight into life at the Ottoman court at the end of an era. Neale was taken to a pavilion where he was entertained to coffee, sherbet, sweetmeats and a smoke from a *naghile*. His host was the Kızlar Ağa, or Master of the Harem, the Chief Black Eunuch. Neale was astounded by the official's exceptional ugliness. Nor was he impressed by the high-ranking doctors of the law, the *ulema*, or the dervish philosophers who were invited in his honour. He did meet the Hekimbaşı, or head physician, who was a Greek and who informed him that the Valide had been ill with the ague for eighteen months. She had got better and then had relapsed and the traditional iced-water cure had proved to be no use at all.

Neale was taken to a second kiosk in order to see the lady. At this door he exchanged his shoes for slippers and was immediately admitted. He found a mattress in the middle of the floor on which lay a figure completely covered by a silk quilt. He was not allowed to see her face or tongue and could only explore her pulse. The old custom of silence in the presence of royalty was strictly observed and the doctor knew nothing about sign language in English let alone that of the Ottoman court. Nor did he know that the sultan was concealed behind a lattice but he did note the gilded lattices of the four large windows, the *divan* round the room with covers richly embroidered in gold and the equally splendid cushions. All of these, in his opinion, were outshone by a magnificent carpet.

The visit could only have lasted fifteen or twenty minutes before the helpless consultant was escorted back to the first kiosk. It was clearly too dangerous to ask a doctor to bleed a patient whom he had never seen and he had to be content to write out an innocent prescription. In the early nineteenth century in Europe, bleeding was still accepted as a sovereign remedy. Judging by the state of English medicine at the time, the whole charade can hardly have mattered except for soothing the sultan, who rewarded Neale with 100 gold sequins. Mihrişah lived eight days more and died at the age of 72. The most humane of sultans, Selim III courteously sent all the doctors messages of thanks for their efforts. From his mother he had received but one request, which was to do all in his power to protect Yusuf Ağa: but within all too short a spell this was beyond him.

Mahmut II, whom Selim had tutored, succeeded to the sultanate in 1808 and patiently achieved many of the hoped-for reforms. When he died in 1839 he left a son, Abdülmecit, who was an intellectual but also delicate. The boy's mother, Bezmialem Valide, who was a Georgian by birth and described as a buxom former *hamam* attendant, was adored by the populace because of her charity. She was as intelligent as her son, whom she loved dearly, and among the many charities which she endowed was a school for girls with a fine library.[7] It was possibly she, as well as her son, who stocked the library at Dolmabahçesaray with handsome editions of French nineteenth-century literature neatly annotated by a succession of readers. It was not just a matter of Hugo or Lamartine: at some point Baudelaire was added to the shelves along with *Madame Bovary*.

The palace of Dolmabahçe was revolutionary. Sultans loathed the pokiness of the Harem at Topkapısaray as well as its tragic memories and sought refuge elsewhere, only visiting it on ceremonial occasions. The advent of the railway in 1872 was to demolish the summer *saray* and signal its end as a residence – except for the pensioned Harems of past sultans who were turned out of the Old Saray at Bayezit, the site of which subsequently became the ministry of war and later the university. These elderly ladies cut the royal apartments up with shoddy party walls and even inserted floors if the rooms were high enough. They were probably better off than before if only because they had the gardens and the park to wander in. Only the Palace School in the Third Court remained of the old order. As for Abdülmecit, he had extravagant plans.

If the Ottomans were to survive into the twentieth century, it was essential to escape the ghosts of Topkapısaray. It was equally important to decide whether the empire faced east or west although great provinces were Arab still. The consequence was that Mahmut II and his son slowly mingled oriental with western protocol and ceremonial. Now there were ceremonial visits of the royal ladies to the Valide, while she along with the princesses and these royal ladies had to attend an ever-increasing number of ceremonies and were officially summoned to watch the military parades. The public even approached the great ladies and the crowds included onlookers of both sexes. On the fifteenth day of Ramazan, for example, Abdülhamit II (1876–1909) paid a state visit to Topkapı in order to pray in the holy room of the relics of the Prophet. The road was covered in white sand and it was the Valide Sultan's carriage which headed the procession, followed by those filled with the ladies of the Harem. When they arrived at the *saray*, the ladies were the first to pay homage to their sultan, but not out of respect for their sex. It was simply in order that they might be sent home as quickly as possible so that the men could partake of the feast that the women were forced to miss.

The Balyan family grew rich building palace after palace and not only on the shores of the Bosporus. One and all were in a flamboyant École des Beaux-Arts style and furnished extravagantly from the chandeliers to the keyholes. Princesses were still not allowed to walk without a pair of ladies-in-waiting or eunuchs to hold each arm, a custom that must have annoyed the younger girls – but then one day a chandelier crashed and only the princess's ladies dragging her back saved her from disaster. By the end of the nineteenth century, however, the princesses were allowed to get out and about and even go to the shops. They married men they chose for themselves – subject to parental approval and provided that they were not required to make a political marriage. Even Enver Pasha (1882–1924), a future member of the triumvirate that led the Young Turks and who was to be minister of war during the First World War, married a princess. Emine Naciye Sultan, aged only 13, was the daughter of Süleyman, a younger son of

Abdülmecit I. She and her husband built a wonderful art nouveau palace at Kuruçeşme, on the Bosporus, which was later brutally destroyed to make way for a coal depot after the establishment of the Republic. Enver Pasha fled to Russia in November 1920 and the now 22-year-old princess never saw him again.

That Harem life went on until the bitter end was surprising, but it did and there were even innovations such as the 'Lady of the Year' (or first favourite of the sultan), who was the victim of intrigues and malice until she became pregnant: when the whole palace held its tongue.[8] No one could scheme against an odalisque who might bear a son, or even a daughter, to the sultan, who was still seen as the Padişah, or Shadow of God upon Earth. At least at the New Saray (Dolmabahçe), the ladies could amuse themselves with visits to the menagerie at the rear, across from the private theatre, or go on up to enjoy the colours of the rare birds on princely perches in the aviary. On the way, they proceeded by a broad quarter-circle of a grand passage where Abdülmecit had started a gallery of pictures of the world's latest inventions cut out of the *Illustrated London News* and similar journals: these included the first submarine. For all that, and in spite of the occasional play, it was a melancholy world where lethargy married lack of any care for worldly things due to the narcotics which the women smoked as well as tobacco. This did not prevent an indelicate greed for cash. The day would come, in 1909, when the Old Saray at Topkapı closed and advertisements called on relatives to collect the helpless old ladies who stood in bewilderment at the palace gates, but it was a gradual process. Whether or not they were taken home, they would have been remarkable if they had adapted to a world with no servants and only the tatters of past glory.

Did the Circassian girls return to the Caucasus and enjoy foothills where cradles still hung in the trees creaking and groaning and a man struck by lightning was instantly a saint?[9] The Circassian men, small hands and feet though they had,[10] were still pirates in 1856, landing and seizing the prettiest girls and handsomest boys. Later in the century, Georgians were still trading in girls.[11] There were other markets in the east.

Possessions and Last Testaments

The eighteenth century saw a harshening of the Ottoman economy, apart from the static and intellectually lethargic agricultural basement on which the house was supported. By the nineteenth century, the loss of Balkan territories added to the decay of revenues while the palace tried to escape the consequences by awarding tax-farms to the great ladies of the Harem. These included numerous princesses dodging from husband to husband like stepping stones over the river of power. The stultification of the countryside was the inevitable consequence of the lack of money to spend on roads and bridges or any other development. This was a depression common to all the semi-feudal states of central Europe and not only an Ottoman misfortune. Princesses on the Bosporus never travelled in the hinterlands and felt no need for bridges when they were handed into their caiques.

In contrast to the wealth of a few, there were those other people who were not regarded as Ottomans at all. In the view of the great *vezirs* or the *kadıs*, just as with Byzantine officials and clergy, Anatolia was a place of exile far from all that made life worth living. There was no one who could read a book or who talked of anything other than the price of oats. The women chattered about other people who had been discussed to death already or exchanged family worries or griefs: sadness at the death of children, the young couple who ran away, the mould on the vine leaves. Flocks and fields fettered people to the land with only the village fool to make them laugh. There was no education for these women whatsoever and the landowner's wife was little better bred. Their possessions reflected this emptiness however fine the wifely needlework might be. It was their passive status which was so demeaning to these women, particularly to those who could not accept the arrogance of many men. All of this can be read into the meagre lists of possessions left behind by the notables of Bosnia. If this were all that the better-off possessed, what did the peasants have?[12]

Some assessments of the value of the estates left by notables in the region of Sarajevo are very detailed, while in others the household effects are simply given as the lump total of the money fetched at their sale. A few list item for item unless, and we cannot tell, some items were left unsold. The registered documents give a clear idea of the way of life of each of the deceased, from bookbinder to *imam*. The *imam*, for example, was a major farmer while one Pino Ibrahim Alemdar was equally involved in town properties and the land. Rich as he certainly was, he had the most meagre of household effects, although they included a kitchen grater and a broom (which do not appear on other lists) and a *gevl*, which was a shaggy garment presumably for country wear. The custom that all soft furnishings were the property of the wife, and all metalware that of the husband, would explain their omission from his list, were it not for their appearance in others. There are two or three others among the twenty estates for which records are available which are so devoid of home comforts as to make one wonder if the deceased were a widower living with his son and daughter-in-law.

The most important list of all the household effects and clothing is that of a senior officer of the janissaries, Mustafa Ağa, whose farmhouse and land would revert to the state on his demise (he died in 1815). His town properties, including the large house that he resided in, perhaps for most of the year, were his own freehold. The rest of the estates varied in value but all implied some income from farming and the rents from modest peasant crofts as well as town houses and shares in shops – the latter are sometimes described as simply an alcove with one door.

Throughout the Bosnian records, it is the modesty of personal possessions that is noteworthy (except in the case of the janissary), implying a lack of comfort from the viewpoint of a wife. A retired judge, for example, was a modest farmer yet his house listed only 2 mattresses, 7 cushions, a copper cauldron and a few copper pots. But he did have a large library, not listed in detail, but certainly of 200 or 300 books. With traders, the contents of their shops are recorded, as one might expect. There was a janissary officer who farmed diligently and raised 15 cows, 55 oxen and 170 sheep. His estate was by far the richest yet, clearly, he was living far above his income and he died deeply in debt. Loans and debts recur with these estates.

The point of making a list of a deceased person's property, and incurring the fees of a judge and his clerk, was that the estate should be divided exactly according to the law. The only way to assess the value of the goods was to sell them at public auction by means of the town crier who brought people to the house. There were no death duties except in the sense that retired officers lost all claim to lands held from the state. In Mustafa Ağa's case there were no children so that the meagre remnant of his estate was divided between his two sisters, his two nephews (one of whom was absent in the country) and his widow, who is not even given a name, which was unusual. One of the sisters would have had to shelter the nearly destitute wife, since she had no children of her own.

The family misfortunes at least permit historians to ask a number of questions although not necessarily to answer them. It is possible to account for every one of the Ağa's possessions – or almost, because brooms, pails and kitchen graters are not recorded. While some are associated with his high rank and his obligation to mount and arm followers in the event of a war, others are inexplicable unless he and his wife entertained lavishly or had a large staff of servants. The cooking and household management was the woman's task. In order to live with largesse, Mustafa Ağa resorted to money-lenders. Perusal of the Bosnian estates reveals that, like farmers everywhere, the Ağa borrowed money, planted crops and restocked the herds and flocks. The state lent large sums involuntarily in the form of unpaid taxes but the chief usurers were the *ulema* and military fief-holders. Of Mustafa Ağa's creditors, 18 belonged to the *ulema* and 18 were retired soldiers or administrators while 9 were landowners. To this one may add 2 Tatars and 2 Jews. A saddler and a barber were owed trifling sums which one may assume were unpaid bills. Of the remaining 21 creditors, their names are listed but not their occupations.

It is not surprising that the Ağa left weapons and horses but he also left 4 *naghiles*, a rack of 36 pipes with 13 spare mouthpieces, ashtrays and 5 packets of tobacco. All these were likely to have been shared with his wife: as would the 2 chiming clocks, 2 desks and 2 wall clocks, with 1 more of considerable value, and 3 pocket watches. The Ottomans had a passion for clocks and it is this rather than military training which was the likely cause of this extravagant collection. The Ağa also left 1 small and 3 large mirrors – since he was clearly a dandy, he may have made more use of them than his wife. He only possessed 15 books: except for a 3-volume history, these were all religious including 6 copies of the Koran.

Now let us move on to the kitchen, the domain of the Ağa's wife. The vast battery of pots could hardly have been needed to feed a childless couple and their household, which was unlikely to exceed in number the dozen who served the governor. Yet there were 19 saucepans, 41 copper dishes with lids and 5 more without, two dozen copper pots and bowls and 5 frying pans, 4 cauldrons, 17 brass *ibriks*, a silver balance, buckets of both wood and metal, metal baskets, a mallet and an old pair of tongs. When cooked, the food could have been served on 2 silver and 12 brass trays with another reserved for serving bonbons. In all, the Ağa possessed 37 trays.

There were only 1 large and 2 small silver knives, however. There were either 18 dozen spoons or only 36: the text is confusing. There were 77 cups of all sizes and only 11 coffee pots. Add various glass and china bowls and 34 china plates, 2 coconuts, a censer, 6 bottles of olive oil in a box and 2 pots of ground musk. If this is the kitchen of a soldier of field rank, what were those of a pasha like? The sultan's, we know, were huge but then he was serving thousands of meals each day.

In this context it is interesting that a former eighteenth-century Chief Black Eunuch, who was exiled to Egypt, not only left 27 properties including houses and mills. He also left numerous metal dishes which were not for his own use but distributed among charities as well as his villages. Charities were exempt from death duties, which were levied on books as well as most other possessions. Books could be of great value and needed to be given away before their owner's demise. The Chief Eunuch advised the Valide on her Egyptian affairs for so long as he was in office; hence, no doubt, his ability to build up a modest fortune by the Nile.

Whereas the kitchen utensils were the property of the husband, the soft furnishings belonged to the wife who, in humbler houses, probably made or at least embroidered them herself. What they establish is that each room was furnished with *divans* along the walls. It can also be assumed that the windows were latticed and shuttered since there is too little fabric for curtains on the list.

There were 20 kilims, but it is impossible to determine whether they were used on *divans* or on the floor. This was spread with special but unspecified coverings and Egyptian mats and almost valueless old felt, perhaps underlay for carpets. The 2 expensive carpets were probably displayed in the middle of a room. There were 10 mattresses of which 3 were of superior quality. Usually there were 2 mattresses, 1 thin and a better stuffed one on top, for each bed ('bed' meaning the floor or a stretch of a *divan*). There were also 17 quilts of which 1 was particularly expensive and flowery while 6 were old and another had worn thin. There were 179 cushions of which 18 were specifically designated for use as pillows. Of the others, 11 were listed as old and 5 more were small; some were thin and 3 were both old and small. There was a set of 18 superior red cushions, enough for an important room, 6 pairs of stuffed velvet and another 6 of white velvet which were the most expensive.

Sartorially, the Ağa was a man of whom his wife could be proud even if she could not join him at his parties. He left 23 waistcoats and 9 fur coats – mainly fox or sable, but 1 of Tatar fox. The list goes on and on, including 2 raincoats, 1 of which cost as much as a small cottage. The remaining items could only belong to a woman and one can only wonder if they were sacrificed by his widow in order to rescue the estate. They included 10 shawls of which 3 were Kashmiri, 1 of which came specifically from Lahore. A red and walnut example cost 5 times the price of the Ağa's old Koran or 3 times that of a large carpet. Also listed were a woman's white dress, a fur overcoat, an embroidered dress and a cheap red mantle or sheet. One item, out of a total of 597, was an expensive bezoar stone to protect the couple against poisoning.

Finally, there were more than 80 kilograms of the best Edirne soap for which that town was famous. (It specialized in making soap animals for children and soap flowers for the ladies.) There were also 61 kilograms of common soap for the house. The 15 candlesticks and 7 old lanterns appear to be few for a large establishment in winter even if the servants could not read. Significantly, there was embroidery but only 1 silver pen case, which would suggest that little writing was done beyond the Ağa's accounts.

By contrast, a cavalry officer and his wife died in the same year as the Ağa, 1815, and on the same day, perhaps as the result of an accident. The officer left a few garments, a watch and some copper trifles besides an old pair of çakşır (trousers with boots attached to them at the ankles) in the peasant style, a little vermicelli, a quantity of cheese and some syrup. It suggests that the food belonged to the man because he either went to market himself or gave his wife the money with which to go herself or send a manservant to buy it. He possessed a mere 4 oxen, 4 cows and 2 calves, a bull and a mare. His wife left a trifle more than he had, including a hovel in their village, but a surprising amount of ready cash. Pieces or bolts of linen cloth were her most valuable possessions and possibly she traded in them. She owned a kilim and a prayer rug, a mattress, quilt and cushion, napkins, shirt and drawers, 5 handkerchiefs, used boots, copper trifles and a box. It is clear that they did not entertain and that she could only just manage one change of clothes.

One thing that emerges predictably (and compatibly with research elsewhere) is that there were large numbers of peasants who were in debt to their landlord. No will mentions a *mangal*, the brazier with a lid that warmed the houses of Anatolia and the Balkans. The peasants could only have kept warm in winter because they had hooded *ocaks*, or hearths, in which to burn wood. The soft felt cap-maker who is recorded as having died in 1777 left a substantial estate unencumbered by debts. It was divided between 4 sons, his mother and then his widow who received least of all. In her case, it might have been sufficient to tempt a widower. One Attar Mustafa Beşe, an exceedingly successful herbalist, was also the deputy governor of the province. Since he had married 3 wives, he left 3 widows. The result was that the inheritance of each of these women was the same as the fee paid the judge to wind up the estate. It was just enough to buy a dress. Attar Mustafa's mother was left a little better off: she could buy 4 such dresses or a large winter overcoat.

One may conclude from this evidence that only her dowry could rescue a widow from dependence or poverty. It was a period in history when numberless households harboured old aunts, widows or spinsters. The situation was the same – and far more financially burdensome – in the crofts of villagers, especially when so many were encumbered with debts. It also emerges that there was little evidence of valuable inheritance from a father unless he were a merchant. However, a father may well have endowed his children during his lifetime apart from such settlements and dowries as were given when his children married.

These questions could be multiplied. There was no conveyance for the Ağa's wife unless she rode a horse, for example. In the town house, she could be escorted when she went out on foot. In the country, one wonders if she were a prisoner although she was a woman of rank. Was it really necessary for whoever wound up an estate to account for a dozen candles, some syrup and a handful of vermicelli? And if it was, why do such items appear with one estate and not another? If a man died, did relatives clear out his larder on the same day? One wonders if, when a housewife made preserves from her own fruit, they too were shared out according to the letter of the law. One must also ask whether a peasant's trifling possessions would be distributed. It is a dangerous mental exercise which leads to the crofter with one cow. It is difficult to believe that his widow, his three sons and his mother solemnly cut the beast up into the portions due if it could not be sold.

More seriously, the Bosnian wills suggest that apart from the grandees, little wealth descended from one generation to the next and that a family was indeed responsible for its own success in life.

The Harem staircase in the Beylerbey Saray, on the Bosporus, where Abdülhamit II died. The architect was Hagop Balyan of the family that built most of the nineteenth-century royal palaces (author)

CHAPTER 7

The Final Decades

Gossip, Scandal and Spoilt Children

Perceptive travellers who visited Istanbul in the latter half of the nineteenth century saw that nothing was as it was supposed to be. The position of women was a great deal less restricted than was asserted in the common gossip of the west. It was not only that Moslem women had always had marriage rights respecting their property – unlike the French, for example, whose property was controlled by their husbands until after the Second World War. It was also that the veil gave women a certain freedom of movement, just as Lady Mary Wortley Montagu had pointed out. When Atatürk forbade the wearing of religious garments in the streets, there were those among the orthodox clergy who were delighted to be able to go to the cinema in suits, undetected. A veil is a protection against the wandering eye. Just how much mothers felt it to be a protection was made clear when they finally had to let their good-looking sons walk to school unattended but their new-blossomed teenager was veiled like his sister and for the same reason. The reserved sections of the newly introduced trams in the 1870s were for women to relax in, secure from men's wandering hands: an enhancement of women's liberty rather than a restraint. There were white silk curtains and covers for the seats and it seemed certain that one would find friends travelling down La Grande Rue Pera as full of chatter as oneself.

Compartments reserved for ladies were to be found all over Europe, especially on trains, at the time. It had long been the rule that men could not share a ferry across the Golden Horn with women who did not belong to their own family. Writing in 1878, Amicis stated that women went about Istanbul just as they would in Europe,[1] with their veils very loosely put on, while older women might be seen unveiled altogether. Not only could women go in and out as they pleased, to visit friends or relatives or to go to the *hamam*, but there was no attempt to check how long they had been out. If they were wealthy, they could order their carriage just as they wished.[2] Yet as late as 1908 a visitor to the city wrote that no Turkish lady of rank would ever walk in the street. Many did so nevertheless, for Europeanization had begun as early as the reign of Abdülmecit I (1839–61). There is now a campaign in the Istanbul press, not by reactionaries but by the liberated women of the intelligentsia, to reintroduce women's sections on ferryboats and trams just as there had been until the Republic.

Clothes, headwear, posture, and manner of walking are elements of the coded language of any society and many foreigners misread the message when that language is not their own; especially one that had been changing as fast as it had in Istanbul when Paris bonnets could create a furore and the great couturiers found it profitable to travel to the city in the early summer in order to display their latest fashions – and not only to royalty, either. The coming upheavals in society may be symbolized by the first general election, which was held in 1908. On 21 December voting booths along the Bosporus were decorated with great bunches of chrysanthemums and branches of magnolia and bay. When the voting was over in the city, policemen took the ballot boxes to the Sublime Porte headed by mounted troops and a band. There were carriages filled with lightly dressed little girls followed by schoolchildren in pinafores and clean white collars and seemingly the whole population of the city on foot singing the new patriotic song, *Vatan* or Fatherland.

In Anatolia and other provinces, change was less easily perceptible. In the last years of the Ottoman caliphate, an Englishwoman called Mrs Ellison, travelling on a slow but sure-footed horse, undismayed by fords, reached a village near Bursa for the night and found the house of the local schoolmaster. The tiny house had two storeys and she was greeted by the master's wife who was only 17. Inside, she found that there were four rooms. Although the garden was minute, it was shared by a cow, a goat and a lamb. The grandmother, almost inevitably in a country village, lived in the house along with a baby and they all came to meet the visitor. The young wife kissed the hem of the traveller's dress in the old style and led her to a ladder up which the guest climbed to her room. It was filled with cushions but, sign of the times to come, there were also a bed and a chair. Strangely, Ellison was stopped from removing her boots. This really was challenging an established custom – which was a wise one: it prevented dirt being brought into the house just as it did into a mosque. Then, as often when all is going well, the guest relaxed and praised the wife's jewellery and immediately had the utmost difficulty in refusing to take it as a gift. Yet the wife only owned the clothes that she wore. As an honour, Ellison was given goat's milk and seven lumps of sugar with home-baked bread. There was no question of ever eating meat in that house. The husband, whose career was a real challenge to the past, would never have seen himself as subversive, yet that indeed was what he was. That there should have been a schoolmaster in a village at all, let alone a small village, was a lantern in the shades departing.[3]

It is no surprise, then, to read that Mrs Harvey of Ickwell also found it difficult to discover a people more kind-hearted or considerate. The nineteenth-century rich continued to treat their servants and slaves as if part of the family. Moreover, slavery was dying out, just as it did in the United States, but without a civil war. And if all mistresses were less than angelic, so some slaves could overcome the spirit of a patient householder who was ignorant of the philosophy of freedom. There were also women of vicious temper, like the previously mentioned cook in the slave market, who could upset a large household and bring misery on a small. For these unfortunates there were final solutions. They could be sold or, more humiliating still, be given away for nothing: but they could not be thrown out onto the street.

Virtue and the Lack of It

Inevitably, there were women who lacked virtue just like the men, however grand their place in society. The easiest way to pleasure was in the back room of a shop. This was why, in theory, no woman would enter farther than the front room; but since their veil hid them it hardly mattered even if they were seen. Their lover was not hidden by his clothes but would hardly care provided that he had a reputation for being a young Don Juan. Indeed, he was probably pleased. If the affair was discovered by ill chance, then retribution might be brutal. It rarely was, however.

There were a number of rules governing women's lives when they were out. Any household of standing would require its mistress to be accompanied by a servant. Istanbul was, after all, full of refugees of all kinds making their bed here or there as best they could: but not in Pera where the best shops tempted. One rule might be called quaint. If a woman took a tram out, then she had to come back from a different terminal and by another route. Virtue was often inconvenient and, equally, theoretical.

Whether there were more scandal in nineteenth-century London, Paris or Istanbul is not known, but Régla, a French social lion, resident in Istanbul during the Belle Epoque, was a keen observer of society. At a grand reception, a wicked old man pointed out to his foreign guest what might be called the sights of the town. A whole host of sinners paraded. There was the husband who had come across a portrait of his wife at a photographer's and a lady who had been recognized entering and, an hour later, leaving a smart shop. There was a pretty divorcée who was waiting for her gentleman to rid himself of one of his four wives. (Since it had become rare to preside over such a household, he must have been rich.) There was an *efendi* who was a clerk at the foreign ministry. He had just married his Arab slave and was having her taught Turkish by his sister. There was the lady who was pining for her husband whom she had twice divorced already. By marrying another man and divorcing him next day, she would be able to return to her first love but, as mentioned previously, this would be for the last time under Koranic law. A man whose way of life had left him elderly at 50 had had ten wives while an old woman in green had had twelve husbands. A former slave had become the concubine of her master: they married, but subsequently divorced. She had married again but was now widowed and so was looking for a third husband. There was a lady who had made a fortune buying 14-year-old girls, educating them and selling them at 500 per cent profit. That travelling merchant had wives in Istanbul, Trabzon, Salonika and Alexandria. This great pasha was only 24 and a month ago had been a cadet. A sister of the sultan had fallen for him: she was as jealous as a nightingale and he was relentlessly spied on. Elsewhere a child of 5 was encountered: she was betrothed to a boy of 8 who was furious when she kissed him.

Unfaithfulness was as common as in any city. Moreover, faithless wives were partly protected by the fact that jealousy provoked ridicule. Nothing in heaven or earth could prevent *harem* jealousies. Middle-class men closeted their wives more strictly than the rich did but in their world the idea of a *harem* or of having more than one wife did not arise.

By 1900 a revolution was in progress. Hardly any man married before he was 30 and only 2 per cent of those living in Istanbul had two wives whereas in Anatolia the figure was 4 per cent.[4] These Anatolian husbands were not just rich citizens but canny peasant landowners in the rough world of the eastern provinces. Overall, fertility was dropping in spite of an absence of old maids since remarriage was fairly frequent. One result was that, in the villages, boys were adopted illegally, and against religious convention.[5] In Istanbul, women were forerunners in a lower level of fertility after 1875.[6] This was a first step towards liberty. As early as 1830, for some rich families marriage was becoming a social and economic event, rather than a matter of individual fulfilment,[7] due to the influence of the French revolution. By the mid-century, novels and plays could be read and seen. More important was that even trivial romances could be taken seriously.[8] A woman's life was no longer concentrated only on her children and there was time for the relationships between happier couples to develop affection and respect. As a concomitant of this revolution, nearly a fifth of all marriages among the well-to-do ended in divorce.[9] Most important of all was that the laws against abortion were ignored, either in an amateur way or at the hands of an experienced gynaecologist. If some women were still eager to rear a large family, the indications are that the majority of those permitted a choice certainly were not.[10]

There were so few women who had never been married, one can only suppose that they were either deformed or spinsters by choice. One girl with a fine dower had reached the age of 28 and her parents were in despair. But she had not waited in vain; she married the man of her own say.[11] Towards the end of the nineteenth century, brides tended to be more mature than before although 28 was still seen as late in life.[12] That there were exceptions to these generalizations, as always, is unquestionable.

Mrs Harvey commented shrewdly on men who did not love their children and who saw their sons as rivals as if they had been born out of the world of *The Golden Bough* or at least Greek mythology. But there were plenty who were fond fathers. The sultan's brother-in-law, who had been forced to divorce his first wife when he was compelled to marry a princess, kept her and his children across the Marmara at Üsküdar and visited them as often as he could in secret. In 1880, when the commander-in-chief in Aleppo, Cemal Pasha, was obliged to live without his wife, he found this a real trial. He read his guest a touching letter from her, announcing the arrival of a little daughter born during his absence. The wife had taken the baby's hand, covered the palm with ink and pressed it on the paper at the end of the letter. The tiny facsimile was placed there like a seal.[13] Had Cemal Pasha been a Sufi he would have known that the true lover never seeks union. His company is separation and his friend is imagination. But Majnun had renounced love in order to achieve divine experience.[14] The pasha happily had not.

The life of a well-to-do wife was no longer centred on the care of her children.[15] She was constantly listening to gossip and she made weekly visits to the *hamam* – unless she was very rich, in which case she entertained friends in her own baths. Late in the century, she could venture out shopping and there were always the valleys of the Sweet Waters of Asia. The grandees had gardens and kiosks to escape to and rooms in each corner of their *konaks* or *yalıs* (mansions beside the Bosporus) that let them follow the sun. There were story-tellers awaiting their defeat by modern fiction and the rebec-player among the slaves. If suitably attended, the great ladies could ride out in their carriages to watch public festivities which included child and adolescent jugglers and acrobats. At the end of the century, the press discovered that many of these youths had been bought off their parents in Liverpool at the age of 5 to be trained by a circus master in Istanbul until they were proficient. The mother was rewarded with £5 but the child received very little at all, if ever, since accidents occurred. These pleasures were strictly (or less and less strictly) interrupted five times a day by prayers for which mats were always at hand. If nothing had changed in 1800, the tide was coming in by stealth, overlapping one custom at a time. There could have been demonstrations and martyrs but the social revolution proceeded with decorum. Townsfolk now sat on chairs and dined off tables. In one bourgeois household, the family's proudest possession was the daughter's piano. One could have been in western suburbia.[16] However, an elite among women got up from their chairs and joined the first freedom movements.

Tides or no tides, wives still had to be dutifully back home in the evening in time to greet their husbands; since they were usually the only wife and without a rival, their only dread was that their husband would arrive with a company of male friends who would keep him from her.

She could not go down to them even in the garden, but the master of the house could enter the *harem* at any time although always with circumspection. If a pair of shoes had been removed at the door, there was clearly a guest in the house so that it was necessary to send a slave to announce the master's presence.

Since the rooms were cleaned and the meals cooked for her, the lady of the house might be said to have only one crowning task, which was to look after her appearance. The *hamam* ensured her creamy white skin tinged with delicious shades of pink and there were innumerable bottles of perfume.[17] She would be as singularly unperturbed by the ill behaviour of her offspring as her guests would be. No one appeared to mind a baby screaming or naked toddlers running around throwing water: their elders just went on chattering as if in a novel by Jane Austen. The women were shrewd and intelligent and often musical. But they lacked education, a lack that was to be overcome not by the few schools founded in the latter half of the century, but by the lycées of the Republic. The year 1900 was approaching before these rich women could escape into serious reading and even develop a little gentle thinking. They were utterly bored, just as Lady Mary Wortley Montagu had discovered at the time of Ahmet III. It was boredom that had driven them to eating sweets, with the result that their teeth decayed at an early age. To avoid this, many were given to chewing mastic long before Wrigley's gum became a symbol of American life. Mastic was said to nourish and purify the gums.[18] An idle life also resulted in rapid ageing in the middle years.

When Games Were Magic

There is little record of indoor games for adults or children, let alone hide-and-seek or blindman's buff. In the country children would use anything to play with, like the stones in the cave near where the great architect Sinan was born and with which children still build 'houses'. But by the age of 7 work intruded. In one Anatolian village in the 1950s, a child had a very simple but comic toy made by his father. A piece of board was painted green and four bottle tops were added for wheels so that the boy could pull it along with a piece of string. In the middle was the wooden silhouette of a man without details, but painted with identical mustachios and grin on both sides. It is impossible to trace toys for girls in the villages. Perhaps they shared with their brothers. In towns, swings and even ferris wheels of a modest but perilous size were popular from before the sixteenth century but were mainly used by adults. Hoops and kites, however, appear common to both town and country but were only for boys.

As for the salons and *hamams*, travellers complained about unruly, spoilt children rushing noisily between their feet. These adults were unable to define what was going on although what appeared to be fracas to them would have been clear and meaningful to the children, whether it were indeed tag or something quite other. Children soon perceive that many grown-ups have no imagination and so escape to a magic world of their own.

It was at Eyüp, the most sanctified suburb of Istanbul, that toyshops were first established after the conquest. The vendors made their own rough-hewn playthings on the premises and they were exported to India and Yemen in the seventeenth century. The last of these wonderlands has only closed recently. The quantity of swords and other weapons, in recent times made of plastic, again makes one wonder whether girls were catered for. The tin trumpets and drums listed by Evliya Çelebi suggest that the musicians, at least, were male though the shops also specialized in tops and humming tops. According to Evliya, the guild of wax bird makers also catered for children. Green parrots and white turtle doves were carried on poles, perhaps revolving, with little boys running and crying, 'Alicim and Balıcım'. Again, since girls of good or modest family were never allowed to run about the streets, one wonders if they were ever given a bird of their own.

Board games were originally symbolic of the fight between good and evil; the skill required in playing chess made it the most prestigious of them. It had been popular all over Asia and since Byzantine times in Istanbul. It, too, appears to have been a man's game. The boards were made of cloth, painted in oil, and could be rolled up and carried around. The Royal Asiatic Society in London has the manuscript of an illustrated teaching manual which shows men playing chess in a meadow. The Mongol conqueror, Timur, played with a circular version which lay dormant for centuries after his death, but there is also a normal square board extant which was probably his and was recently auctioned. It has one curious feature: the middle squares are darker than the rest. One must assume that draughts, backgammon and dominoes were played in Ottoman territories just as they were the world over. Knuckle-bones are still used for telling fortunes in Mongolia, especially at the New Year. Yet there is no record of playing with these or with ancient board games, apart from the board dug into the door-step to a room next to the sultan's box at the Green Mosque in Bursa, which was probably reserved for women. We have seen, however, that girls played ball games in Topkapısaray.

It must be remembered that the popularity of most games was related to gambling, another form of magic; indeed, one has the impression that practically nothing happened in the Ottoman and Arab world without a bet being placed, just like it was in eighteenth-century Europe. This was despite the Prophet having banned the game of *meisir* along with the drinking of wine. The former was a gambling game which determined the size of the portions of a newly slaughtered camel that the players won by drawing arrows of different lengths from a quiver. Wine and *meisir* were deemed the work of the devil. Although an ancient sport of nomads, it is one in which women were unlikely to have taken part.

Status in the Village

Like the ladies of a *harem*, the struggling populace also aged but at least it was for a purpose. These women not only brought the water from the fountain and watched over their children. They could obtain humble or menial work which, though disgracefully badly paid, yet meant some-thing to them because it gave them status. But their way of life was also changing even if even less obviously. The ending of plural marriages, for example, left more women alone or the prisoners of the relatives who sheltered them. It should not be assumed that having two wives was an unmitigated evil. The first wife, when she became middle-aged, needed a young, strong girl to help with the daily tasks. And at night, she did not have to suffer the appetites of a husband who was still demanding. Nor did the first wife lose her seniority or her standing in her village. Of course, this is to talk of marriage as if that represented some form of civilization. It did not. But it would take time for the concept of mutual esteem to be accepted; indeed, it is taking genera-tions still.

At Home with the Grandees

Unexpectedly, it was Ahmet III who first broke the taboos by sending the former janissary, Yermisekiz[19] (Çelebi) Mehmet Efendi, as ambassador to France in 1720 with the mission of discovering all that he could about French architecture and culture. The envoy was unprecedented in his success and popularity with the great ladies of Versailles. He not only returned with architectural drawings of that palace and, more particularly, of the pavilions of Marley-le-Roy and with cases of Burgundy and champagne, but he wrote enthusiastically about Paris society, declaring that in the land of the French the women enjoyed higher status than men and were free to go anywhere they wished. A nobleman of the topmost rank showed the highest consideration and respect for a woman even if she belonged to the lowest class.[20]

By the end of the nineteenth century, life for prosperous Turkish families was changing more rapidly than ever. The younger generation of women could read and write while continuing to dance and sing for their pleasure. The polka, Lancers and quadrilles arrived in the Yildiz[21] Harem along with the telephone,[22] with which the princesses amused themselves all day in who knows what gossip, since they were incredibly ignorant and pathetic[23] according to the shrewd wife of the Sherif of Mecca. Quadrilles and polkas were one thing but dancing the Lancers was reckless. The circles turned faster and faster, girls were swung off their feet and could be flung across a ballroom and be injured.

There was a tragic incentive for women and girls to learn to read and write in the mid-nineteenth century: wives, mothers and sisters wanted to write to their husbands, sons and brothers who were fighting in the Crimean war. Many of them still had to go to a public letter-writer.[24] If the letters ever arrived, they may have had to be read aloud by another scribe. Thus they consisted of formulas which lacked intimacy although they were full of stilted poetry or some other substitute for love.

Once there were increasing numbers of literate women in the *harem*, family life was changed and the lives of the children most of all. Foreign guests were welcomed with their news of the world. They were nobly received and some were quite as observant as any Lady Mary. There is a remarkable record by Mme Vaka of life in one Selim Pasha's household at the end of the nineteenth century.[25] His first wife lived on the first floor because it had most rooms, but the house had only one bathroom or modest *hamam* which was used by everybody. The fourth wife had to be content with the top floor. Since the pasha was supposed to have had fourteen wives, one wonders where they were all fitted in.

However, there were sixty-five rooms for the women, though no bedrooms since the salons were convertible.

The Valide Pasha was queen of the household and ruled it, although only aged 38; she was remarkable since she spoke Arabic, Persian, French and Greek besides Turkish. Absolutely no overt jealousy was permitted any one of the young wives or the servants. The Valide had a passion for Sophocles and had doubtless read other playwrights and philosophers. The whole Harem had to go to bed early and wake early.[26] The Valide was a suffragette and therefore enlightened friends like Hilmi Pasha visited her even when a female guest was present. She wore a transparent veil that hid none of her beauty. She was addicted to cigarettes, which she rolled herself and smoked while holding them by a pair of golden tongs. At dinner, her guests were brought scented water and towels before eating, as was the custom anywhere. The courses were served in profusion, carried on brass trays on the heads of the servants.

The Valide's company was amusing and the women of Istanbul were natural comediennes. So great a household was hard to run but she managed it and her family as well, just as she would manage a great enterprise today. Her only son had to go down on his knees and beg to be allowed to marry before she reluctantly agreed. That she was fastidious was unquestionable – she daily washed her hair, which was then rubbed sweet with rose petals. No doubt her son would never have found a bride of whom she could really approve because none could be her match.

Thomas Thornton was a merchant of long standing in Turkey during the last half of the eighteenth century. His book, published in 1809, is the most authoritative of the period and covers every subject concerned with the structure of Ottoman government, including the army. Thornton remarked that the husband was the only real male acquaintance of the wife but in a household such as Selim Pasha's or Şakir Pasha's on Prinkipo (now Büyükada), the largest of the Prince's Islands, at the end of the nineteenth century this was no longer true because uncles and brothers were permitted to visit, particularly in the garden. The old restrictions faded away. The Şakir Pasha *konak* had a dining table with chairs for forty people; the family and three governesses sat down together along with the passing guest. Similarly, the great drawing-room was neither *selamlık* nor *harem* but a salon in the Parisian style, except for the fact that the south wall had been turned into a grotto with gliding waterfalls and ferns. Again, the distinction between indoors and out was blurred – until this room became a cinema sixty years later.

Grottoes were temptations: one grotto in the garden belonging to the master of the sultan's household was reached by jumping through a gentle fall of water. It was a place of assignation, where the youngest known malefactor was a boy who had that year reached his teens. It should be remembered that this was a period when the young were never left alone in Europe for fear that they would be under the dining-table, hidden by its cloth, while grand pianos wore frills to mask their suggestive legs.

It was the turn of the century and visits had become parties, when the Sherif of Mecca's English wife, Princess Musbah Haidar, frequented the mostly vanished gardens of the Bosporus. These were romantic settings of shade and dripping fountains with the sea hastening past. In it were reflected hundreds of lamps of bronze and oiled parchment which moved in the breeze and sparkled on every ripple.[27] There was music to accompany the al fresco banquet and the sherbet except where champagne had already conquered. At a party given at his mother's residence by the Khedive of Egypt, at Bebek on the European shore, the gardens and woods stretched up the hillside behind. This was reached from a first-floor salon by a bridge across the public road. There, on one occasion, the royal orchestra played. The ladies were no hirelings or demure amateurs. Many of the princesses of the last royal families were gifted instrumentalists and they were trained by notable, and patient, masters. If polkas and waltzes, Schubert and Saint-Saens dominated their repertoire, this was only to be expected.

Such parties were long after the 1830s, when Miss Pardoe[28] had resided in the city. Pardoe had accompanied her father when he was posted to Istanbul from Lisbon; she wrote two famous accounts of the former city and one about the latter. In particular, she had been overwhelmed by the cleanliness of the *harems* that she visited in Istanbul. There was not a grain of dust or a footmark on the parquet flooring of the great halls off which the private apartments lay. These halls were used as dormitories for palace women even at the waterside palaces. Anyone who arrived late at night had to skip over this prostrate host, according to Princess Musbah.

Lott's account of the Khedive's *harem*, where she took a post as governess in the 1860s, is amusing for anyone to read, except for the prim spinster herself and her wounded pride.[29] Her hauteur set all the women of the palace against her even when the prince and his mother tried to soothe their, and her, mutual detestation. As governess to the heir, she could escape by taking him out whereas the other women were effectively the prisoners of his mother and his grandmother and their whims. Lott was taken aback on the first Wednesday of their stay on the Bosporus because all the languid, scheming women came to life, furniture was stacked, carpets shaken from every window, matting scrubbed and ornaments polished into mirrors. It took a day, but then the place was spotless for another week. Since this was the routine everywhere, the sultan and the lesser husbands took care to keep well clear of their homes on Wednesdays.

When Miss Pardoe stayed at a particularly grand house she found that the palatial rooms were divided by tapestries while on all the three sides that were not windows there were closets for bedding. The nineteenth century took the window to its climax in Ottoman domestic architecture, creating walls of glass so far as wooden structure would permit. Such rooms were brilliant from the earliest light and invited the visitor to rise. No sooner had she done so than the servants removed the bedding: mattresses of embroidered satin, sheets of gauze or worked muslin, and half a dozen cushions of brocaded silk were replaced by the proper daytime furnishings of the *divans* down the sides of the room.

However, economics were almost imperceptibly influencing the social mores. Between 1901 and 1909 household expenses rose gently and so did house prices. This continued until the savage inflation of the war years and after. The number of servants was cut back but not the expenditure on pleasure which, however, was relatively modest.[30]

Talking of Flowers

> *The crystal streams of Paradise*
> *Flow, the name of God repeating,*
> *The nightingales of Islam there*
> *Sing, the name of God repeating . . .*[31]

It is said that there is only one tree that cannot grow in an Ottoman garden and that is the tuba which only grows in paradise. In the poem by the mystic poet Yunus Emre, parent of Ottoman literature, there are the ingredients of the ideal Ottoman garden – water, birdsong, trees, fruit and flowers. The mystical nature of a garden was expressed by the master of a dervish monastery, Abdal Sultan, who wrote that the crocuses are as one with the dervishes. Scents took precedence over looks, although the spreading of a rug could create an instant garden, but not the ideal enclosed space of Egypt, Iran or, above all, Mughal India. Kiosks overlooking a pool were decked with jasmine and honeysuckle: all thoughts had to be sweet for these bowers were meant for lovers.

The Ottoman garden was neither a vegetable nor a flower garden, nor an orchard – but all three. There were borders of herbs and mustard. Onions and garlic protected the rose-bushes against greenfly. Cypresses along the Bosporus were symbols of hope but they also cut off a view of the ladies, even in winter, while the Judas tree in spring bled among the white magnolia the length of the Straits. Few people other than the Ottomans realized that its flower is a culinary delicacy. For a humble few there were, and still are, allotments such as those either side of the Theodosian walls of Istanbul where the most fertile soil is in the dry bed of the moat. But the expansion of the city has overwhelmed most of the rest, the women dig no more and there are no free vegetables for them to harvest.

Doubtless, wild flowers were enough for the first *beys* like Orhan and Murat I. In spite of urban development, these are still profuse all over Anatolia, including the spiky and spotted tulip that inspired designs sent from the *saray* studios to Iznik. As a symbolic precaution against ill fortune, each sultan learned a trade – symbolic because when a sultan fell from power, there could be no escape from strangling, however silken the cord. Goldsmith, maker of archers' rings or what you will, the skilled trades were honoured. It was Mehmet II, the conqueror of Constantinople, who chose gardening. He not only planned and supervised the plantings at the palace at Edirne and the Old and New Sarays in Istanbul but he urged his *vezirs* to create gardens too and these were for the benefit of the citizens of the capital. They were meant to delight the women of Mehmet's household whose presence was essential for the beauty of the glades. Flowers were confined to precise areas set apart in order to escape the gazelles which were free to wander at will. This meant that young trees too had to be protected. But flowers there were in astonishing abundance: hence the 600 or so *bostancis*, or gardeners, at Topkapısaray.

The extravagance of the orders for the Topkapı palace gardens in the sixteenth century was astounding. It was not simply a matter of growing the tens of thousands of plants required in the market gardens of Manisa and elsewhere, but of transporting the bulbs great distances, which meant that they were carried for weeks on the backs of camels. In 1587, 50,000 crocus bulbs were ordered from Maraş in the south-east of

Anatolia, after which an order for 4,000 young trees from nearby Izmit seems modest. The saplings included elm, ash, lime, judas, laurel, oak, plane and terebinth. What is one to make of an order for 24 tons of red and 16 tons of white roses from Edirne?[32] Lady Mary Wortley Montagu visited the Harem garden at the island palace at Edirne. It was filled with trees but no flowers, and in the middle were fountains and a kiosk, raised some 9 or 10 steps, with its gilded lattices entwined with vines, jasmine and honeysuckle to make a green wall. This was something that she was to see often.[33]

One of the most astonishing sights in Istanbul is described by Maurand,[34] who travelled there with Hayrettin Barbaros Pasha in the sixteenth century: it was the array of Parma violets that blanketed the terrace of the palace of the Grand Vezir Ibrahim Pasha, overlooking the Hippodrome. They were in flower in August whereas in France they only blossomed in the spring. Their scent was overwhelming as an antidote to the smell of the crowds that came to the *Divan*, or hall of justice, above the terrace: like Cardinal Wolsey sniffing his half of orange when faced with the far worse stench of English crowds.[35] The Ottomans had even been to war to cull violets from Greece and the transplanting of trees in season was a clause in many of their treaties with defeated countries.

In the country, gardens were not meant to last and women worked hard to cull their crops in all too short a season.[36] Many of them were for practical use, like dock leaves where there were no vine leaves to stuff or the seeds of love-in-the-mist which flavoured cream. The herbs of the pastures were culled with the knowledge inherited from millennia.[37] An aphrodisiac was made from the syrup of orchis roots: other plants supplied medicines besides dyes and reeds for matting. At Nisi in Laconia baskets of truffles were found by tapping the ground with a rod and listening to the sound: skilled diviners could even tell which species were buried there.[38]

Ladies of wealthy families travelled to the Sweet Waters of Asia in carriages attended by black eunuchs. It was their ostrich-feather fans that protected them from the gaze of the idle rather than veils – but only in so much as they wished. The village women who came to fill their pails at the fountain beside the little palace of Küçüksu were ignored. It was the young bloods of society – and especially the secretaries from foreign embassies – who mattered when they were rowed past in their skiffs and caiques, providentially slowed down as the rowers fought the six-knot current of the Bosporus. For them, veils slipped and fans were momentarily lowered. The ladies sat on cushions shaded by the elegant plane trees, cosseted by their slaves. A pale pink *ferace*, or light cloak, would contrast with the yellow or scarlet of the servitors and no notice seems to have been taken of Abdülhamit II's order that women might only go out in black, on the grounds of religion. The days were past when one or two sinners could be put to death by a monarch such as Murat IV to make an example of them. Young girls would even let their *ferace* slip off their shoulders to reveal their velvet jacket embroidered in gold and fastened with a jewelled clasp.

From the eighteenth century, carriages were of two main types. There was a *telek*, or pumpkin coach worthy of Cinderella, except that it had no springs; and the large and much more comfortable *araba* – a grandiose carriage full of cushions under a canopy of scarlet cloth, sometimes of velvet, on which languished parasols, fans and merriment. The fields beyond the ruined castle of Yıldırım Bayezit were increasingly filled by the populace and the number of portable stalls grew and grew. There were even bubbling cauldrons out of tune with popular music. Archers competed at the butts and story-tellers drew their knots of listeners. For the romantic or for botanists in search of peace, the stream that gave its name to the locality meandered round the village to hillsides which in spring were woven with wild flowers.

It was in this setting that the language of flowers grew up – it eventually achieved a vocabulary requiring a dictionary that was defeated by the idiosyncrasy of the dialects of different lovers. This may partly have arisen from the inconvenience of having a word cut out of the language because a flower was out of season. In Lady Mary Wortley Montagu's day, the sending of a rose asked the loved one to be pleased and let all her sorrows be his: and a jonquil meant that she should have pity on his passion. A grape, or presumably two, more obviously meant '*My eyes*' but why cinnamon should mean that the gallant was offering all his fortune is no more obvious than that a pear should beg for hope. Every flower spoke but there were not enough and pearls ('*You are the fairest of the young*'), soap, paper, straw ('*May I be your slave?*'), hair, gold wire and gold thread head a second list. Gold thread begging the girl not to turn away her face should not be confused with gold wire, which declared that the gentleman was dying and that she should come quickly. Later there were daffodils ('*Can you love me?*'); and a rosebud pulled into two ('*Would you die for me?*') to which the answer was to pull the head off a geranium ('*My neck is ready for the bowstring*'). But what happened if there was no geranium in the garden? To fill such gaps, all languages expand and so it is no surprise that walnuts, pistachios and bits of coal became meaningful.[39]

The other great pleasure ground at Kağıthane was the favourite resort of Ahmet III in the early eighteenth century.[40] In imitation of Marley-le-Roi, he had his *vezirs* build pavilions beside the artificial lagoon, filled by little streams that drifted over a miniature weir, but all these were ruthlessly destroyed upon his overthrow. The meadows and groves survived until late into the twentieth century, when roads and building lots finally destroyed them. In the eighteenth century, they lay between the royal parterres and the source of the waters of the Golden Horn and remained a retreat for any who could afford to hire a boat and even had servants to bring cushions and baskets of food. Like the Sweet Waters of Asia, there were plenty of vendors for the ordinary folk in search of relaxation for themselves and their children while, in the main, their husbands were at work. Besides the caiques, the *arabas* drawn by cream-coloured oxen ambled along from villages nearby or a landing stage. In the fields behind, the finest Arab horses grazed under the guard of Bulgarian grooms whose tents were pitched in the valley.

On Fridays, all the world came, including the men, to celebrate the holiday. The greensward was covered in mats and carpets. Bagpipes and the ungainly dances of the Slavonians contrasted with groups of lively children and the water-melon vendors wandering up and down. When Miss Pardoe visited, the sultan, Mahmut II, had not been seen for two years because his most favoured and beautiful odalisque had died. He had her buried under a weeping willow. Similar meadows on the banks of Edirne's two principal rivers were havens for the townsfolk to wander in at evening, picnic and sing with a freedom which would have been impossible at any other time. This is one more piece of evidence that the sultans certainly, and most of their subjects besides, were happiest in open places and preferred tents to their internment in hovel, house or palace.

The Survival of the Family

Today all has changed, but in Ottoman times it was modestly true that, as with many societies, great wealth divides families while poverty unites.[41] This was no law in Istanbul in the nineteenth century, but there and elsewhere in the Ottoman world members of a humble family were always in close company with each other, the husband as well as the children. Leaving monsters aside, and there were many, necessity drew a family together. In their intimate world, the mother had neither slave nor servant but had to do her own work and her labour enhanced her authority and importance. There were those who had to drag their lazy husbands from the coffee-house or tavern and drive them home with blows from their slipper. But not every wife nor on every night. What was remarked on was that husbands and wives treated each other very much as equals and would pass the evening together in gossip at the door of their house. They even went to the shops together, since for them there was no back room, which implies mutual consultation. At holiday times, they might picnic together at the grave of a relative or in the nearest piece of country.

That Istanbul was filled with numbers of roving men did not attract the attention of foreign observers, who never visited many of the quarters of the city. But they were amused by the street vendors selling glasses of water, *simit* (a ring of bread encrusted with sesame seed)[42] or other delights. The streets were thronged, and noisy with cries and children running. There was also laughter and it was a custom to throw a flower at the feet of a foreigner but no cuckolding was meant.[43] Foreigners were astounded by the *hamals*, or porters, who had a specially shaped human saddle on their back on which they carried loads that eventually killed them. They lived in dormitories and bought love when they could afford it, joining the throng at the door of a house of ill-fame so humble that there was only one room and ten minutes per client.

All this was a very different world from that of the grandees. They, for example, could escape the city when the plague arrived with the spring, although it died out due to the strict quarantine measures taken by successive governments just as they were in Venice. But if bubonic plague was defeated, there were new enemies. Malaria flourished in the countryside, debilitating whole areas. Typhus arrived without a visa in 1892 and in 1893 the *hajj* brought the plague back again: the caravan lost 40,000 of the faithful on their journey. After this, the crop failures which led to famine in 1906 and 1908, and the massacre of flocks and herds by disease, was only excelled by the even worse massacre of young men between 1914 and 1918.

Orga[44] was to lose his father in this war but also his comfortable home and garden due to one more devastating fire. His mother's savings were in jewels, which were lost as well, and it was only because his grandmother married again that they were able to move into a humble flat in a humble neighbourhood. It was a strange new world for the boy where street vendors had a monopoly since they were used to keep women off the streets. Typically, when his mother was very ill, the whole street rallied to help her and the family because she had been kind to them in the past. But when she was better, she had no money left in face of rising prices and she had to go to work for a pittance sewing in bad light. It changed her character irrevocably. If the grandmother had not returned to them, the family would have collapsed and, as it was, the children had to be sent to orphanages. The grandmother kept the home going by will-power succoured by her piety but also by her glass of forbidden wine in the evening, which she never abandoned. It was, indeed, the end of an era for all classes and the past was made irretrievable by defeat.

Women and the Caprices of Capital

The peasant woman's day was filled with labour and so was her spare time because she would be spinning wool if only to make clothes for the family. Two comments may be made about the latter. It is possible to spin walking about, as many Turkish women still do, and talk to fellow villagers. It is also true that before television insinuated itself so far as to affect agrarian life, there was nothing for anyone to do with their spare time except gossip or improve the home by work done for pride and pleasure. Education might have helped but it would have also increased the frustration of a people enslaved by nature. Moreover, men also spun both wool and cotton if the yarns were of a quality that would find a buyer. The tribal women weaving their narrow kilims on portable looms were living the life of conservative artists because they preserved the culture of their people by continuing to create traditional patterns from designs of long-forgotten significance, except the comfort of familiarity.

The archaeologist James Melaart realized the significance of the tells (or mounds) that abound on the plain near Konya. Having chosen to excavate one which had later archaeological detritus on its surface, he unearthed one of the oldest known human towns. With his discovery of Çatal Hüyük, it is clear that the origins of kilim weave patterns go back at least 7,000 years. The dyes from local plants or those culled along transhumant routes were essential to the chastity, if one may use the term, of the pattern. This would die in the later decades of the nineteenth century with the flush of commercial dyes. Not that the women appear to have minded this, provided the kilims were bought and one was saved the expense of making one's own dye or of going to buy it from the great vats in the market of a far-off town.

At the end of the nineteenth century, Mrs Scott-Stevenson[45] found that the kilims of Tarsus were an ugly white with an inferior geometric pattern but that one could order finer work to be specially woven. These traditional works were beautiful because of their smaller designs and the delicacy of colours which were never gaudy. The new kilims were the monopoly of Armenian merchants who had no interest in Turcoman culture although employing Turcoman women. The old motifs were woven at home in the old way: if not for long.

Not every part of the Ottoman provinces produced fine workmanship. The Balkans, in particular, wove quantities of coarse cloth such as *aba* which was used for rough woollen cloaks.[46] In the Morea, the coarse cloth was made into head shawls, girdles and towels. These found a market and the Balkans were lucky to be near to Europe, whose traders came to the two or three great fairs held each year in order to import timber (in the case of Venice) or cheap cloth. In a Greek village like Agrafa, the women worked full time weaving for a living. Villages specialized in particular items and many in Greece were employed in embroidering coarse German muslin in cheap imitation of the work done in Istanbul.[47] The old had to work too since there was never enough money – and because the Greeks, in some travellers' minds, had no respect for the aged such as was inbred in the Turks.

A foretaste of the future backwash of the industrial revolution in the Ottoman empire was observed in the seventeenth century by Busbecq, who noted spinning yards in Ankara and specially trained women washing angora wool in the rivers near the town. He also noted that women spun wherever they went out of doors. It was necessary, therefore, to have workshops in the town and by 1600 there were thirty there, each with two to three looms. This was not universal – as can be seen in many villages where the crofts were bigger than usual because the main room now contained a loom. (This could be seen until recently at Side, in the south of Anatolia, to quote an example.) The home loom certainly saved time but not necessarily the drudgery of long and tiring work, tiring because it required vigilant eyes and disciplined fingers which did not disturb the even tempo of their rhythm.

The Death of Natural Dyes

Change is inevitable and it is foolish to lay the blame on one incident. Nevertheless Anatolia was deeply affected by the 1851 Exhibition in London's Hyde Park, the first of the great commercial exhibitions in Europe. Later, there were the influences of great exhibitions elsewhere. The export of carpets soared and the annual export from Turkey was to double.

In a hamlet near Kayseri, an old Ottoman carpet-weaving yard still exists behind the headman's house. Here seven girls aged between 10 and 14 still work on a broadloom producing about twenty carpets each year. They follow the Gordes pattern, which has nothing to do with Kayseri, because, as the mistress of the yard explains, that is the pattern that is fashionable and which sells. And even so, although in step with the market, the girls work for a little food and so little money that one wonders why they smile and are eager to show their skills. The dyes are commercial because cheaper but also because they are brighter.

The death of natural dyes came on the tail of a high wind after 1851. Kula workers used a natural yellow berry to produce a distinctive dye. This was culled from an area near Konya and the berries cost enough to make it worthwhile for village women to gather them. By the end of the century the price had dropped to one-sixtieth and would not even pay for a child if she worked day and night. Uşak gave up making kilims altogether and Gordes gave up weaving coarse cotton cloth. Hundreds of villages were hit by the change to broad looms which could only be used in factories, although there were still rush jobs which were farmed out with the likelihood of poor knotting and cotton woof replaced wool. The women now used wheels although spinning is better by hand, if wanted for carpets, because it is looser.

Eventually, men took over the spinning, giving women more time to knot. At least by working at home they could also follow the demands of agriculture, and groups of women would combine to install a wider loom. Light prevented them working more than seven hours in winter but in the summer they could work as many as twelve. If they worked under a master, they received daily wages and not piece rates. A master would frequently employ 7- or 8-year-old girls for two to three years as apprentices. After this, he might take them on his roll or merely replace them with new apprentices who cost him relatively nothing and whose eyes had not been weakened by fine work – if fine work does in fact weaken eyes, a subject on which oculists now express doubts.

The carpet factories dominated the market. Uşak still led the way for others like Kula, Gordes, Isparta and Demirci. For one thing they employed only women and girls whereas the other centres also employed some men. The work grew rapidly until by 1900, 6,000 weavers worked 1,200 looms. By 1895 the important state factory at Hereke employed 1,000 women knotting to order. This has continued in that furnishing patterns imported from abroad in the mid-nineteenth century are still being meticulously copied for the palaces of the Bosporus. In the nineteenth century girls aged from 4 to 14 worked at Hereke on 150 or more knotting frames of varying sizes. Only the youngest escaped an 11-hour day. The girls either lived in a furnished dormitory with a medical room or, if lucky, walked home. The dormitories were under the supervision of old women who were themselves prisoners of the system. By 1900 the state also owned water-works, public utilities and the arsenals. Half the production of crude cloth for workers was woven at a huge mill at Bakırköy.[48] In 1897 it appears to have employed only women, girls and children, but it is not clear how many men worked in the managerial offices. In 1908 the Oriental Carpet Manufacturers set up their base in Izmir; by 1913 the company controlled three-quarters of Turkey's carpet manufacture and employed 50,000 knitters. The profits went to London.

The history of cotton weaving is not much different.[49] But there was one important step taken by the government, which was to found the Ziraat Bank in 1888. This bank let looms to the peasants at a modest 6 per cent until there were 800,000 in use in Anatolia alone: but the export of cotton fell steadily throughout the nineteenth century. Sickness like malaria, droughts and locusts were a scourge but the grimmest fate of all struck the unfortunate Kurds. In 1858 there was a benevolent attempt to settle these quasi-nomadic peoples who met with violence and the hostility of the villagers whether Christian or Moslem. The problem was the undercutting of prices by women who lived on the poverty line in Kurdish regions.

There were also problems with cultivation itself besides the trend to settle in towns like Dıyarbekir. The ultimate problem was that Lancashire and other western centres could produce better cloth more cheaply on commercial looms. The consequences for Ottoman trade were dire. At Ankara, for example, the guild had bought mohair for a fixed price but now women bought it cheaply at local markets, spun it and sold it for what they could get, which had to be below the European market price. The need for cheap labour was such that even the traditionally introverted guilds employed female labour, though only as hirelings.[50] The furniture and clothing guilds employed embroiderers and there were 5,000 women working for bonnet-makers. It was a picture painted across Europe. The abolition of monopolies was premature and resulted in the export of raw materials, which proved a disaster for many local artisans.

Bursa had traditionally been the centre of the silk trade together with Dıyarbekir, Amasya and Istanbul besides some smaller towns. Their looms had always depended on Iran for their silk until inconceivable harm resulted from Selim I's closure of the frontier in the sixteenth century, turning the looms into coffins in a mortuary. The harm done proved to be long-lasting. By the early nineteenth century, however, 6 caravans a year brought 120 metric tons of silk to Bursa on the backs of 1,200 camels and the population rose steadily throughout the century. Home-bred silkworms led to the planting of mulberry trees: the women were responsible for the highly skilled task of rearing the cocoons.[51] In the 1860s the worms were smitten with a disease for which Pasteur was to find a remedy.

Once again, girls were housed in dormitories and female labour filled the factories. The labour was seasonal and a worker was lucky to be employed for 100 days in a year, a third of the number worked by cotton spinners. Moslem and Christian women worked side by side and the girls ceased to be employed when they married. With all the work from shoe-making to brocade, the reliance on cheap labour meant that a skilled workforce could not be achieved. Child labour was exploited everywhere, including the tobacco factories at Izmir, Salonika and Samsun. The Salonika factory employed 1,400 women. At the Cibhalı factory, the 180 sorters were men while the rest of the 1,600 employees (who were packagers) were women or children. Sexual harassment of the women was common.

New Toil

At the end of the nineteenth century, conditions in the mines of Anatolia varied from region to region but the worst were in the great lead mines of Banya Luka in the Balkans.[52] In the Azap Dağ, near Izmir, men and women provided unskilled labour from 2 nearby villages, the men earning 4 or 5 times the wages of a woman. During the Crimean war, the Ereğli mines employed 500 workers who were mainly Croats.

A few English miners were brought in to teach these and the Montenegrans how to work but they were rapid victims of disease. The Croats
and Montenegrans survived and some settled there. The regime was
brutal and youths were employed to carry coal on their backs in baskets
from the face to the carts outside. None of these appears to have been
girls since, in 1867, headmen had to list all the men in their villages, and
they then had to work in 2-day stretches. There were regulations about
shifts and hours and some medical services. The men slept in barracks
– except for the locals who made their way back to their villages and
their wives. Bulgars and Italians enlisted in the mining force in the
1870s and joined the rest in their dormitories. The local women suffered
from the intermittent absences of their husbands and sons, which could
only mean more labour on the land; worse was the inevitable search for
prostitutes by men unnaturally penned.

The result of the grim working conditions in the towns and the
increasing impoverishment of village life was emigration. The traffic
was not one-way: Moslems fleeing the Russians in the Crimea and
Caucasia were hotly followed by others from Greece and the Balkans as
the Ottoman empire shrivelled up. By the turn of the nineteenth
century, these amounted to as many as 5–7 million people. They were
given good land, sometimes with disastrous results (as with the
arrogant Circassians, in particular).

Another example in the last days of Ottoman government, before
the Republic was created in 1924, was the transfer of Moslems from
Yugoslavia to Pasha Liman island in the Sea of Marmara in place of
Greeks. The Greeks had cultivated vines and olive trees besides
exploiting the rich fishing, but the newcomers were farmers who had
not seen the sea and they brought with them a completely alien outlook.
Years of struggle followed before sufficient crops were reaped to
support a family. It was an achievement deserving compassion. The
tragedy was that they learnt to use the sea successfully just when motor
trawlers arrived to pillage their waters. The women worked in the fields;
a youth was the shepherd who took the village flock to the hill by day;
and one courageous girl had her own boat, leaving the men hopelessly
confused by a mixture of admiration and disapproval. If the women
made money out of their vegetables, then they were off across the island
to the only village that had a shop and bought cloth to make into
clothing. There was no longer any question of weaving their own.

With the coming of the twentieth century the lure of America
attracted the ablest men. The new reforms gave the Christian

population equal rights with the Moslems but also equal obligations, including the much dreaded military service. Only some 20 per cent of the emigrants were Moslem: and only 16 per cent were women. Three-quarters of the emigrants were men in the prime of life or youths, and the balance between Moslems and Christians in Turkey was completely altered. The high number of women and children left behind was as sad as bereavement, but in the end as many as 400,000 husbands and sons and brothers returned. Homesickness was one reason, while only a small proportion of emigrants eventually found good wages and set themselves up in their new country. Sons and brothers were gone and only husbands might summon their wives to join them. As a consequence, one third of all single-person families were forsaken women. Again, this was not simply an Ottoman tragedy: 6 million, or nearly a fifth of the population of Italy, emigrated at this time.

The professions of midwife – honoured as always – and nurse saw no changes in the nineteenth century, but with the slow emergence of education for girls there grew a need for women teachers, a challenge which was gladly accepted. A school needs a directress and by the nineteenth century there were skilled female administrators who were able to pass on their knowledge. Moreover, some of the esteem in which educators were held throughout the Moslem world could not but be transferred to a woman teacher unless she had an exceptional personality. It was the most important development in the sexual structure of the country and a secret revolution was in progress by the turn of the century. On graduating from their schools, those who were inspired among the new generation of women could aspire to entering other professions than education. Within a generation, women became doctors, lawyers and even managers under the Republic. But this is not a book about Atatürk's singular revolution or only in so far as the events under the sultan that preceded it can be seen as part of its inspiration. It is better personified by women's entry into the civil service, and therefore government, than by the casting off of the veil. Women were no longer beating at the door because of injustice: it was they who had to open it. But not in the nineteenth century.

Women against Authority

The nineteenth century saw wives of clerks, who could not in any way be denigrated as a mob, relentlessly battling for justice for their husbands and family. At the end of the century, there was the usual delay in paying the salaries of civil servants. A large body of women marched on the ministry of finance and invaded it, swarming up every stairway, filling every corridor and blocking every door with their lamentations and demands for payment. The minister escaped out of the back door but his staff were trapped because the women refused to budge. The authorities could not manhandle such a crowd without causing a scandal and so terms had to be reached. As in the past, with the mutinies and riots egged on by the janissaries, it was not a revolution. There was no suggestion that the state as such was threatened. But the stoning of ministers' carriages and other modest rioting occurred throughout the century.

On one occasion, the owner of some land in the village of Rumeli Hısar decided that he wanted to enclose it right up to the village fountain. From earliest memories, the land had been a pleasant resort for the women and children of the village where they could sit under trees and enjoy the fresh air and the beautiful views of the Bosporus and the Asian shore. The women were furious at the threat to their haven and resorted to the law but their case failed. Work began and they sulkily looked on when going to draw water, for the building works soon approached the fountain. New negotiations failed and the wall grew. Soon afterwards, a band of militant women appeared led by the widow of the late (and mother of the present) *imam*, dark of face and sharp of tongue. Armed with sticks and stones, they drove the alarmed workmen off but the police arrived and obliged the women to retreat. They then retired and the women held a council of war.

When the workmen arrived in the morning, they found that the women were already there and that the *imam*'s mother and a friend were sitting in the trench. There was a lull for the authorities to consider the crisis. In the dark that evening, the women then pulled down what had been built of the wall. A police guard was assigned by day and the watch by night. The matter was out of hand and even the government was involved. A deputation of the women was summoned to the palace, where a veteran minister scolded the law-breakers. More effectively, he told the young *imam* that he was about to lose his position. Thus, in a sense, he had to torpedo his militant mother if he were to keep his job: this he did. Protests stopped but the builders were threatened with being stoned. The fountain is still well clear of the wall 100 years later. This was not a fight on behalf of husbands, from whom the women appear to have had little support, but for the women themselves. It is an aspect which adds significance to the event in the history of women's fight for liberty in Ottoman territories.

It was also significant of the way that rules were breaking down even more than they had always done under Ottoman rule. Thus the bridges across the Golden Horn (completed at the end of the nineteenth century) were paid for by toll but the women got away tax-free because their veils hid their identities and could not be lifted: but more because toll-keepers, like other men, were unwilling to hassle a woman. Thus laws become games and even pastimes. Women may have had to walk behind their husbands if they came from humble backgrounds but in the home they were on their own ground. Unhappily, this cheerful supposition makes no allowances for brutal or merely uncouth husbands, nor the weariness of penury.

The world of tit-for-tat that rules conjure up is nicely caught in Van Millingen's anecdote about a respectable foreign couple who sat in an empty women's shelter while waiting for their ferry across the Bosporus. When a motherly old woman and a 14-year-old boy arrived, the boy fetched the pier master and had the foreign gentleman thrown out. Whereupon the wife had the 14-year-old thrown out too.[53]

'Constantinople' by Hubert Sattler (1817–1904): Istanbul in 1848

CHAPTER 8

The Seeding of Western Culture

Women in the Arts

In the seventeenth century there were paintings of women but no portraits and they principally appeared as characters in a story or anecdote. The pornography of exposure, curiously enough, pertains to males rather than women. There is, for example, a miniature of a couple who have come in distress to the *kadı* because their marriage is in ruins since there have been no children. This is a reminder of how important fertility was to a woman. In the story, the judge is old, but fortunately not too old, and he can diagnose the problem: the young couple have no idea how to have intercourse. The judge draws back his robe in order to expose himself in splendid form since the dimensions of his manhood would have made the most lascivious of sultans jealous. The couple presumably hurried home to bed.[1] As an educational instrument, the miniature was not pornographic since there is nothing obscene implied in the event. That is to say, for so long as one does not stop to attribute the judge's performance to the presence of a pretty girl or see the unusual size of his rampant member as either comic or erotic.

Love stories were only rarely illustrated by nudity, and the adolescent lover was still beardless in most miniatures, leaning with his beloved against a symbolic tree. Men were encouraged to grow beards because these were said to put off nubile girls by hiding the men's good looks. Otherwise, such a character as the starving Majnun reveals bones and nothing more and, although his story gives the illustration a subdued erotic overglow, there is no pornographic interest. By the eighteenth century, however, Levni and Buhari were creating erotic miniatures which were always subdued by the traditional formality of definition that was integral to the technique. It is almost as if the artists were perversely refusing to study anatomy seriously.[2] Yet the two artists were no amateurs and they depicted breasts which were no longer the shallow yoghurt bowls that were frequently depicted in *hamam* scenes. The breasts might claim to be the first part of the body after the face that was studied by the Ottoman miniaturist. The innovators were also aware of what they were about because they would often – often enough to be no accident – expose the woman's breasts while leaving the rest of her body fully dressed. Pornography is always in the eye of the beholder.

There was now a sense of freedom. Subjects such as Adam and Eve freckled by leaves in the shadow of the interfering serpent were no longer daring. It is not so much the square metres of naked flesh in the miniatures of Vehbi, like those of festivals in the 1720s, but the ambiguities which are pornographic.[3] His miniatures of scenes with dancing girls, who must have been played by boys in girls' clothing, are ambiguous twice over. The miniatures themselves are suggestive in modern terms, but when they were painted there were dancing boys in any mildly disreputable drinking house and they were meant to provoke desire. A portrait of a woman seated in childbirth, on the other hand, was a record without any erotic overtones. The seventeenth century was a period when no woman except a prostitute would go out in the street provocatively dressed. Even seductive glances that were not accidental were inconceivable. No woman gave way to the temptation of lifting her veils anywhere near bottom-pinching men who ambled by unburdened by their repressions, ready to accept anything which seemed to them to be an invitation.

In the nineteenth century, European artists were hard at work in the Ottoman empire. Their influence was bound to affect local artists, among whom there were many men but very few women until the turn of the nineteenth century when one or two emerged out of the privacy of their homes. Mihri Hanim is an example of them all in that the pasha, her father, had her educated in the western manner and she received private lessons to become a skilled and charming portrait painter.[4] She is representative of those few higher-class girls who painted modestly but with skill and who opened the gate for the women who were to appear in the middle of the twentieth century. It was the camera that underscored a revolution in the educated public's attitude to art partly because, once people were used to photographs, pictures were easier for everybody to read.

In the rococo apartment of Mihrişah Sultan at Topkapısaray there is an important landscape which well serves to typify a whole genre of Ottoman painting. In the manner that one reads miniatures, the admirer looks down on the scene, which is of a basin or pool dominated at one end by a large but frail pavilion and surrounded by immaculate little flower-beds inset in the stone terraces alongside the water in several ranks. These halt at a relatively high wall beyond which is the wild world of trees, seemingly entangled one with the other to form that wilderness, by contrast with the order and immaculate pruning of the formal garden within, which is the other Eden. This was a contrast well known in the west. Here, however, it is not used simply to enhance the beauty of both the inward garden and the outward freedom but to make a statement, which is further underlined by the long view over estuaries to a seemingly open sea. The popularity of the genre would support Professor Arık's contention that women did not simply see an idyllic landscape but knew the deep emotion that those who are confined feel for the free world beyond their walls.[5]

In the nineteenth century, there grew up a tradition of wandering artists who came to village or town to paint the inside of public buildings and the main rooms of wealthy burghers' *konaks*. There are examples in more modest village houses and the work was particularly popular in Karaman. The mosque of Şerefettin at Konya, for example, has a very large depiction of the Süleymaniye mosque above the mihrab. The Çakır Ağa Konak at Birgi has views of a red-roofed Istanbul, and a house in Karaman has a light-hearted paddle-steamer probably riding on the Bosporus. Under the wooden dome of Kara Mustafa Pasha's large fountain at Merzifon is a scene full of as many trains, coaches and all the roads and byways, not to mention guns and hills, as anyone could desire. And desire may be the correct word because it does not take long to realize that this is escapist and not just decorative art.

A significant date in the history of education in Istanbul was the opening of the Imperial Museum in 1875. There was a home at last for the treasures of Anatolia and the start of a modest control of the pillaging of sites by western archaeologists and unscrupulous traders on the grounds – not entirely unjust – that the sultan and his government were glad to be paid for these objects and had nowhere to store them. At last, innumerable treasures were on view to the public. Women were only admitted on Wednesdays[6] when men were excluded, however, because they might misbehave even in museums and they had the right to go there all the other days of the week.

Literature

Apart from the *One Thousand and One Nights*, which are not Ottoman, poetry and popular prose literature will not be touched on in this book. This is because the subject needs to be seen as a whole else the continuing strength of Turkish poetry is accepted without reference to its roots. However, it would be wrong not to mention one popular prose work which came to western Ottoman society after passing through Iran. This is because *The History of the Forty Vezirs*[7] is an almost, but not quite, unbridled attack on women. It is all the more powerful because it is a complete story in itself and not a jumble of folk, court or even French fancy in the manner of the *Nights*. In one sense, it is more damning of many men's attitude towards women than any rival book simply because of its assumptions even though disguised as humour. It is also important as the record of what nineteenth-century writers had to contend with.

The Ottoman version of *The Forty Vezirs* was dedicated to the sultan Murat II and therefore dates from the mid-fifteenth century. Forty of the stories are attempts to persuade the king not to behead his son and forty are the stepmother's responses to these stories and were intended to keep her husband's axe sharp. The stories may have been trimmed to suit the most extreme Ottoman attitudes towards women, attitudes that did not differ greatly from those throughout fifteenth-century Europe. The values, like those of the Urals and north Asian folk-tales, were universal at the time and the book expresses male paranoia about the powers of women. It is noteworthy that, once again, the number forty, weighed down by its symbolism, at least cuts short what otherwise would have been a fatiguing procession of improbable events stretching out to the end of time. The number forty in itself implies infinity, but fortunately also acts as a buffer.

The story is that of the son of a king, a king for whom we can have little respect. He is merely a stage property who, one hopes, has never been a real person and certainly had nothing in common with the mystic Murat II to whom the tale was offered. The incredibly handsome youth is taught by a noble scholar who educates him in astronomy and astrology. One day, this tutor is alarmed to see a fearful gap of forty days in the boy's horoscope and, in his wisdom, declares that the prince must not speak for forty days else he will die by the sword. Grievously, as it turns out, and as he might have foreseen, he tells no one else about his admonition. So when the king speaks to his son, the dutiful student is silent until his father sends him to his stepmother in the hope that she will persuade him to speak. It is of passing interest that stepson and stepmother should have free access to each other although she is young. She has lusted after him from the day that she entered the Harem.

When he still will not speak, the queen flings her arms around him and proposes that she should murder his useless old father and then delude the court into thinking that someone else has done the deed. Then she can marry this dazzling youth on the verge of his sexual prime. Horrified, the prince strikes her on the mouth in order to free himself of her hot embrace and thus arouses her pathological hatred. She tears her face and covers her rent clothes with blood so that when the king comes she can accuse the prince of attempting to ravish her, saying that he would murder his father in order to marry her. She successfully pleads with the king that the boy should be executed else murder will ensue. After a restless night, the king orders the execution.

After pleading for the prince's life, the shocked Grand Vezir distracts the king with the story of a holy man whose death was contrived by a wicked old woman who sent tempting damsels into his cave. He was portrayed as a sinner who was no match for St Antony. The *vezir* then warns the king to beware the wiles of women. But the queen counters with her own story about a fair prince who was not beaten for ill-conduct when a child and so grew up to be a brutal tyrant. Her will prevails so that the prince is again faced with execution in the morning. He has to be saved by the second *vezir*'s tale, based on the evil done by women. Again, the queen has to riposte with an equally prejudiced tale of man's vileness; only her tale is palpably untrue. And so the story proceeds from day to day until all forty *vezirs* have told their tales of women's shame while the queen behaves like a rival of Sheherazade night after night.

The queen finally wins and on the forty-first morning the scaffold is set up in the public square and the king orders the execution not only of his son but of all the *vezirs* as well. The prince is blindfolded and forced onto his knees. The executioner draws his sword, walks twice round the scaffold and asks if he is really to behead the youth – once the head has been severed from the body, it cannot be put back and after death it will be too late for repentance. The king fiercely orders the execution a second time. Fortunately, the indomitable executioner asks the question a third time and the king passes his final sentence – or he would have done had not the prince's tutor arrived in a fluster to order the hapless and obedient boy to speak. This he does succinctly and creditably. Now, at last, the girls of the Harem bear witness against the queen. The king repents and the queen is tied to the tail of an ass to be driven out and torn to pieces in the desert. The palace is given over to forty days of revelry and delight. The envoi begs God to keep men good and so preserve them from the guile of crafty women.

A number of interesting references to women occur in the stories. At one point[8] the Grand Vezir correctly reminds the king that there is no permission in Koranic law to act on the word of a woman alone. Later, we are told how many are the lies and tricks of women. If a woman but looks at her great toe she will hatch from two to seventy tricks and plots. We are reminded that the caliph Ömer advised that nobody should take the council of a woman but should do the opposite of what she says. In the fourth story, the holy man has a cunning, brawling wife.

The twelfth *vezir* tells of women's dishonesty and why one should never confide in them about business or anything else; nor should women ever be allowed to act of their own free will. The queen answers with a story of a weaver that belongs to the tradition of 'The emperor has no clothes'. She appears to understand that her story is thin; proving herself a woman indeed, she resorts to tears. And so on.

It would be impossible to list all the derogatory references to women – or the inverted examples inherent in the queen's defence of her own sex – in Ottoman legends, though there are some fair girls to be found in the stories who are even worthy of marriage. What is more germane is that there are ill-begotten men involved. These include the probably wicked but certainly unlucky Frank, who buys two sons of a prince as his slaves and dies a horrible death for his tactlessness. It does no credit to either prince or purchaser. In another story, the queen who locks her lover in a chest is certainly an adulteress but then what is the youth who serves her? In a curious way, it is difficult to slander one sex without belittling the other.

The supposed inferior standing of women, in spite of the queen of Sheba, was accepted almost universally by men. There were exceptions but they were clothed in the attributes of men. By the nineteenth century, the Ottomans were no more than 100 years behind the developed countries of the west. It is the ambiguities in *The History of the Forty Vezirs* that are fascinating, rather more than the fornicating fiction of the present day.[9]

There had been poets and story-tellers from Seljuk times and before. The latter were often thinly disguised popular spokesmen who used jingles to express discontent. They remained an important outlet for news that mattered to the common folk until the twentieth century. They included the *meddahs*, who were nearer to jesters than minstrels. The hero of their tales was often the orphan whose step-parents would personify both innocence and rascality. Nothing in these stories ever happens by chance. It is as if the Fates are cooking in the background.

The Theatre

The most famous of the popular Ottoman entertainments were the shadow puppets. The genre originated in Java, China and India but there is evidence that the plays travelled through Central Asia into the Ottoman lands and there acquired shamanist elements.[10] That there is a debt to Dionysus is equally apparent with the mother figure of Demeter, together with Persephone and the underworld of Pluto, where the girl is abducted to return with the spring to her grieving mother, relations and friends. The stories, however, lack the dignity of classical legends.

As one example, a rich man dies, leaving his property to the first person to win his daughter. Karagöz – who is not called Black Eye for nothing – manages to achieve this. When things do not go well between the couple, the wife leaves him. He marries for the second time, but the first wife returns and he is pestered by his mother-in-law. He tries to soothe her but both wives are women of determination and claim their rights over him. It is time for Karagöz to run away. The theme of cuckolding is constant. Karagöz abandons his wife and escapes to Yalova with his sweetheart but does not know that she has two lovers. Since his wife has abandoned him, he brings his sweetheart home and his jealousy feeds on a train of lovers until the last, who is a ruffianly drunkard, chases him out of his own house.

It is difficult to claim that these stories have a moral. The women in the plays range from young to old and are either flighty, loyal or scheming gossips. If they personify anything, it is intrigue. The *orta oyunu*, or open-air theatre,[11] was acted by real people in the middle of a field or open space but the female parts had to be played by boys. In a sense, the puppets had an advantage there although their voices were not those of women. In the nineteenth century, children came to performances just as they did to Punch and Judy in the Tuilleries gardens. Karagöz was somewhat more obscene than Punch's baton and a foreign friend was appalled at the sight of two little girls enjoying the spectacle. He asked his elderly and dignified Ottoman host how he could expose children to such degradation – to receive the answer that they would sooner or later have to know about the facts of life.

The *meddah* plays employed a stream-of-consciousness technique long before it returned to Turkey at the turn of the nineteenth century with the books of western novelists.[12] The popular dramas can therefore be seen as one of the influences on the first Ottoman theatre as well as the first Ottoman novels. The earliest fiction was awash with fantasy but soon merged into realism because books which were for 'the public good' or for 'progress' became the ideal. By 1842 European novels were used as models: they included such popular works as *Robinson Crusoe*, *Les Misérables* or *Monte Cristo*. In spite of French Romanticism, Ottoman authors were down to earth and some wrote very factual or photographic descriptions. The work of Halide Edip Adivar, who published her first novel in 1912, was remarkable for its opposition to the oriental tradition. Simple and static, it was equally opposed to the dynamic of the west.[13]

At a similar serious level, Ahmet Midhat was one of several writers whose novels made clear that there would be a continuing fight for the right of women to be rid of any sense of inferior status, although he admitted that there could be limits.[14] Ahmet Cevdet was equally courageous but more passionate in his fight against the cult of hatred and with it the diseases of inertia, ignorance and fanaticism. It was a battle between the old order and the more dynamic members of a new generation who were not afraid of female emancipation. They were threatened with hellfire and ruin if women were to be treated as if they were the equals of men. This was a curiously disguised compliment to the supposedly inferior sex. Indeed, the *ulema*'s fears resulted in many outbursts and the prediction of disasters but Cevdet was unswerving in his belief that Turkey's decline was due to the abominable status of women as late as 1908. Meanwhile, the contrast in cultures between east and west was a matter of moods and modes: they may be summed up in musical terms as melodic in the east and symphonic in the west.

In 1872 the first Ottoman play was published but it was not performed: *The Marriage of a Poet* discussed relationships between the sexes in a serious manner. Three years later, Namik Kemal had his play *Fatherland or Silistria* performed with Armenian women actresses since Moslem women still could not appear on the stage.[15] Again, it was about sex and the status of women and asked questions about the concept of marriage. Kemal's newspaper, *Ibret* [Warning], was radical enough but this play went beyond the tolerance of the conservatives and was banned on 10 April 1873: its author, who was the foremost Ottoman prose writer, was exiled.[16] With these few exceptions, the popular dramas usually followed the western fashion for light comedy and had no serious content whatsoever.

Costume

Meanwhile, oblivious of social, let alone republican revolutions, court life continued with its women in splendid jewels and Paris gowns. The jewels were so heavy that one wonders how they put up with them and it is not a surprise that one of Abdülhamit II's daughters rebelled because her grandmother had given her a surfeit.[17] It was a period when special attention was paid to hair and there was no more eager market for Paris hats than Istanbul. In the past, the costume of the Valide had been no different from the rest except that the fabrics were finer and the jewels more gorgeous. Now, fashion had created a mock democracy since great wealth opened the doors of the leading couturiers like Worth without distinction other than price. It is significant that in the 1890s a fashion journal appeared entitled *Hanımlara Mahsus Malumat* intended exclusively for women. Clothes had always been politically important in the Ottoman empire since their colours and styles were meant to differentiate one section of a complex society from another, whether on grounds of religion, race, profession, trade or beggardom. A revolution often affected styles from the sans-culottes to jeans and the fantasies of pop stars.

With the arrival of Worth came a change in attitude. The great ladies were not simply displaying their wealth but their position in an international society. This outlook could only affect the shopkeepers gradually and the poor hardly at all except for those given handed-down garments by the charitable grandes dames. It was for them that, in 1878, Abdülhamit II created a special order of chivalry for compassionate women engaged in charity. The pretty gold, enamel and rose diamond star of the order of Nişane-Şefkat was awarded to one or two foreign women as well as Ottoman but most often to favourites in the sultan's Harem.

These splendid, if often bored, ladies were still surrounded by embroidered velvet cushions and pearl-clotted bedspreads. Their coffee tables were covered by silk circles emblazoned with embroidery and held fast by a fringe of metal thread at the hem. Such rich designs on rich fabrics were the hallmark of a grandee but, as with all such symbols of importance, they were hankered after by the parvenus out of some Ottoman *À la Recherche du Temps Perdu* by, so to speak, Rüstem Proust. The embroidery section of Topkapısaray contains examples of the ornate squares of velvet cloth in which wedding presents were bundled. There were, inevitably, silk prayer rugs but these at least would be painful if studded with gems.

By way of contrast to this heavy magnificence, produced by many sore fingers, are the fine works associated with the capital, the coasts and the islands. The cotton towels or scarves were too frail to support thick clusters of metal or gems, the linen or the silk examples even less robust. Instead, they were embroidered in silk with elegant borders of a refreshing refinement after all the plush pomp of the velvets. Hand towels predominated over sashes and the rest and it seemed sad to visitors like Lady Mary Wortley Montagu, as we have seen, to wipe one's hands and soil gossamer or stain a napkin for fear that they would not survive even sensitive washing by hand. A surprising number did: enough to identify local patterns.

In what is left of the once great house in the fabulous park at Bowood in Wiltshire, there is a portrait of Mrs Baldwin painted by Sir Joshua Reynolds. She is in the dress which she had brought back with her from Turkey. Her husband spent much of his life as a merchant all over the Near East and wrote a copious number of books of little value. Indeed, one was declared to be the work of a maniac. Egypt and Alexandria were his chief interests.

Turkish clothes entranced eighteenth-century women in Europe because they were so free, and by the turn of the century the world of stays and other instruments of conformity was in disarray partly because of the liberalizing elements within the philosophic outlook of the more humane protagonists of the French revolution. Now, at the very end of the Ottoman period, the glamour of Parisian clothes encompassed Turkish women in bodices and stays else they could not have worn these creations which demanded a slender waist. The natural form and the loose belt were abandoned and no doubt Mrs Baldwin turned in her grave.

From the sixteenth century the basic costume in Turkish towns had been an undergown which was enveloped in another when the women went into the streets.[18] The veil remained a constant feature and simply consisted of white cotton bound round the forehead and hair and fastened at the back. The bottom half was fastened in the same way. It was concealing but women could speak simply by altering the position of the lower half in particular. In the nineteenth century, the material became finer and finer among the rich until it was transparent gauze – this became so frail as almost to disappear and then its only use was to enhance rather than disguise. For peasants and humbler wives, where it had a hold, the veil was steadfastly thick enough to remain a real mask. Because it was not worn by the Christian or Jewish communities, one wishes that one had a record over the centuries of how Moslem women felt as opposed to the opinions of the pontificating husbands.

They were, unhappily, the victims of more than convention because the government, due above all to the power of the *ulema*, continued to issue edicts about dress into the twentieth century. It was not just that the medieval customs of western Europe were continued so that materials and colours conformed to a complex social register which permitted an official to tell the nationality and worth of any woman at a glance; it was that any change in custom was a challenge to the stability of the ruling regime. The colours of houses were also regulated so that only a believer could paint his house or *yalı* red. It was, however, common practice to keep the exterior of a home shabby in order to deceive the tax-collector as to the worth within. One may suppose that this custom did not apply to either the householder or his wife and family.

Women nevertheless managed to circumvent dress regulations increasingly during the nineteenth century. The black shoes of a Jewess became dark blue and all colours appeared among Christian women; nor were the rules about a plain *ferace*, or light cloak, taken seriously. But when the Egyptian Ismail Pasha was governor of Damascus he forbade the wearing of fashionable bonnets.[19]

Lady Mary Wortley Montagu was an authority on Ottoman clothes and bought them for herself. That is to say, she had them made but not sewn up any more than the wife of a grandee would have done. As in Europe, this was a job for the lady's maid and her needle or tiny gold safety pins. Lady Mary's drawers were of rose-coloured damask which went with brocaded shoes: kid embellished with gold. Over her drawers she wore a smock of fine silk gauze edged with embroidery; its wide sleeves reached halfway down her arms. She then put on a waistcoat with equally wide sleeves which were folded back to display a deep gold fringe and over it a damask kaftan reached to the ground. It was, so to speak, to dress in layers. She could also wear a loose robe in cold weather. All this was engirdled with precious stones. On her head she wore a *kalpak*, or velvet cap,[20] adorned with gems and with a gold tassel worn on one side.

There were variations of costumes, including the *entari*, or loose gown, which was tight at the back and wide open in front with jewel buttons at the waist. Buttons of diamonds or rubies or emeralds set in gold or diamonds were remarked on by many travellers and pearl buttons were commonplace to the rich. All of this was extravagant compared with the fine linen chemise and *şalvar*, ample trousers ideal for sitting on a *divan*, and a gown which was covered with a second one of silk on going out: this was the humbler version of the *ferace*, but was sometimes used like a cloak, even by women. With the *ulema* it was a cloak that was worn everywhere. It was almost universally made of green cloth while the rich might have a silk hood. In the sixteenth century, it had been more of a gown made of rich materials and worn with a cape over head and shoulders. When the woman walked, the front of the *ferace* opened to show the fine lining and the dress beneath. In the nineteenth century the best *feraces* were of the richest shot poplin. The best sleeves were of Bursa brocade and were purchased separately. At this period black hair was the fashion and henna was used in profusion.[21]

An enchanting fashion which survived from the sixteenth century was the gown with the triple skirt.[22] Previously worn at weddings, it was clearly also donned on other important occasions by the nineteenth century. The embroidered gown opened down the front to reveal a traditional heavy silver belt and semi-precious stones, including amber and cornelians, worn at the waist over the *şalvar*. Two other vents sprang from under the arms, thus creating a long skirt which was indeed divided into three. The grace was in the wearing because only someone with poise could make the panels flow when walking and fall in a cascade when seated. Worn by a woman who had no dress sense, they exposed her clumsiness with each step and, since the long panels spread out as much as 1 metre over the floor, could even trip her or have her floundering.

Associated with the bride's visit to the *hamam* were the Baidalli jacket and complete dress of velvet on heavy silk which was enriched with braid and embroidery. The fabrics themselves were heavy but were made all the more so by the gold and silver thread used in their decoration; again these could only be worn by a woman with a stately posture, since there were no corsets.

A lady should be seen in her setting. In the 1860s Lady Hornby described a visit to a pasha's wife and took careful note of her clothes.[23] The great lady received her in a *selma*, the wide-sleeved underdress. Her *şalvar* were a delicate shade of violet and bound round the waist by a richly embroidered scarf: above this she wore a shirt of silvery Bursa gauze. Over this again was a magnificent jacket of amber-coloured cashmere, lined with the richest sable. On her head she wore a fez bound round with a plait of hair, fastened here and there with an immense rose of diamonds. A purple lily-flower was stuck straight down the plait and shaded her forehead. Her earrings were of a single pendant emerald set in a small spray of brilliants. She must once have been of a surprising beauty and she was still strikingly handsome. Household women constantly came in to see the group without rebuke and the pasha's second wife, a Circassian, brought a present from him. The meal ended with *naghiles* and a woman jester.

Shoes were a special delight and cobblers' shops were among the first that a respectable woman could visit. Even modest craftsmen worked from a last. *Çedik* were little slipper boots that rode high in front. *Papuç*, the best known of all Ottoman shoes, carried soft uppers on strong soles and were much embroidered in gold. There was also a version without heels where the toes curled over in the manner of the foppish points of the early Renaissance in Europe. There were wooden pattens of walnut or box for use in the *hamam*: for the rich they were inlaid with mother-of-pearl and tortoise shell and held by silver nails. They required experience and skill to walk in, high above a wet and slippery marble floor.[24]

When women wore caps, they were often wound round with a muslin scarf.[25] Indoors, a grand lady's hair could be elaborately braided to form a semi-circle in front and fall in long braided tresses down her back. A quaint form of cap was the coy, because miniature, version perched on top of the head and secured by a scarf. This fashion had ended by the eighteenth century as had the Venetian-type mask which covered the whole face except for the eyeholes. There was a form of miniature turban shaped like half a pleated melon which seems to have evolved for dignitaries of the royal Harem just as they wore kaftans which were very much men's attire. Yet another style of headgear used in the seventeenth century was the tall hat that had echoes of Venetian styles partly because of its brocading. Mischievously, it could be seen as a predecessor of the hats of French judges or cooks and scullions. Another popular fashion was for a padded cap which flopped backwards, somewhat in the manner of those worn by the *bostancıs* (royal gardeners and guards) at one period.

Almost the last beautiful Ottoman fashion was for a long dress once again made up of three panels which fell to the floor. It could only be worn by the young and slim but no doubt stouter ladies were tempted. Fat was not unsightly and it did not need disguising because the real form of a woman mattered more than the contortions of bony foundation garments. Above all, a young woman needed to carry a single bud or bloom to complete her dress.

She also needed jewellery and of that the Ottomans had an astonishing abundance: as we have seen for the daughter of Abdülhamit II. It appeared as necklaces and earrings as well as rings. It weighed down headgear, bosom and belt. Stones tended to be cabochon set in gold or clusters of diamonds which set the hair alight. The greatest fantasy was the wearing of quivering blooms of diamonds and gems in the hair – these were cunningly set on wire so that when the wearer walked, they jostled and sparkled magically in candle or lamplight. There is something of a Fabergé taste about Ottoman jewellery. The toiletry was elegant and a delight to use. Ivory combs inset with gold and tiny gems were kept in slim inlaid boxes. Every woman had her own *hamam* bowl and, again, for the rich it was of chased silver. Even pumice stone had its silver holder. But the most beautiful objects were those handkerchiefs and towels enriched with hours of patient embroidery and of a linen so fine that it could be seen through.[26]

On occasion, the black intendant of the royal Harem went out shopping for the inmates: doubtless a great amount of trouble had been taken over drawing up his list of purchases. In the mid-nineteenth century, White observed him buying quantities of cotton stockings and cambric kerchiefs. There were also orders for artificial flowers of which the Ottomans were fond. Ahmet III had great flower festivals at Topkapısaray in the spring when massed blooms flowed in and out of the kiosks and the pavilions. Tortoises carried little lanterns on their backs and wandered among them in the evening. When by the third day some flowers wilted, they were replaced by artificial understudies. Cutting out paper flowers became a specialist craft because it called for great skill. Other presents on the intendant's list were Windsor soaps and English pins. He chose perfumes and orange water together with cold cream. He also bought quantities of cats'-hair toothbrushes. Toothbrushes were regarded with suspicion since they might come from some unclean beast.

The poor did not buy artificial flowers, white cotton stockings or toothbrushes, although the middle class did. There was good green Turkish soap made of olive oil and henna was not extravagant. Peasant clothes were largely home-made (including the spinning and weaving), even in the nineteenth century. Women from Abasia and Georgia wove prettily striped shawls and rugs made with the hair of Circassian goats which was long and soft. Their success was due to their ability to produce excellent dark blue and red dyes.[27] On the Side coast, women were still weaving kerchiefs in the Pharaonic Egyptian manner and on the Black Sea coast cottons were stamped with black patterns inherited from the Hittites.

The Circassians wove as they had always done. This was also true of the Tatars, who still wore their hair in innumerable plaits below their fez caps. They had begun to hide their faces when a stranger passed. Clothes are always a question of posture for which the carrying of weights on the head is the finest training. All Ottoman women carried themselves with poise and dignity until the working women were bowed by childbirth and ever bending to work in the fields or, for that matter, washing clothes in the stream.

The Last Course

The basis of Ottoman cooking during the nineteenth century remained leavened bread with sour dough or unleavened on religious occasions like Ramazan, the month of the fast. There was a greater yield of rice than before and this was the centre of any feast. The more that was needed, the better, since the best rice comes from the largest cauldron. Meat was still a luxury: the poor ate it only at great holidays when they would receive the gift of part, at least, of the sacrificial sheep of the rich or well-to-do. The women's vegetable plots produced greenstuff and a little fruit which was supplemented from the woods and hedgerows. In Bulgaria, in particular, there was a trade in rose-petal jam which married happily with crumbling goats' cheese. If one single article of diet contributed to the long life of the peoples of the mountains in particular, it was yoghurt. When made from buffalo milk, it was known as *kaymak* (a sort of clotted cream), but when made from goats' milk and heavily salted it was too pungent for any west European to eat, except the brave. Women would share ovens in the poorer villages but in the towns the bakers were the foremost citizens. If there were several of them, the guild rule was that they each baked the same quantity of loaves as the others – thus the master craftsman was sold out early and the worst and most heavy-handed loaves of the ungifted baker were all sold to sluggards or late arrivals. It was not a competitive, capitalist system. Bakeries as such were the monopoly of men, as were all public shops and eating houses.

A great empire acquires dishes from every province but these are modified by the quality of the materials and also their variety. As has been mentioned, this was why the market at Bursa was unrivalled either in Ottoman territories or any other. The food was mainly stewed rather than baked or fried because fat was valuable. Grilling meat on skewers to produce kebabs was not usually work for the home. It is doubtful that villagers ever ate kebabs, but there were kebab houses in the towns with their specialities just as there are today. Nor did peasant women make any of the puddings which townsfolk and the *saray* enjoyed. Those servants who ate at the *saray* were mainly served stewed vegetables and there was rice on special occasions.

Meat dishes acquired local names: Ankara, Bursa or Talas *börek*, which was meat in puff pastry: the pastry that conquered Vienna, when Kara Mustafa Pasha failed to do so in 1683, and gave Europe the croissant for breakfast. The Turks had always been mistresses of layered bread, which came to be made as thin as muslin. The development of this *yuvka* pastry came about because of the lack of an oven. Its perfection calls for genius in the building of layer upon layer of pastry brushed with butter and honey, pistachio nuts and any other predilection. Whether such *böreks*, or cheese-filled triangles (*muskas*), were invented by the Turks of Central Asia or not, their equivalents are known all over the Moslem world.

The grandest vegetable dishes could carry a proud title such as *imam bayıldı* ('The *imam* fainted'), which was made with aubergine, rich oil and tomato. But the names of sweet desserts were largely reserved for women so that one might enjoy a pastry such as *kadın göbeği* ('ladies' navels'), although their thighs were a meat course. The great pastries depended on their lightness and the quality of the honey.

The very finest Ottoman dishes can no longer be found and *çerkeştavun* (Circassian chicken) bears little relationship to what the great dish once was. An eminent surgeon, who founded the first children's hospital in Istanbul, explained that it was necessary to start with eight grandmothers who had an earthenware flowerpot the size of a brick between them. On one side were the ladies crushing walnuts so fresh that they were black and on the other a team taking chicken breasts to pieces hair by hair. The bottom of the pot was painted with the walnut juice and then a layer of cotton-thin shreds of breast rested on it. And so on until, at the end of the day, the pot was full. A brick was laid on top all night and this ambrosia was ready to be eaten for lunch on the next day: and never to be forgotten.

Western influence on cuisine was slight because Istanbul and Edirne enjoyed fine supplies of fruit and vegetables from season to season. They inherited ideas from the Byzantines, but it was in Asia that they had learnt how to preserve meat and fruit for winter use. They had also learnt to make stews like *güveç*, with or without meat. Milk puddings were important just as were sweets of nuts and honey or the august *lokum* ('delight'), which powders the eager eater's nose. Eggs were unimportant if only because a hen had difficulty scraping a living from the dust of an impoverished village. Fish abounded, but the Turks were an inland people who were adept enough with river fish but then learnt Mediterranean ways of cooking anything from the sea such as turbot, swordfish or octopus. Red caviare still came from streams into the twentieth century but sturgeon had become rare in the estuaries of the Black Sea coasts where once they had been abundant.

The spices of the east continued to be important but by the nineteenth century a great number of peppers, saffron and even unguents grew in Anatolia. There is a continuing trade in the products of Egypt and Arabia – the most considerable being coffee, especially from Yemen and Arabia (or it was until the end of the Ottoman dynasty, but now comes from Brazil and other, cheaper sources). Nor does prize honey now come from the Nile; Turkey produces fine honey of its own, from Trabzon for example. It was and is a gourmet's world but is still very regional. The trout of Erzerum, the crayfish of Apolyant, the giant prawns of Iskenderun and the truffles of Antep are examples of this – or were until western greed looted these sources.

Wines were produced at village level except in Erzerum or Trakya (Thrace), often by single farmers. Cyprus had long exported wine on a commercial scale to Europe as well as to the *saray* and wherever the janissaries penetrated. Water was a specialized art and there was fierce competition between springs. Before the end of the Ottoman period, when restaurants developed, their water menus took precedence over the wine lists, which were shorter if they existed at all.

Postscript

Eton[28] was as prejudiced an observer as one could hope to find, but his report on the condition of the women and children captured at Ochakof[29] is thought-provoking. They were crowded into one large tent suffering from the freezing cold, their nakedness and their wounds. Eton, who spoke some Turkish, was left in charge. All had lost a parent, a husband or a child yet none lamented aloud but spoke calmly and firmly. He was astonished at the patience and resignation inculcated by their religion although, being Eton, he had to say that their behaviour might be due to insensibility.

Then he saw a woman who was silently, but openly, grieving. She told him that she had lost all her family except one child. She then pointed to a child by her side who had just expired. Eton wept but not the mother. Looking back over the years of endurance that Ottoman women experienced through five centuries, their capacity to face grief was not astonishing.

Giladi[30] has dealt sensitively with the problem at an earlier period of Islam. It was true that parents had many children, knowing that only a few were likely to survive. It was felt that people should not become attached to something which could only be regarded as a probable loss. Children, for example, were the first victims of the plague. The precept did not work. The loss of a loved one could release such sadness that a debilitating melancholy resulted. Parents were distraught at seeing the toys of a deceased child. Some would not eat or drink and others could not sleep. One man said that he had nine children. When challenged that he had only one, he replied, 'I had ten, nine of whom died and only one survived. Now I wonder whether I am his or he is mine.' What then did the mother feel? In the Ottoman world, resignation could go so far, but no farther, than it went in those of Macduff or Aegeus.

It is not enough to praise the strength of character of Ottoman women: it was deliberately wasted. That this was equally true in much of Europe excuses no one. Men suffered as badly as women from lack of education and the impoverishment of the imagination. But this was worse for women because they were burdened by the accepted belief of both sexes in the male right to dominate. Even those women who established their own authority within the home could not confront men other than their husbands. Only nomadic women managed to achieve such liberty because they subdued arrogance with their versatility.

Before the coming of machines, a struggling peasant farmer had little spare time, and his wife had less. Thinking was restricted to the gossip of a village made up of, perhaps, a couple of hundred households. Like the Byzantines before them, their 'headlines' were the disease that had struck the oat crop or the death of one more infant. There were no schools until after the Second World War in such villages. Wisdom was learned through the fingers and not the ears. Ibn Battuta noted peasants in southern Anatolia who did not even know the names of the days of the week. Sadly, what had in the past been a flight from the land became, by the end of the nineteenth century, a flight from the country of the liveliest minds and strongest wills. They would emigrate and never come back. The widows lost their sons and the wives any hope in the future.

In the cities, the women of the well-to-do had comforts such as no villager could imagine. Yet wealth putrefies when too much leisure becomes a burden and not a delight. Here were women with a wealth of hours but nothing to do with them except pomade their hair.

Education was a revolution in the nineteenth century, before the opening of the first lycée for girls in 1911. Its progress kept in step with the fall of the Ottoman empire.[31] In Europe change was more rapid but no more explosive. Women, it is true, might study at English universities but no amount of brilliance could earn them a degree until 1920. Men clung to their dominance everywhere just as much as they did in western Asia. Nothing was more improbable, and nothing more disastrous to contemplate, than an attack on their divine right to ordain the rules of a society. Their weakness was that as power dissolved all around them, and the cities filled with refugees because of the poverty of a government of men, there seemed no reason why anyone should be deluded as to the quality of their minds. Women too had been to blame in earlier periods but it was for exactly the same reason: a Valide Sultan might intrigue and influence governments but her power could not influence the basic errors of administration or the sapping of vitality that comes from policies of perpetual hand-to-mouth solutions in the name of expediency. If education would make better men, it would certainly make better women. Nor did they have to be recruited from the sultan's bed. In the end, intellectually dishevelled men could only claim that the hand that fired the harquebus had stronger rights to rule than the hand that swung the cradle. How odd! The turban was big but there was no head in it.

To rule is not simply to take a single-sex view of the needs of any society. In that sense, the government of the Amazons was a disaster. Partly because they were not taught to read and write, women under Ottoman rule took no part in government at any level. There were exceptions such as Kösem at the *saray* in the sixteenth century or strong-willed village women, but the previously mentioned report on Hal shows how weak even these women were when faced by arrogant and, sometimes, brutal males who were entitled to beat their wives. There were the protective influences of relatives and there was the disapproval of some neighbours just as in Christian Europe. But nothing could make up for the loss that resulted from the absence of intellectual training for women and the need to balance the reasoning of men with that of women.

Any society requires an equal contribution to the solution of its problems if valid policies are to prevail. In the evolution of most societies, women were not to achieve equality anywhere before the first half of the twentieth century else social and political history would have been very different. That half the brains of a society were uncultivated or extended is a tragedy in itself, in particular because women were responsible for rearing children even after they were 7 years old. But much more poignant was the stultifying of the intellects of intelligent women. It was bad for the poor who worked themselves, literally, into the ground. It was a more refined cruelty for the rich who had nothing to do and who could not even write a letter. In one sense, this book is a record of the 650 years of letters that were never written by women who would have outshone the gossip of western travellers. To be truly poor is to die and leave behind neither a word nor footprint: nor a name. Such poverty made beggars of nearly all of them and, as St John of Damascus said, a beggar is an insult to God. With this even an atheist can agree.

The end of an era (R. E. Chorley)

Notes

Of the most important works which have contributed to the substance of this book, H. Inalcık and D. Quataert, *An Economic and Social History of the Ottoman Empire*, has been essential. S. Faroqhi, a contributor to this major publication, is also the author of several scholarly works on Anatolian social history. Other historical sources include C. Kafadar, 'Seljuk to Ottoman Period' in *9000 Years of Anatolian Women*, and *Between Two Worlds*; H. A. R. Gibb and H. Bowen, *Islamic Society and the West*; Ibn Battuta's *Travels*; Busbecq's *Turkish Letters*; Evliya Çelebi's *Travels*; I. M. Lapidus, *Muslim Cities* and, also, *Islamic Societies*; R. Mantran, *La Vie Quotidienne*; A. Alderson, *The Structure of the Ottoman Dynasty*; J. S. Trimingham, *The Sufi Dervishes*; D. DeWeese, *Islamization and Native Religion in the Golden Horde*; the works of Mrs M. J. Garnett, especially *Turkish Life in Town and Country*, *Balkan Home Life* and *Mysticism and Magic in Turkey*. F. W. Hasluck, *Christianity and Islam under the Sultans*, is the outstanding work on magic and superstition. C. F. Coxwell, *Siberian and Other Folk Tales*, is a major source which, sadly, is still out of print. Of the nineteenth-century travellers, Mrs Scott-Stevenson, *Our Ride through Anatolia*, is informative and witty. W. Wilkinson, *Moldavie et Valachie*, is also important and the novels of Yaşar Kemal are invaluable sources of information on Anatolian peasant life and on that of the Kurds in particular.

Apart from these, other major sources are listed below at the start of the chapter in which their first references are made.

For full publishing details of the works referred to in the notes, the reader is referred to the Bibliography.

The abbreviation *EI* has been used for *Encyclopaedia of Islam* throughout.

Notes

Introduction

1. In this book, 'Harem' refers only to royal palaces, and to Topkapısaray in particular, whereas '*harem*' simply means private or family area.

Chapter 1

Works include A. K. S. Lambton, *Landlord and Peasant in Persia*; T. Talbot Rice, *The Seljuks*; and H. Moser, *A Travers l'Asie Centrale*.

1. Harvey, *Economic Expansion in the Byzantine Empire*. See Farmer's Law and *morte*, pp 16ff.
2. Kafadar, 'Seljuk to Ottoman Period', p. 203.
3. Lindner, *Nomads and Ottomans*, p. 27.
4. They still do.
5. Coxwell, *Siberian and Other Folk Tales*; for tall tales from Central Asia, see pp. 232ff.
6. Hyland, *Medieval Warhorse*, p. 133.
7. Moser, *A Travers l'Asie Centrale*, p. 74.
8. Ibid., p. 246.
9. Ibid., p. 28.
10. Lambton, *Landlord and Peasant*, pp. 79ff.
11. Ibid., p. 350.
12. Ibn Battuta, *Travels*, p. 335.
13. Ibid., p. 482.
14. Ibid., p. 451.
15. Talbot Rice, *Seljuks*, pp. 91ff.
16. Shaw, *History of the Ottoman Empire*, vol. 1, p. 13.
17. Lindner, *Nomads and Ottomans*, p. 25.
18. *EI*, vol. VIII, 1993, p. 180: 'Othman'.
19. Kafadar, *Between Two Worlds*, pp. 66ff.

Chapter 2

H. H. G. Danişman, 'Yayla Settlements'; and M. Gough, *The Plain and the Rough Places*.

1. Garnett, *Turkish Life*, p. 198; Coxwell, *Siberian and Other Folk Tales*, p. 52.
2. Lindner, *Nomads and Ottomans*, p. 1.
3. Lambton, *Landlord and Peasant*, p. 156.
4. Mainly in the form of family quarrels.
5. Garnett, *Turkish Life*, p. 200.
6. Danişman, 'Yayla Settlements', p. 25.
7. The concept was urban and alien to nomad culture.
8. Inalcık, *Ottoman Empire*, p. 32.
9. Lapidus, *History of Islamic Societies*, p. 282.

10.   Lindner, *Nomads and Ottomans*, p. 66.
11.   See Shaw, *History of the Ottoman Empire*, pp 80ff, on the subjugation of eastern Anatolia.
12.   Lindner, *Nomads and Ottomans*, pp. 63ff.
13.   Ibid., p. viii.
14.   Shaw, *History of the Ottoman Empire*, pp. 150–1.
15.   Lindner, *Nomads and Ottomans*, p. vii.
16.   Ibid., p. 88.
17.   Scott-Stevenson, *Our Ride through Anatolia*, passim.
18.   Danişman, 'Yayla Settlements', p. 21.
19.   Lapidus, *History of Islamic Societies*, p. 275.
20.   Scott-Stevenson, *Our Ride through Anatolia*, p. 291.
21.   Ibid., p. 137.
22.   Danişman, 'Yaya Settlements', pp. 21ff.
23.   Coxwell, *Siberian and Other Folk Tales*, p. 381.
24.   Bourdieu, 'La Maison Kabyle', pp. 745ff.
25.   DeWeese, *Islamization and Native Religion*, pp. 43ff.
26.   Ibid.
27.   Lindner, *Nomads and Ottomans*, p. 59.
28.   Garnett, *Turkish Life*, p. 198.
29.   Lindner, *Nomads and Ottomans*, p. 59.
30.   Garnett, *Turkish Life*, p. 24.
31.   Gough, *The Plain and the Rough Places*, p. 43.
32.   Garnett, *Turkish Life*, p. 201.
33.   Ibid., p. 257.
34.   Scott-Stevenson, *Our Ride through Anatolia*, pp. 265, 294.
35.   Ibn Battuta, *Travels*, p. 480.
36.   Coxwell, *Siberian and Other Folk Tales*, p. 381.
37.   Grigor of Akanc, *History of the Nation of the Archers*, pp. 205ff.
38.   Garnett, *Turkish Life*, p. 203.
39.   Possibly in order to conserve them.
40.   Lapidus, *History of Islamic Societies*, p. 390; Hasluck, *Christianity and Islam*, p. 131.
41.   Coxwell, *Siberian and Other Folk Tales*, p. 262.
42.   Hasluck, *Christianity and Islam*, pp. 143ff.
43.   See DeWeese, *Islamization and Native Religion*, pp. 44ff, on The World Tree (feminine).
44.   Ibid., p. 131.
45.   They were no more superstitious than hordes in the west today reading horoscopes in newsprint and, if rich enough, consulting necromancers.

Chapter 3

P. Stirling, *Turkish Village* and *Village in Anatolia*, are important sources. N. N. Ambraseys and C. F. Finkel, *The Seismicity of Turkey*, is invaluable for its review of the great number of earthquakes but also for its asides. M. Eliade, *Shamanism*, is a standard work. Payne's work on Ankara housing has yet to be published; E. Kalças, *Food from the Fields*, is a unique contribution; I. Orga's well-known *Portrait of a Turkish Family* is equally timeless. This chapter introduces the works of many travellers, including R. Chandler, E. Chishull, J. Jackson, W. M. Leake (*Travels in Northern Greece*), C. MacFarlane, E. Pears, Earl Percy and J. de Thevenot.

1. See Gibb and Bowen, *Islamic Society and the West*, vol. II, p. 166, on *tapu* as 'advance rent' and also 'periodic rent'.
2. Walpole, *Memoirs*, p. 113. Turkish farmers continue to help each other at harvest time and at the vintage.
3. It is not clear at what age a youth was considered a man. It must to some extent have depended on his maturity.
4. Researched by the author, who made frequent visits to the Marmara in the 1960s.
5. Nagata, 'Bosnian Notables', pp 86ff. A croft could cost less than a coat.
6. Walpole, *Memoirs*, p. 136.
7. Kemal, *Undying Green*, pp. 20ff.
8. Pierce, *Life in a Turkish Village*, p. 28.
9. Ibid., p. 86.
10. Presumably levied on Christians.
11. Ambraseys and Finkel, *Seismicity of Turkey*, pp. 87, 89–90.
12. Kemal, *Undying Green*, p. 279.
13. Garnett, *Turkish Life*, p. 15.
14. Kemal, *Undying Green*, passim. The cunning of the untrained peasant mind was weakened by fatalism.
15. Barkey, *Bandits and Bureaucrats*, passim.
16. See Gibb and Bowen, *Islamic Society and the West*, pp. 114ff, on the reliability of Ottoman lawcourts and p. 130 on there being separate courts for women.
17. Exactly as it was in Europe until women's property acts protected them from rapacious husbands.
18. A policy of slash and burn which, in some areas of Britain, has done serious damage to the countryside.
19. Faroqhi, 'Peasants, Dervishes and Traders', p. 62.
20. Faroqhi, 'Towns and Townsmen', p. 686.
21. Inalcık, *Ottoman Empire*, p. 135.
22. Baer, *Fellah and Townsman*, p. 21.
23. Ibid., p. 16.
24. Inalcık, *Ottoman Empire*, p. 127.
25. Ibid., p. 25.
26. This was one factor that contributed to the Armenian massacres of the First World War.
27. Faroqhi, 'Peasants, Dervishes and Traders', p. 236; Inalcık, *Ottoman Empire*, p. 135.
28. Inalcık, *Ottoman Empire*, p. 77.
29. Beldiceanu, *Recherches sur la Ville Ottomane*, p. 39.
30. Inalcık, *Ottoman Empire*, p. 96; Faroqhi, '16th-Century Periodic Markets', p. 124. It supported the army along campaign routes.
31. Baer, *Fellah and Townsman*, pp. 15ff.
32. Kemal, *Undying Green*, p. 115.
33. So foolish a policy would be incredible if it were not for equally blind policies

pursued today.
34. *EI*, vol. II, 1965, p. 238: 'Djalālī (Celali)', writes of idle and dissident officers.
35. Faroqhi, 'Peasants, Dervishes and Traders', XI, p. 220.
36. Inalcık, *Ottoman Empire*, pp. 165ff.
37. Ibid., p. 174.
38. Ambraseys and Finkel, *Seismicity of Turkey*, pp. 87–9.
39. Stirling, *Turkish Village*, p. 183; Gough, *The Plain and the Rough Places*, p. 5.
40. Thevenot, *Travels*, p. 34.
41. The author has feasted on the steps of the mosque at Pertek.
42. Macfarlane, *Constantinople*, pp. 110ff.
43. Known as a hubble-bubble pipe because the smoke is cooled through water.
44. Gough, *The Plain and the Rough Places*, pp. 40–1. Strangers who camped were visited partly out of curiosity and partly out of politeness until interest was lost. As many as twenty villagers might come at a time.
45. Macfarlane, *Constantinople*, p. 217.
46. Baer, *Fellah and Townsman*, p. 7. Ibn Battuta, *Travels*, p. 416, states that the women of Alanya were the cleanest in dress and the kindest of God's creatures, and neighbours asked after his needs. When bidding farewell, the women – who were unveiled – wept.
47. Chandler, *Travels*, p. 330.
48. Ibid., p. 87.
49. Pierce, *Life in a Turkish Village*, p. 65.
50. Abbott, *Under the Turk*, pp. 4ff.
51. Even in the winter cold, poor interior light drove women to work outside.
52. Wilkinson, *Moldavie et Valachie*, p. 157.
53. Bryer, *Peoples and Settlement*, p. 4.
54. Percy, *Highlands of Asiatic Turkey*, passim.
55. Chandler, *Travels*, p. 273.
56. Jackson, *Journey from India*, p. 206.
57. Busbecq, *Turkish Letters*, p. 200. When in Amasya, he wrote that the Turks avoided display and built huts to protect them from robbers and the weather, and to keep warm. They only had rugs because linen was a luxury.
58. Thevenot, *Travels*, p. 26.
59. Garnett, *Balkan Home Life*, p. 5.
60. Wilkinson, *Moldavie et Valachie*, p. 684.
61. Chishull, *Travels*, p. 6.
62. Walpole, *Memoirs*, p. 113.
63. Gough, *The Plain and the Rough Places*, p. 47.
64. Ibid., p. 46.
65. Erdentuğ, *Social Structure of a Turkish Village*, passim.
66. Ibid., p. 46.
67. Ibid., p. 34, n. 49.
68. Kafadar, *Between Two Worlds*, pp. 42ff.
69. Hasluck, *Christianity and Islam*, vol. I, pp. 194ff.
70. Erdentuğ, *Social Structure of a Turkish Village*, pp. 43ff.
71. Ibid., p. 26.
72. Ibid., p. 54.

73. Payne, *Ankara Housing*, p. 97.
74. Ibid., p. 162.
75. Garnett, *Turkish Life*, p. 71.
76. Kingsley, 'Greeks, Shamans and Magi', p. 189.
77. Ibid., p. 193.
78. Eliade, *Shamanism*, p. 89.
79. Slade, *Records of Travels*, p. 121.
80. Eliade, *Shamanism*, p. 273.
81. Hasluck, *Christianity and Islam*, p. 580.
82. Garnett, *Balkan Home Life*, p. 34.
83   Orga, *Portrait of a Turkish Family*, pp. 294ff.
84. Oral communication from H. E. the late Emin Divanı-Kibrizli.
85. Author's own experience.
86. Kafadar, *Between Two Worlds*, p. 201. There were no witch hunts under Ottoman rule.
87. Garnett, *Balkan Home Life*, p. 63.
88. Ibid., p. 188.
89. Hasluck, *Christianity and Islam*, pp. 81–2.
90. Garnett, *Balkan Home Life*, pp. 62ff.
91. Kakouri, *Death and Resurrection*, pp. 13ff.
92. E. Savage Smith, oral communication, British Museum, 20.1.1995.
93. V. Porter, as above.
94. Hasluck, *Christianity and Islam*, p. 106.
95. Eliade, *Shamanism*, p. 135.
96. Ibid., p. 175.
97. Hasluck, *Christianity and Islam*, p. 106.
98. White, *Three Years in Constantinople*, p. 21.
99. Fadl Allah, *Successors of Genghis Khan*, p. 48.
100. Hasluck, *Christianity and Islam*, p. 109.
101. Erdentuğ, *Social Structure of a Turkish Village*, p. 6.
102. Pierce, *Life in a Turkish Village*, p. 83.
103. Lopasic, *Turks of Bosnia*, pp. 17ff.
104. Garnett, *Balkan Home Life*, pp. 25ff.
105. Stirling, *Turkish Village*, p. 40.
106. Garnett, *Balkan Home Life*, p. 25. In Albania, for example, the father's consent was essential and lack of it the cause of elopements.
107. Erdentuğ, *Family Structure and Marriage Customs*, p. 15.
108. Stirling, *Turkish Village*, p. 179.
109. Ibid., p. 261. The term 'cousin' is of recent use in villages, where most people are cousins anyway.
110. Pears, *Turkey and its People*, p. 67. The selection of men and women was as it was in France. The property bond was better than in England until the Married Woman's Property Acts.
111. Kemal, *Undying Green*, p. 53.
112. Stirling, *Turkish Village*, p. 53.
113. Lopasic, *Turks of Bosnia*, p. 14.
114. Wilkinson, *Moldavie et Valachie*, pp. 144ff.

115. Khadduri and Liebesny, *Law in the Middle East*, p. 104.
116. Ibid., p. 138.
117. Pears, *Turkey and its People*, p. 59. The girl entertained her friends alone.
118. Beldiceanu, *Recherches sur la Ville Ottomane*, p. 19.
119. The bride's family only supplied sweets and *pekmez*.
120. Erdentuğ, *Social Structure of a Turkish Village*, p. 13. One may ponder the symbolism of this gift.
121. Stirling, *Turkish Village*, p. 193. Both might have to flee the district.
122. Erdentuğ, *Social Structure of a Turkish Village*, p. 14.
123. Lopasic, *Turks of Bosnia*, p. 15. The proud, pretty child of a noble repented and drowned herself on the way to the man's house. Her father shut himself up for life. The man married later.
124. Garnett, *Balkan Home Life*, p. 24.
125. Gough, *The Plain and the Rough Places*, pp. 82ff.
126. Garnett, *Turkish Life*, pp. 178ff. There was a grim contrast between the condition of rich and poor.
127. Wilkinson, *Moldavie et Valachie*, p. 170.
128. Heffening, *Shorter EI*, pp. 418–20. See also Lambton, 'al-Mar'a', *EI*, vol. VI, p. 477. Into recent times *mut'a*, or temporary marriage, was alive even in Mecca itself. On the revitalized existence of *mut'a* in Iran, see Haeri, *Law of Desire*.
129. Kafadar, *Between Two Worlds*, p. 202.
130. Busbecq, *Turkish Letters*, p. 203; Kafadar, *Between Two Worlds*, p. 202.
131. Erdentuğ, *Family Structure and Marriage Customs*, p. 9.
132. Kemal, *Undying Green*, p. 52.
133. *EI*, vol. IV, 1934, p. 636: 'Talak'.
134. Erdentuğ, *Social Structure of a Turkish Village*, p. 11.
135. Hasluck, *Christianity and Islam*, pp. 535ff.
136. Stirling, *Turkish Village*, p. 41.
137. Garnett, *Balkan Home Life*, pp. 83ff.
138. Ibid., p. 39.
139. Lopasic, *Turks of Bosnia*, p. 18.
140. Author's observation.
141. Goodwin, *Janissaries*, p. 34.
142. Ibn Battuta, *Travels*, pp. 416ff.
143. Bryer, *Peoples and Settlement*, pp. 1–2.
144. Ibid., p. xiii.
145. Walpole, *Memoirs*, p. 138.
146. Beldiceanu, *Recherches sur la Ville Ottomane*, p. 178, n. 7.
147. Kemal, *Undying Green*, p. 16.
148. Erdentuğ, *Social Structure of a Turkish Village*, p. 41.
149. Scott-Stevenson, *Our Ride through Anatolia*, p. 70.
150. Busbecq, *Turkish Letters*, p. 596.
151. Scott-Stevenson, *Our Ride through Anatolia*, p. 259.
152. Kalças, *Food from the Fields*, p. 75.
153. Calvert, *Tour to the East*, pp. 216ff.
154. A scandal probably circulated by their enemies.
155. Rosenthal, *Politics and Thought*, p. 191.

156. Soorma, *Islam's Attitude*, pp. 16ff.
157. Marius, 'Men, Women and Property', p. 146.
158. Erdentuğ, *Social Structure of a Turkish Village*, passim.
159. Garnett, *Balkan Home Life*, pp. 9ff.
160. Slade, *Records of Travels*, pp. 437ff.
161. Forbes, Hogarth, et al., *Balkans*, p. 247.
162. There had been Menteşe pirates in the Aegean from before Ottoman rule.
163. Faroqhi, '16th-Century Periodic Markets', p. 180.
164. Garnett, *Turkish Life*, pp. 208ff.
165. Leake, *Travels*, pp. 666ff.
166. Trimingham, *Sufi Dervishes*, passim.
167. Ibid., p. 175.
168. Yunus Emre, the fourteenth-century Turkish mystic poet, in Menemencioğlu (ed.), *Penguin Book of Turkish Verse*, p. 123.
169. See Koran, IV, 'Women', and chastisement.
170. Heyd, *Ottoman Criminal Law*, passim.
171. Unsal, *Chronique*, passim.

Chapter 4

The contribution of F. W. Carter to economic and social history is introduced; M. Cezar, 'Osmanlı Devrinde', is particularly useful as a source for the great fires and their damage in Istanbul; M. Bainbridge, 'Life-cycle Rituals of the Turks', is a vital source. Works on slavery and slave markets include reference to the contribution of M. I. Finlay towards a definition of slavery, 'Between Slavery and Freedom'. Other contributions include A. Fisher, 'Studies in Ottoman Slavery'; P. G. Forand, 'The Relation of Slave and the Client'; C. White, *Three Years in Constantinople*; and R. Jennings, 'Women in Early 17th-Century Ottoman Judicial Records'. Travellers include J. C. Hobhouse, R. Walsh, G. Keppel and J. Dalloway. Miss Pardoe's two famous works can hardly be listed under 'travellers'. G. Jarring, 'Dervish and Qalandar', is revealing.

1. Inalcık, *Ottoman Empire*, p. 256.
2. Lapidus, *History of Islamic Societies*, p. 86.
3. Inalcık, *Ottoman Empire*, p. 602.
4. Ibid., p. 601.
5. Today, the finest example is Safranbolu.
6. Garnett, *Balkan Home Life*, pp. 4ff.
7. Ibid., pp. 34ff.
8. Küçükgerman, *Türk Evi*, passim.
9. Faroqhi, 'Peasants, Dervishes and Traders'. Towns were famous for their specialist crafts: Vize for wagons, Ankara for mohair, Konya for shoes, skins and kilims; but by the nineteenth century Kütahya had lost its tile market to Europe (ibid., p. 530).
10. Scott-Stevenson, *Our Ride through Anatolia*, pp. 36–7.
11. Ibn Battuta, *Travels*, p. 454.
12. Inalcık, *Ottoman Empire*, p. 652.
13. Ibid., 941.

14. Cezar, 'Osman Devrinde', p. 361.
15. Ibid., p. 343.
16. Lapidus, *History of Islamic Societies*, p. 147.
17. Laoust, *Gouverneurs de Damas*, p. 707. Famine was so bad at Dıyarbekir one year that a mother ate her seven children, one after the other.
18. Lapidus, *History of Islamic Societies*, p. 176.
19. Carter, 'Ottoman Empire', p. 25.
20. Lapidus, *History of Islamic Societies*, p. 176.
21. Dalloway, *Constantinople*, p. 132.
22. Jarring, 'Dervish and Qalandar', pp. 8ff.
23. Lapidus, *History of Islamic Societies*, p. 178.
24. Johnson, *Constantinople*, pp. 356ff.
25. Dols, *Majnun*, p. 297.
26. Peri, 'Waqf and Ottoman Welfare', pp. 167ff.
27. Lapidus, *History of Islamic Societies*, p. 83.
28. Forand, 'Relation of Slave and Client'.
29. Ibid., p. 66.
30. Fisher, 'Studies in Ottoman Slavery', pp. 49ff; Finlay, 'Between Slavery and Freedom', pp. 234ff.
31. Forand, 'Relation of Slave and Client', p. 61.
32. Tritton, *Materials on Muslim Education*, pp. 146–7.
33. Jennings, 'Women': black slaves, pp. 295ff.
34. Sahillioğu, 'Slaves', passim.
35. Fisher, 'Studies in Ottoman Slavery', p. 54.
36. Inalcık, *Ottoman Empire*, p. 284.
37. Ibid., p. 596.
38. White, *Three Years in Constantinople*, p. 609.
39. Mantran, *La Vie Quotidienne*, p. 149.
40. Keppel, *Narrative*, passim. Keppel was in the country in wartime when conditions were near to famine. He was offered what the locals ate.
41. Walsh, *Journey from Constantinople*, p. 58.
42. Mantran, *La Vie Quotidienne*, p. 141.
43. B. Lewis, *Islam from the Prophet Muhammad*, vol. II, pp. 243ff.
44. Toledano, *Ottoman Slave Trade*, passim.
45. Mantran, *La Vie Quotidienne*, pp. 201ff.
46. The logic which endows men with twice the wisdom and perception of women surely precludes the First Woman from making so vital a decision?
47. Bainbridge, 'Life-cycle Rituals', passim.
48. Chandler, *Travels*, p. 355.
49. Lopasic, *Turks of Bosnia*, p. 143.
50. Mantran, *La Vie Quotidienne*, p. 199.
51. Castellan, *Histoire Pittoresque*, pp. 223–4.
52. DeWeese, 'Baba Kamal Jandi'.
53. Bainbridge, 'Life-cycle Rituals', p. 8.
54. Pardoe, *City of the Sultan*, p. 133.
55. Hobhouse, *Journey through Albania*, p. 837.
56. Alderson, *Structure of the Ottoman Dynasty*, pp. 125–6.

57.   *Sürre Alay*: procession of gifts.

Chapter 5

The outstanding recent work on Topkapısaray is G. Necipoğlu, *Architecture, Ceremonial and Power*. Earlier sources include T. Dallam, J. B. Tavernier, J. P. de Tournefort and, more recently, N. M. Penzer. The invaluable contribution of S. Skilliter includes 'Catherine de Medici's Turkish Ladies-in-Waiting', the 'Letters of Nūr Bānū' and 'Three Letters from "Sultana" Safiye to Queen Elizabeth I'. Related to government are C. H. Fleischer, *Bureaucrat and Intellectual*; and Evliya Çelebi (intro. Rhoads Murphy), *Melek Ahmed Pasha*. The *Letters* of Lady Mary Wortley Montagu remain unique.

1.   Alderson, *Structure of the Ottoman Dynasty*, tables XXIV and XXV. Bayezit I had nine recorded sons. Ertuğrul, Kasim (probably blinded), Korkud and Ömer were politically unimportant while the Emir Isa (Jesus) may have been a Christian. Musa died in 1402 and Mustafa was either executed in 1402 or was not a Pretender and died in 1422. Süleyman died in 1415 and was the future Sultan Mehmet I's foremost enemy.
2.   *EI*, vol. II, 1965, p. 66.
3.   Now Sadrazam as opposed to Vezir Azam.
4.   Necipoğlu, *Architecture*, p. 159.
5.   *EI*, vol. V, 1986, p. 66: 'Khurrem'. There is a well-researched record in the Bank of St George, Genoa.
6.   Necipoğlu, *Architecture*, p. 163.
7.   Alderson, *Structure of the Ottoman Dynasty*, p. 82, expresses doubt but her letters had not yet been published.
8.   Skilliter, 'Letters of the Venetian "Sultana"', p. 516.
9.   And presumably well educated at home.
10.   Skilliter, 'Letters of the Venetian "Sultana"', passim.
11.   Ibid., p. 519. Nurbanu had Selim's body put on ice until Murat III could be brought from Manisa.
12.   Gibb and Bowen, *Islamic Society and the West*, vol. II, pp. 73ff. The important source of information on the structure of the Harem; Necipoğlu, *Architecture*, pp. 180ff; Hierosolitano, Austen ms., passim.
13.   Dallam, 'Diary', passim.
14.   Necipoğlu, *Architecture*, p. 180.
15.   Ibid., p. 78.
16.   Bon, *Sultan's Seraglio*, pp. 47, 57.
17.   Tavernier, *Nouvelle Relation*, pp. 89–90.
18.   Fadl Allah, *Successors of Genghis Khan*, pp. 120–1; *EI*, vol. V, 1986, p. 1112.
19.   *EI*, vol. IV, 1934, p. 1113: 'Kösem Walide'.
20.   Tournefort, *Relation d'un Voyage*, p. 81.
21.   Skilliter, 'Letters of the Venetian "Sultana"', p. 119.
22.   Abbott, *Under the Turk*, p. 4.
23.   Skilliter, 'Letters of the Venetian "Sultana"', p. 148.
24.   Baysun, *Ottoman History*, vol. V, p. 272; Mantran, *La Vie Quotidienne*, p. 194.

25. Alderson, *Structure of the Ottoman Dynasty*, table XXXIV, spelt Anastasya.
26. Shaw, *History of the Ottoman Empire*, vol. I, pp. 190ff.
27. Alderson, *Structure of the Ottoman Dynasty*, p. 11.
28. Fleischer, *Bureaucrat and Intellectual*, p. 175.
29. *EI*, vol. IV, 1934, p. 1113: 'Kösem Walide'.
30. Inalcık, *Ottoman Empire*, p. 64. On 18 August.
31. *EI*, vol.V, 1986, p. 273. Not with a silken cord, but strangling was probably a mark of respect.
32. Murphy, *Intimate Life*, p. 89.
33. Shaw, *History of the Ottoman Empire*, vol. I, pp. 207ff; *EI*, vol.V, 1986, pp. 256ff.
34. Van Crayesteyn, 'Letter to Jacob David'.
35. De la Jonquière, 'Histoire de l'Empire Ottoman', p. 177.
36. Shaw, *History of the Ottoman Empire*, vol. I, p. 101.
37. Ibid.
38. Murphy, *Intimate Life*, pp. 5ff.
39. Alderson, *Structure of the Ottoman Dynasty*, table XXXVI; Evliya Çelebi, *Melek Ahmed Pasha*. p. 231.
40. Alderson, *Structure of the Ottoman Dynasty*, table XXXIV.
41. Bon, *Sultan's Seraglio*, p. 144.
42. *EI*, vol. VI, 1991, pp. 860ff: 'Mawakib'.
43. Nütku, ' "Nahil" ', passim.
44. Montagu, *Letters*, vol. VI, pp. 105ff.
45. By now the Valide had a residence of her own.
46. Skilliter, 'Catherine de Medici's Turkish Ladies-in-Waiting', pp. 188ff.

Chapter 6

This chapter relies heavily on previous works cited. E. Lott, *Harem Life*, is an extraordinary story which one must accept as true if only because this governess has such an elevated opinion of herself that she reveals her lack of understanding – of which she was unaware; more conventional is J. Thornton, *The Present State of Turkey*. The most important new source in this chapter is V. Nagata, *Bosnian Notables*, which is a revealing record of possessions (or lack of them).

1. Howard, 'Ottoman Historiography', p. 243.
2. Nichol, *Byzantine Lady*, passim.
3. Merriman, *Suleiman the Magnificent*, p. 24.
4. Ibid., p. 153.
5. Her portrait in mosaic can be found in the gallery of Haghia Sophia.
6. Neale, *Travels*, pp. 198ff.
7. Thornton, *Present State of Turkey*, p. 228; Kafadar, 'Seljuk to Ottoman Period', p. 237.
8. Lott, *Harem Life*, pp. 257ff.
9. Forbes, Hogarth, et al., *Balkans*, p. 178.
10. Mrs Harvey, *Turkish Harems*, p. 217.
11. Ibid., p. 244.

12.   Nagata, 'Bosnian Notables', passim.

Chapter 7

Ahmet Refik, *Eski Istanbul*, is still a primary source as is A. Duben and C. Behar, *Istanbul Households*. Views of their society in the nineteenth century are given in the works of O. Dalvimart; P. de Régla, *Constantinople* – a masterpiece of gossip; G. Ellison; Princess Musbah Haidar; Mrs Harvey; and the long-respected A. Van Millingen, *Constantinople*. N. Berkes, *The Development of Secularism in Turkey*, is invaluable.

1.   Amicis, *Constantinople*, passim.
2.   Duben and Behar, *Istanbul Households*, passim.
3.   Ellison, *Englishwoman in Angora*, p. 145.
4.   Duben and Behar, *Istanbul Households*, p. 155.
5.   Stirling, *Turkish Village*, p. 41.
6.   Duben and Behar, *Istanbul Households*, p. 4.
7.   Stirling, *Turkish Village*, pp. 112–13.
8.   Duben and Behar, *Istanbul Households*, pp. 87ff.
9.   Ibid., p. 155.
10.   Ibid., pp. 181ff.
11.   Thornton, *Present State of Turkey*, p. 252.
12.   Faroqhi, 'Towns and Townsmen', p. 786.
13.   Scott-Stevenson, *Our Ride through Anatolia*, p. 64.
14.   Huri, *Leyla and Majnun*, p. 63.
15.   Mrs Harvey, *Turkish Harems*, pp. 11ff.
16.   And at this time a lady would not go out of her home unescorted.
17.   However, Dalvimart, in *Dress and Manners of the Turks*, p. 14, attributes indolence to the way of life in the *harem*.
18.   Thornton, *Present State of Turkey*, pp. 246–7.
19.   Twenty-six: the number of his janissary battalion. The credit for his mission is likely to belong to the cultivated, but spendthrift, Grand Vezir Damat Nevşehirli Ibrahim Pasha.
20.   Berkes, *Development of Secularism*, p. 34.
21.   Musbah Haidar, *Arabesque*, p. 41.
22.   Ibid., p. 63.
23.   Ibid., p. 231.
24.   Méry, *Constantinople*, p. 357.
25.   Vaka, *Unveiled Ladies*, pp. 16ff.
26.   Ibid., p. 63.
27.   Musbah Haidar, *Arabesque*, p. 64.
28.   Pardoe, *City of the Sultan*, pp. 125ff.
29.   Lott, *Harem Life*, passim.
30.   This excludes gambling, which does not appear to have been a part of the lives of women.
31.   Yunus Emre. See Menemencioğlu (ed.), *Turkish Verse*, p. 123.
32.   Ahmet Refik, *Eski Istanbul*, passim.

33. Montagu, *Letters*, p. 143.
34. Diez, *Itinéraire*, pp. 195ff.
35. Who did not wash their faces, hands and feet several times a day or go to the baths once a week.
36. Walpole, *Memoirs*, pp. 243ff.
37. Kalças, *Food from the Fields*, passim.
38. Walpole, *Memoirs*, p. 284.
39. Kafadar, *Between Two Worlds*, p. 198.
40. Pardoe, *City of the Sultan*, pp. 125ff.
41. Amicis, *Constantinople*, p. 221.
42. Still popular on Turkish streets today.
43. Busbecq was presented with flowers by janissaries as a similar expression of goodwill.
44. Orga, *Portrait of a Turkish Family*, passim.
45. Scott-Stevenson, *Our Ride through Anatolia*, p. 130.
46. Faroqhi, 'Peasants, Dervishes and Traders', p. 699.
47. Ibid., p. 700.
48. Once Hebdomen, suburb of Istanbul and crowning place of the very early Byzantine emperors.
49. B. Lewis, *Emergence of Modern Turkey*, p. 469.
50. Faroqhi, 'Towns and Townsmen', pp. 872ff.
51. Ibid., p. 893.
52. Ibid., p. 911.
53. Van Millingen, *Constantinople*, pp. 249ff.

Chapter 8

R. Arık, *Anadolu Tasvır Sanatı*, is a standard work. Other sources include E. J. W. Gibb, *The Forty Vezirs*; A. Evin, *Turkish Novel*; A. Bombaci, *Littérature Turque*; Bassano di Zara, *I Costumi*; Lady Hornby, *Constantinople during the Crimean War*; and A. Giladi, 'Concepts of Childhood'.

1. Titley, *Detailed Catalogue of Islamic Miniatures*.
2. And, *Turkish Miniature Painting*, p. 14.
3. Ibid., p. 59.
4. Kafadar, 'Seljuk to Ottoman Period', p. 254.
5. Arık, *Anadolu Tasvır Sanatı*, p. 154.
6. Ergil, *Müzeleri*, p. 10.
7. Sheykh-zada, *Forty Vezirs*, passim.
8. Ibid., p. 15.
9. Evin, *Turkish Novel*, passim.
10. And, *Karagöz*, passim.
11. Martinovitch, *Turkish Theatre*, p. 18.
12. Evin, *Turkish Novel*, pp. 29ff.
13. Bombaci, *Littérature Turque*, p. 392.
14. Berkes, *Development of Secularism*, p. 283.

15. Ibid., p. 380.
16. B. Lewis, *Emergence of Modern Turkey*, pp. 154ff.
17. Hanoum and Ellison, *Abdul Hamid's Daughter*, pp. 42ff.
18. Bassano di Zara, *I Costumi*, passim; Dalvimart, *Dress and Manners of the Turks*, passim.
19. Laoust, *Gouverneurs de Damas*, p. 707. They were built like a gold tiara.
20. Later, a fur or astrakhan hat like a large fez.
21. Hornby, *Constantinople*, pp. 239ff.
22. Gonül, *Sadberk Hanim Museum*, passim.
23. Hornby, *Constantinople*, p. 239.
24. White, *Three Years in Constantinople*, pp. 82ff.
25. Mrs Harvey, *Turkish Harems*, pp. 244ff.
26. White, *Three Years in Constantinople*, pp. 95ff.
27. Mrs Harvey, *Turkish Harems*, pp. 244ff.
28. Eton, *Survey*, pp. 123–4.
29. Ochakof (Oczakow) was a stronghold at the mouth of the Dneiper during the Russo-Crimean war of 1791.
30. Giladi, 'Concepts of Childhood', pp. 625ff.
31. When women could still not enter restaurants even with their husbands. Berkes, *Development of Secularism*, pp. 386ff.

Wealthy woman of the eighteenth century (T.S.K.)

Glossary

acemi	cadet or female slave new to the Harem
ağa	chief; landowner
akçe	silver coin long used in the Ottoman empire
Anadolu Kadıasker	second most senior judge in the Ottoman empire
araba	carriage
baba	holy man; head of a dervish lodge
Bailo	Venetian ambassador to the sultan
Baş Hasseki or Kadın	mother of the sultan's eldest son
bedesten or *bedestan*	market hall for valuables
bey	(originally) ruler, chieftain; (then) man of rank; (now) any man
beylerbey	viceroy; 'lord of lords'
börek	filled pastry triangle
bostancı	gardener; royal gardener and guard
boyar	Christian landowner, especially of large estates
boza	drink of fermented millet
Büyük Valide	Great Valide (only imposed by Kösem)
cariye	humblest rank of slave girls in Saray
celalı	rebels made of up dervishes, disbanded soldiers, students and the dispossessed

Glossary

çerkeştavun	Circassian chicken
Damat	son-in-law of the sultan
divan	fitted sofa
Divan	the council of state; hall of justice
efendi	gentleman
funduq	market area; shop
gazi	heroic leader; warrior fighting for the Faith
gecekondu	house roofed in one night. The squatter could appropriate the land that it was built on. In time, the initial shack was greatly improved.
gedik	the 'privileged'; girl not yet chosen by the sultan
gelin	newly married daughter-in-law
gözde	'girl in the sultan's eye': term related to possible relationship with the sultan
güveç	casserole; hot pot; earthenware pot
hajj	pilgrimage to Mecca
hamal	porter
hamam	hot public bath house
han	hostel or inn for merchants
harem	women's or any private area
Harem	[in the present book] the royal palaces, and Topkapısaray in particular
Hasseki Kadın	mother of daughters born to the sultan
Hasseki Sultan	mother of sons born to the sultan
hassodalik	fortunate or chosen one; paramour of the sultan (hence 'odalisque')
Hatun	woman of rank
hayat	(a) life; (b) verandah
Hazinedar Usta	Lady Treasurer of Harem with rank of *kadın*
Hekimbaşı	head physician
helva	sweet made of sesame flour, butter and honey
hoca	Moslem religious teacher; tutor and chaplain
ibrik	slender spouted jug (usually metal)
idda	waiting period of three months after divorce to see if the wife is pregnant
ikbal	paramour of the sultan but not yet promoted to be a *kadın*
imam	prayer leader
kadı	judge

kadın	lady of rank (one of the four senior women in the Harem)
Kahya Kadın	Lady Intendant in charge of the Harem
kaif	'quintessence of the soul' (can relate to hashish, opium or other drugs)
kalpak	tall cap, usually of astrakhan or fur
Kapudan Paşa	Grand Admiral
kaymak	thick cream made with buffalo milk
kervansaray	Turkish spelling of caravanserai; fortified hostel
kira	business agent working for the Valide Sultan and the Harem in particular
Kızlar Ağa	Master of the Harem; Chief Eunuch
konak	mansion
kral (or *kıral*) *kızı*	royal lady
kul	slaves of the sultan, seen as members of the sultan's greater family (applies to both sexes). A servant of the state
kumiss	fermented mare's milk
lala	nurse and tutor
lokum	Turkish delight (the sweet)
mahalle	quarter (of a town)
mangal	brazier
meddah	jester; public story-teller
medrese	religious college
mescit	small mosque; in Ottoman vocabulary, a mosque without a pulpit
meydan	square; open space
molla	doctor of Islamic law
muhtar	headman of a village or town
muska	cheese-filled triangle
naghile	hubble-bubble pipe
nahil	marriage palm made of gold and silver, etc
ocak	hearth
orta oyunu	open-air theatre
Padişah	God's Shadow upon Earth (usual title of the sultan)
paşmakluk	slipper money
pastırma	meat preserved with garlic and spices
pekmez	concentrated grape juice
peri	fairy

peyk	royal guard
saray	palace
Şariat	Koranic law
selamlık	male guests' reception rooms
şeyh	master of a dervish convent; elder; head of a Moslem religious order
Şeyhülislam	Grand Mufti
Shia	sect believing Ali to be the first authentic caliph after Mohammed
simit	ring of bread encrusted with sesame seed
sipahi	cavalry officer; horseman; feudal cavalry
sultana	princess
talak	divorce
tarhana	dish made of dried curds and flour
tekke	Sufi monastery; dervish lodge
telek	large coach
türbe	tomb; mausoleum
ulema	members of the judicial class; Fathers of the Law
Vakuf, Vakıf	grant of property to produce income to maintain a charitable foundation (Arabic: *Waqf*)
Valide Sultan	queen mother
vezir	minister of state (Turkish spelling of vizier)
vila	neutral spirit who could be hostile or friendly
yalı	mansion beside the Bosporus
yayla	camp
yurt	nomad's hut
yuvka	paper-thin pastry
zaptiye	police
zaviye	dervish monastery; dervish convent accommodating travellers

The Wardrobe

aba	coarse woollen cloth
arakçın	tall cap made of fine-quality silk
bürümçük	gauze skirt to wear over trousers
çakşır	trousers with boots attached, worn by men in the country

çarşaf	(in late nineteenth century) a voluminous outer coat or cape and skirt
çedik	slipper boots; light indoor shoes
çepken	long-sleeved version of bumfreezer jacket (for page-boys) worn with plain long dress of same colour
enselik	wide band at back of head worn with *hotoz*
entari	gown; loose robe; state robe
ferace	light cloak; outdoor mantle
hotoz	coloured headdress shaped like a cushion and bound in place by a scarf round the forehead
kalpak	tall hat of fur or astrakhan in Cossack fashion
nalın	high-heeled wooden sandals worn in *hamam* in particular
paçalık	nineteenth-century two-piece outfit showing Parisian influence
papuç	slippers
peçe	dark veil
peş	gusset
şalvar	baggy trousers reaching to the ankles
selma	wide-sleeved underdress
serpuş	frivolous cap (banned by the eighteenth century)
sorguç	plumed aigrette
terpuş	fez-shaped cap, tapering by the sixteenth century
tırtıl	chenille
torba çarşaf	large hood with a circle cut out for the face (country wear)
üç etek	three-panelled skirt
yaşmak	veil of two pieces worn above and below the eyes

Mother and daughter in the hamam, *Raphael, eighteenth century* (T.S.M.K.)

Bibliography

Abbreviations

BMGS	*Byzantine and Modern Greek Studies* (London)
BSOAS	*Bulletin of the School of Oriental and African Studies* (London)
EI	*Encyclopaedia of Islam* (Leiden)
IJMES	*International Journal of Middle East Studies* (Cambridge)
IJTS	*International Journal of Turkish Studies* (Wisconsin)
JAOS	*Journal of the American Oriental Society* (Ann Arbor, Michigan)
JESHO	*Journal of Economic and Social History of the Orient* (Leiden)
JRAS	*Journal of the Royal Asiatic Society* (London)

Abbott, G. F., *Under the Turk in Constantinople*, London, 1920

Abou El Hajj: *see* El Hajj, A.

Adjarian, H., *Hayots dere Osmanian Koysratyean Medj Banber Erevani Hamalsarani*, Yerevan, 1967

Afetinan, A., *The Emancipation of Turkish Women*, The Hague, 1962

Ahmet Refik, *Eski Istanbul, 1553–1839*, Istanbul, 1931

Alcock, T., *Travels in Russia, Persia, Turkey and Greece*, London, 1831

Alderson, A. D., *The Structure of the Ottoman Dynasty*, Oxford, 1956

Alexander, J., *Brigandage and Public Order in the Morea, 1685–1806*, Athens, 1986

Allom, T., *Constantinople and the Seven Churches of Asia Minor*, London, 1838

Altinoluk, Ü., 'The Old Turkish House and the Traditional Way of Life', *Ilgi* (Istanbul), no. 56 (winter 1989)

Ambraseys, N. N., and Finkel, C. F., *The Seismicity of Turkey and Adjacent Areas*, Istanbul, 1995

Bibliography

Amicis, E. de, *Constantinople* (trans. C. Tilton), London, 1878

And, M., *Turkish Miniature Painting. The Ottoman Period*, Istanbul, 1974

——*Karagöz*, Ankara, 1975

——'Ösmanli Düginleriade Natullar', *Tarik Mecmuası* (2 Jan. 1968)

Anderson, S. P., *An English Consul in Turkey . . . Paul Rycault at Smyrna, 1667-78*, Oxford, 1989

Angiolello, G. N., 'Breve Narratione . . .', in G. B. Ramusio, *Viaggi*, vol. 2 (no place), 1554

Archer, A., *The Mutual Efforts*, New York, n.d.

Arık, R., *Batililaaşma Dönermi Anadolu Tasvır Sanatı*, Ankara, 1976

Armstrong, T. B., *Journals of Travels in the Seat of War*, London, 1831

Arnold, T. W., *Painting in Islam*, New York, 1965

Artan, T., 'The Kadırga Palace: An Architectural Reconstruction', *Maqarnas* (Leiden), vol. 10 (1993)

Ascoli, G. J., *Documenti Orientali . . . Italia, I. Federigo II di Gonzaga*, Rome, 1859

Atasoy, N., *Ibrahim Pasha Saray*, Istanbul, n.d.

Atil, E., 'Islamic Women as Rulers and Patrons', *Asian Art* (Oxford), vol. VI, no. 2 (1993)

Baer, G., *Fellah and Townsman in the Middle East*, Ottowa, 1982

Bainbridge, M., 'Life-cycle Rituals of the Turks of Turkey', *Research Papers* 16 (Centre for the Study of Islam and Christian–Muslim Relations, Birmingham) (Dec. 1982)

Barbaro, N., *Diary of the Siege of Constantinople, 1453* (ed. and trans. T. R. Jones), New York, 1969

Barkey, K., *Bandits and Bureaucrats*, Ithaca, N.Y., 1994

Bassano di Zara, L., *I Costumi et i Particolari della Vita de Turchi*, Rome, 1545

Baysun, M. C., *Ottoman History*, vol. 5, Paris, 1980

Beauvoisins, J. E., *Notice sur la Cour du Grand-Seigneur*, Paris, 1809

Beck, L., and Keddie, N. (eds), *Women in the Muslim World*, Cambridge, Mass., 1978

Beldiceanu, N., *Recherches sur la Ville Ottomane au XVe siècle*, Paris, 1973

Beldiceanu, N., and Steinherr, I., *Le Monde Ottoman des Balkans (1402-1566)*, London, 1976

——*Le Monde Ottoman des Balkans (1402-1566)*, London, 1936

——*Recherches sur la Province de Qaraman au XVI siècle*, London, n.d.

Bell, R. C., *Board and Table Games from Many Civilizations*, London, 1960

Berkes, N., *The Development of Secularism in Turkey*, Montreal, 1964

Birge, J. K., *The Bektashi Order of Dervishes*, London, 1937

Blount, H., *A Voyage into the Levant*, London, 1638

Bombaci, A., *Histoire de la Littérature Turque*, Paris, 1968

Bon, O., *La Relazione degli Stati Europei . . .* (ed. G. Goodwin and publ. in English as *The Sultan's Seraglio*), London, 1996

Bos, G., 'Maimonides on the Preservation of Health', *JRAS*, 3rd series, vol. 4, part 2 (July 1994)

Bourdieu, P., 'La Maison Kabyle ou Le Monde Renversé', *Sociologie de l'Algérie* (Paris) (1961)

Brown, A., 'Introduction to Geo. Eliot', in *Romola*, London, 1944

Brown, J. P., *The Darvishes; or Oriental Spiritualism*, London, 1927

Bryer, A., *Peoples and Settlement in Anatolia and the Caucasus, 800-1900*, London, 1988

Busbecq, O. G., *The Turkish Letters of Ogier Ghiselin de Busbequius* (trans. E. S. Forster), Oxford, 1927

Bibliography

Cahen, C., 'Economy, Society, Institutions', in *Cambridge History of Islam*, Cambridge, 1970

Çakiroglu, N., *Kayseri Evleri*, Istanbul, 1952

Calvert, E., *A Tour to the East*, London, 1767

Cantemir, D., *History of the Growth and Decay of the Ottoman Empire*, London, 1734

Carbugnano, C. C. de, *Topografica dello Stato Presente de Constantinopli*, Bassano, 1744

Carswell, J., 'Lemon Squeezer', *Proceedings of the IV International Congress of Turkish Art*, Aix-en-Provence, 1976

Carter, F. W., 'Ottoman Empire. A Historical Geography of the Balkans', in H. Inalcik and D. Quataert (eds), *An Economic and Social History of the Ottoman Empire in the Classical Age, 1300–1914*, London, 1973

Castellan, A. L., *Histoire Pittoresque de la Turquie*, Paris, n.d.

Cerasi, M. M., 'Open Space, Water and Trees', *Environmental Design* (Rome), no. 2 (1935)

Cezar, M., 'Osmanlı Devrinde Istanbul Yapilarinda . . . ', in *Türk Sanatı Tarihi Arastırma ve Incelemeleri I*, Istanbul, 1963

Chandler, R., *Travels in Asia Minor*, Dublin, 1775

Chayanov, A. M., *The Theory of Peasant Economy*, London, 1966

Cheyne, T. K., and Sutherland-Black, J., 'Deuteronomy', in *Encyclopaedia Biblica*, vol. II, London, 1901

Chishull, E., *Travels in Turkey and Back to England*, London, 1747

Cochran, W., *Pen and Pencil in Asia Minor*, London, 1887

Colton, W., *A Visit to Constantinople and Athens*, New York, 1836

Cook, M. A., *Studies in the Economic History of the Middle East*, London, 1970

——*Population Pressure in Rural Anatolia, 1450–1600*, London, 1972

Coulson, N. J., *A History of Islamic Law*, Edinburgh, 1964

Coxwell, C. F., *Siberian and Other Folk Tales*, London, 1925

Crane, H., 'Notes on Seljuq Architectural Patronage', *JESHO*, vol. XXXVI, part 1 (Feb. 1993)

Culin, S., *Games of the Orient*, Vermont, 1958 (originally pub. Pennsylvania, 1895)

Dallam, T., 'The Diary of Master Thomas Dallam, 1599–1600', in J. T. Bent (ed.), *Early Voyages and Travels in the Levant*, London, 1893

Dalloway, J., *Constantinople . . .* , London, 1797

Dalvimart, O., *The Dress and Manners of the Turks*, London, 1814

Daneshvari, A., *Animal Symbolism*, Oxford, 1986

Danişman, H. H. G., 'Yayla Settlements', in *Boğazici Üniversitesi Dergisi*, vols. 4–5, Istanbul, 1976–77

Davey, R., *The Sultan and His Subjects*, London, 1957

Dengler, I. C., 'Turkish Women in the Ottoman Empire in the Classical Age', in L. Beck and N. Keddie (eds), *Women in the Muslim World*, Cambridge, Mass., 1978

Devrim, S., *A Turkish Tapestry*, London, 1994

DeWeese, D., 'Baba Kamal Jandi', *Der Islam* (Berlin), vol. 171 (1994)

——*Islamization and Native Religion in the Golden Horde*, Pennsylvania State University, 1994

——*Islamization and Native Religion in the Golden Horde. Baba Tükles and Conversion to Islam in Historical and Epic Tradition*, Pennsylvania State University Press, 1994

Dols, M. W., *Majnun: The Madman in Medieval Islamic Society*, Oxford, 1992

Duben, A., 'Turkish Families and Households in Historical Perspective', *Journal of Family History* (spring 1983)

Bibliography

Duben, A., and Behar, C., *Istanbul Households: Marriage, Family and Fertility*, Cambridge, 1994

Dunlop, D. M., *Arabian Civilization to AD 1500*, London, 1971

Edip, H., *Memoirs*, London, 1940

El Hajj, A., 'The Ottoman Vezir and Pasha Households, 1680–1703: A Preliminary Report', *JAOS*, vol. XCIV (1974)

Eldem, S. H., *Türk Bacheleri*, Istanbul, 1978

Eliade, M., *Shamanism* (trans. W. R. Trask), Bollinger Series, vol. LXXVI, New York, 1964

Ellison, G., *An Englishwoman in a Turkish Harem*, London, 1915

——*An Englishwoman in Angora*, London, 1923

Erdentuğ, N., *A Study of the Social Structure of a Turkish Village*, Ankara, 1959

——*Family Structure and Marriage Customs of a Turkish Village*, Ankara, 1963

Ergil, T., *Müzeleri*, Istanbul, 1993

Esin, E., 'Influences de l'Art Nomade et l'Art du Turkestan pre-Islamique', in *1st International Congress of Turkish Art 1959*, Ankara, 1961

Eton, W., *Survey of the Turkish Empire*, London, 1799

Ettinghausen, R., 'The Dance with Zoomorphic Masks', in *Arabic and Islamic Studies in Honour of Hamilton A. R. Gibb*, Leiden, 1956

Evin, A., *Origin and Development of the Turkish Novel*, Minneapolis, 1989

Evliya Çelebi, *The Intimate Life of an Ottoman Statesman, Melek Ahmed Pasha (1588–1662)* (trans. and commentary, R. Dankoff; intro., Rhoads Murphy), New York, 1991

——*Narrative of Travels in Europe, Asia, and Africa in the Seventeenth Century* (trans. Joseph von Hammer), London, 1834

Evlyapan, G. A., *Eski Türk Bacheleri*, Ankara, 1972

Fadl Allah, Rashid al-Din, *The Successors of Genghis Khan* (trans. V. A., Boyle), Irvington, N.Y., 1977

Faroqhi, S., 'Towns and Townsmen of Ottoman Anatolia', in H. Inalcık and D. Quataert (eds), *An Economic and Social History of the Ottoman Empire in the Classical Age, 1300–1914*, Section IV: 1550–60, London, 1973

——*Men of Modest Substance . . .*, Cambridge, 1987

——'Urban Society and Domestic Architecture in 17th-Century Anatolia', *IJMES*, vol. 2 (1971)

——*Pilgrims and Sultans: The Hajj under the Ottomans*, London, 1994

——'Vakufadin in 16th-Century Konya', *Vakuflar Dergisi* (Ankara), vol. XVIII, part 2 (1974)

——'16th-Century Periodic Markets in Various Anatolian Sanjaks', *JESHO*, vol. XXII, no. 1 (1979)

——'Camels, Wagons and the Ottoman State in the 16th and 17th Centuries', *IJMES*, vol. 14 (1982)

——'Development of the Anatolian Urban Network . . .', *JESHO*, vol. XXIII, no. 3 (1980)

——'Peasants, Dervishes and Traders in the Ottoman Empire. The Peasants of Saideli in the Late 16th Century', *IJMES*, vol. 14 (1982)

Finlay, M. I., 'Between Slavery and Freedom', *Comparative Studies in Society and History* (The Hague), vol. VI, no. 3 (April 1964)

Fisher, A., 'Studies in Ottoman Slavery and Slave Trade', vol. II, *Journal of Turkish Studies* (Harvard), vol. 4 (1988)

Fleischer, C. H., *Bureaucrat and Intellectual in the Ottoman Empire: The Historian Mustafa*

Ali, Princeton, N.J., 1986

Forand, P. G., 'The Relation of Slave and the Client. . .', *IJMES*, vol. 2 (1971)

Forbes, N., Hogarth, G. D., Mitany, D., and Toynbee, A. J., *The Balkans*, London, 1915

Fuzūli, *Leyla and Majnūn* (trans. S. Huri), London, 1970

Fyzee, A. A. A., *Outline of Muhammadan Law*, Oxford, 1964

Galland, G., *Journal d'Antoine Galland pendant son Séjour à Constantinople, 1672–3* (annoted C. Schefer), Paris, 1881

Garnett, Mrs M. J., *Turkish Life in Town and Country*, London, 1896

——*The Turkish People*, London, 1909

——*Mysticism and Magic in Turkey*, London, 1912

——*Balkan Home Life*, London, 1917

Gerber, H., 'Social and Economic Position of Women in an Ottoman City, Bursa, 1600–1700', *IJMES*, vol. 12 (1981)

Gibb, E. J. W. (trans.): *see* Sheykh-zada

Gibb, H. A. R., 'Lutfi Pasha on the Ottoman Caliphate', *Oriens* (Leiden), vol. XV (1962)

Gibb, H. A. R., and Bowen, H., *Islamic Society and the West*, Oxford, 1950

Giese, F., *Settlement Process of Nomads of Sultan Daği in Summer*, Berlin, 1904

Giladi, A., 'Concepts of Childhood. . .', *JESHO*, vol. XXXI (1989)

Goitein, S. D., *A Mediterranean Society*, vol. 1: *Economic Foundations*, Studies in Islamic History and Institutions, Leiden, 1966

Gonül, *Sadberk Hanim Museum*, Istanbul, 1989

Goodwin, G., *The Janissaries*, London, 1994

——'The Ottoman Garden', *The Garden* [journal of the Royal Horticultural Society, London], vol. III, part II (Nov. 1986)

Görecki, D. M., 'Land Tenure in Byzantine Property', *Greek, Roman and Byzantine Studies* (London), vol. XXII, no. 2

Gough, M., *The Plain and the Rough Places*, London, 1954

Grigor of Akanc, *History of the Nation of the Archers (Tatars)*, Cambridge, Mass., 1954

Griswold, W. J., 'Djalālī', *EI*, Supp. 3–4 (1961)

——*The Great Anatolian Rebellion, 100–1020, 1591–1611*, Berlin, 1983

Guillaume, A., *Islam*, Harmondsworth, 1954

Güran, T., 'The State Role in the Grain Supply of Istanbul: The Grain Administrations, 1793–1839', *IJTS*, vol. III (1985)

Haeri, S., *Law of Desire: Temporary Marriage in Islam*, London, 1989

Haidar, Princess Musbah, *Arabesque*, London, 1944

Hallaway, J., 'The Wealth and Influence of an Exiled Eunuch . . .', *JESHO*, vol. XXXIII (1991)

Hanna, N., 'Introduction to the Cairene Middle Class House of the Ottoman Period', *Annales Islamogiques*, vol. 16 (1980)

Hanoum, M., and Ellison, G., *Abdul Hamid's Daughter*, London, 1913

Harvey, A. *Economic Expansion in the Byzantine Empire, 900–1200*, Cambridge, 1989

Harvey, J. H., 'Florist Flowers', in *Garden History*, vol. IV, no. 3 (1976)

Harvey, Mrs, of Ickwell, Bury, *Turkish Harems and Circassian Homes*, London, 1871

Hasluck, F. W., *Christianity and Islam under the Sultans*, 2 vols, Oxford, 1923

Hastings, J., *Encyclopaedia of Religion and Ethics*, vol. IV, London, 1908

Heffening, W., *A Shorter EI*, Leiden, 1953

Heyd, U., *Studies in Ottoman Criminal Law*, Oxford, 1973

Bibliography

Heywood, C., 'Between Historical Myth and Mythohistory', *BMGS*, vol. 12 (1988)

Hierosolitano, D. (trans. M. Austen), c.1552–1622, unpublished ms.

Hills, D., *My Travels in Turkey*, London, 1964

Hobhouse, J. C., *A Journey through Albania . . . 1809–10*, London, 1813

Holt, P. M., 'The Beylicate in Ottoman Egypt during the 17th Century', *BSOAS*, vol. XXIV (1961)

Hopwood, K., 'Türkmen, Bandits and Nomads . . .', in *Proceedings of CIEPO*, 6th Symposium, Istanbul, 1987

Hornby, Lady, *Constantinople during the Crimean War*, London, 1863

Hourani A., and Stern, S. M., *The Islamic City*, Oxford, 1970

Howard, D. A., 'Ottoman Historiography and the Literature of "Decline" of the 16th and 17th Centuries', *Journal of Asian History* (Wiesbaden), vol. 22, no. 1 (1988)

Huri, S., 'Leyla and Majnun', in A. Bombaci, *Histoire de la Littérature Turque*, Paris, 1968

Hyland, A., *The Medieval Warhorse from Byzantium to the Crusades*, Frome, 1994

Ibn Battuta, *The Travels of Ibn Battuta, AD 1325–1354* (ed. H. A. R. Gibb), vol. II, London, 1962

Ibn Iskender, Kai Ka'us, *A Mirror for Princes: the Qābus Nāme* (trans. R. Levy), London, 1957

Ibrahim Pasha [called Damat], *Feste fatti in Constantinopoli*, Rome, 1586

Imber, C., 'Involuntary Annulment of Marriage', *Turcica* (Paris), vol. XXV (1993)

Inalcık, H., 'Ottoman Methods of Conquest', *Studia Islamica* (Paris), vol. V (1957)

—— *The Ottoman Empire: Conquest, Organization and Economy*, London, 1978

Inalcık, H., and Quataert, D. (eds), *An Economic and Social History of the Ottoman Empire in the Classical Age, 1300–1914*, London, 1973

Irwin, R., *The Arabian Nights*, London, 1944

—— *The Middle East in the Middle Ages*, London, 1986

Jackson, J., *Journey from India towards England in the Year 1797*, London, 1799

Jarring, G., 'Dervish and Qalandar', in *Scripta Minora Regiae Societatis Humaniorum Litterarum Ludensis*, Rome, 1985–86

Jennings, R., 'Women in Early 17th-Century Ottoman Judicial Records', *JESHO*, vol. XVIII, no. 1 (1975)

—— 'Black Slaves and Free Blacks in Ottoman Cyprus', *JESHO*, vol. XXX

Johnson, C. R., *Constantinople Today*, New York, 1922

la Jonquière, Vicomte A. de, 'Histoire de l'Empire Ottoman', in V. Duruy, *Histoire Universelle*, Paris, 1846

Kabzińska-Stawarz, I., *Games of Mongolian Shepherds*, Warsaw, 1991

Kafadar, C., 'Seljuk to Ottoman Period', in *9000 Years of Anatolian Women*, Istanbul, 1994

—— *Between Two Worlds, the Construction of the Ottoman State*, Berkeley, Calif., 1995

Kakouri, K. J., *Death and Resurrection* (trans. W. D. Cousin), Athens, 1963

Kalças, E., *Food from the Fields*, Bornova, 1974

Katib Çelebi, *The Balance of Truth* (trans. G. L. Lewis), London, 1957

Keddie, N. R., 'Problems in the Study of Middle Eastern Women', *IJMES*, vol. 10 (1979)

Kemal, Y., *Mehmed, My Hawk*, London, 1966

—— *Undying Green*, London, 1977

Keppel, G., *Narrative of a Journey across the Balcan*, London, 1831

Khadduri, M., and Liebesny, H. J., *Law in the Middle East*, vol. 1, Washington, D.C. 1955

Kiel, A., *Art and Society of Bulgaria in the Ottoman Period*, Assan, 1985

Bibliography

Kingsley, P., 'Greeks, Shamans and Magi', *Studia Iranica*, vol. 23, fasc. 2 (1994)

Kinnane, D., *The Kurds and Kurdistan*, London, 1964

Kinnear, J. M., *Journey through Asia Minor . . .*, London, 1818

Kömürcüoğlu, *Ankara Evleri*, Istanbul, 1950

Köprülü, F., 'Ottoman Inheritance. Royal Lands Return to Sultan', *Vakuflar Dergisi* (Istanbul), vol. II (1942)

Kortepeter, C. M., 'Ottoman Imperial Policy and the Economy of the Black Sea Region in the 16th Century', *JAOS*, vol. LXXXVI (1966)

Kritoboulos, M., *History of Mehmed the Conqueror* (trans. C. T. Riggs), Princeton, N.J., 1954

Kruk, R., *Aristoteles Semitico-Latinus*, Amsterdam, 1979

Küçükgerman, Ö., *Kendi Metaninin Arayisi icinde Türk Evi*, Istanbul, 1978

Kunt, I. M., *The Sultan's Servants. The Transformation of Ottoman Provincial Government, 1550–1650*, Columbia, N.Y., 1983

Kuran, A., 'Haseki Külliyasi', *Boğazici Üniversitesi Dergisi* (Istanbul), vol. 2 (1974)

La Boullaye le Goulz, Sieur de [Ibrahim Bey], *Les Voyages et Observations*, Paris, 1653

Lambton, A. K. S., *Landlord and Peasant in Persia*, Oxford, 1953

——'al-Mar'a', *EI*, vol. VI (1991), p. 477

Laoust, H., *Les Gouverneurs de Damas sous les Mamlouks et les Premiers Ottomanes*, Damascus, 1952

Lapidus, I. M., *Muslim Cities in the Later Middle Ages*, Cambridge, 1984

——*A History of Islamic Societies*, Cambridge, 1988

Lazarev, I. V., *Kurdistan: Kurdskaya Problema*, Moscow, 1964

Leake, W. M., *Travels in Northern Greece*, 4 vols, London, 1835

Leila, A., *Women and Gender in Islam*, Yale, 1992

Lerner, D., *The Passing of Traditional Society*, New York, 1958

Lewis, B., *The Emergence of Modern Turkey*, Oxford, 1961

——*Islam from the Prophet Muhammad to the Capture of Constantinople*, 2 vols, New York, 1974

Lewis, G., 'Modern Turkish Attitudes to Europe', in S. Iyer (ed.), *The Glass Curtain . . .*, Oxford, 1985

Lewis, R., *Everyday Life in Ottoman Turkey*, London, 1971

Leyla, Saz, *Le Harem Impérial* (no place or date)

da Lezze, D., *Historia Turchesca, 1300–1514*, Bucharest, 1909

Lindner, R. P., *Nomads and Ottomans in Medieval Anatolia*, Bloomington, Ind., 1983 [*Indiana University Uralic and Altaic Series*, vol. 144]

Lopasic, R., *The Turks of Bosnia* (Zagreb, n.d.)

Lott, E., *Harem Life*, London, 1867

Lybyer, A. H., *The Ottoman Empire*, Harvard, 1986 [*Harvard Historical Series*, vol. 18]

McCullagh, F., and Ramsay, A., *Constantinople*, London, 1914

MacFarlane, C., *Constantinople in 1828*, London, 1829

McGowan, B., *Economic Life in Ottoman Europe: Taxation, Trade and the Struggle for Land, 1600–1800*, Cambridge, 1981

Malik Khanam and Ellison, G., *Abdul Hamid's Daughter*, London, 1913

Mantran, R., *Istanbul dans la Seconde Moitié du XVIIe Siecle*, Paris, 1962

——*La Vie Quotidienne à Constantinople au Temps de Soliman le Magnifique*, Paris, 1965

Manzoni, R., *El Yemen*, Rome, 1884

Marius, A., 'Men, Women and Property', *JESHO*, vol. XXVI (1983)

Martinovitch, N. N., *The Turkish Theatre*, New York, 1933

Maurand, J. *Itinéraire de Jérôme Maurand d'Antibes a Constantinople, 1544* (trans. L. Daez), Paris, 1901

Melek Hanım, *Thirty Years in the Harem*, New York, 1872

Menavino, G. A., *Tratto de' Costumi, et la Vita de' Turchi*, Florence, 1551

Menemencioğlu, N. (ed.), *The Penguin Book of Turkish Verse*, Harmondsworth, 1978

Merriman, R. B., *Suleiman the Magnificent, 1520–1566*, Cambridge, Mass., 1944

Méry, *Constantinople et la Mer Noire*, Paris, n.d.

Micklewright, N., 'Late 19th-Century Ottoman Wedding Costumes . . .', *Maqarnas* (Leiden), vol. VI (1990)

Miller, B., *Beyond the Sublime Porte . . .*, New Haven, Conn., 1931

—— *The Palace School of Muhammad the Conqueror*, Cambridge, Mass., 1941

Montagu, Lady Mary Wortley, *Letters* (ed. R. Halsband), London, 1968

Moser, H., *A Travers l'Asie Centrale*, Paris, 1885

Motraye, A. de la, *Travels in Europe, Asia, and in Parts of Africa*, vol. 1, London, 1732

Muhammad, Sari, Pasha, *Ottoman Statecraft* (trans. W. L. Wright), Princeton, N.J., 1935

Nagata, V., 'Materials on the Bosnian Notables', *Studia Culturae Islamicae* (Tokyo), no. 11 (1979)

Neale, A., *Travels through Some Parts of Germany, Poland, Moldavia and Turkey*, London, 1918

Neave, D. L., *Twenty-six Years on the Bosphorus*, London, 1933

Necipoğlu, G., *Architecture, Ceremonial and Power*, Cambridge, Mass., 1991

——'The Account Book of a 15th-Century Ottoman Royal Kiosk', *Journal of Turkish Studies*, vol. II (1987)

Nichol, D. M., *The Byzantine Lady*, Cambridge, 1994

Nicolay, N. de, *Navigations into Turkie* (ed. I. Stell; trans. T. Washington the Younger), London, 1585

Nütku, Ö., 'The "Nahil": A Symbol of Fertility in Ottoman Festivities', *Rocznik Orientalistyczny*, T.XLVIII, Z.I. (1992)

d'Ohsson, M., *L'Empire Othoman*, 3 vols, Paris, 1787–1820

Orga, I., *Portrait of a Turkish Family*, New York, 1950

Osman Bey [Major Vladimir Andrejevitch], *Les Femmes en Turquie*, Paris, 1878

Pallis, A. A., *Greek Miscellany*, London, 1951

Panzac, D., *La Peste dans l'Empire Ottoman, 1700–1850*, Louvain, 1985

Pardoe, Miss, *The City of the Sultan, and the Domestic Manners of the Turks in 1836*, 3 vols, London, 1838

——*The Beauties of the Bosphorus*, London, 1840

Payne, G. K., *Ankara Housing and Planning in an Expanding City*, vol. 3, London, 1978 (circulated privately)

Pears, E., *Turkey and its People*, London, 1911

Peirce, L. P., *The Imperial Harem: Women and Sovereignty in the Ottoman Empire*, New York/Oxford, 1993

——'Shifting Boundaries: Images of Ottoman Royal Women in the 16th and 17th Centuries', *Critical Matrix*, vol. 4 (1988)

Penzer, N. M., *The Harem*, London, 1965

Percy, Earl, *Notes from a Diary*, London, 1898

Bibliography

——*Highlands of Asiatic Turkey*, London, 1901

Peri, O., 'Waqf and Ottoman Welfare Policy . . .', *JESHO*, vol. XXXV (1992)

Pian de Carpini, Friar John of, *The Journey of . . . 1245-47* (trans. M. Komroff), New York, 1928

Pierce, J. E., *Life in a Turkish Village*, New York, 1964

Pococke, R., *A Description of the East*, Book 2, London, 1738

Poynter, M. A., *When Turkey was Turkey*, London, 1921

Quataert, D., *Social Disintegration and Popular Resistance in the Ottoman Empire, 1881–1908*, London, 1941

Ramsay, Lady (Agnes Dick), *Everyday Life in Turkey*, London, 1897

Ramsay, Sir William M., *Impressions of Turkey*, London, 1897

——*The Revolution in Constantinople*, London, 1909

Régla, P. de, *La Turquie Officielle*, Paris, 1890

——*Les Basfonds de Constantinople*, Paris, 1891

——*Constantinople*, Paris, 1897

Rosenthal, E. I. J., *Political Thought in Medieval Islam*, Cambridge, 1962

Rosenthal, F., *The Muslim Concept of Freedom prior to the 19th Century*, Leiden, 1960

——*Politics and Thought in Medieval Islam*, Leiden, 1962

——*The Hab-Hashish versus Medieval Society*, Leiden, 1971

——'Significant Uses of Arabic Writing', *Ars Orientalis*, vol. IV (1961)

Roux, J. P., *La Mort chez les Peuples Altaiques . . .*, Paris, 1963

——*Le Livre dans la Tradition Turque*, Paris, n.d.

Rubeck, Friar William of, 'Journey', in M. Komroff (ed.), *Contemporaries of Marco Polo*, New York, 1928

Russell, K. W., 'Ethnographic History of the Becal Bedouin of Petra', *Annual of the Department of Antiquities of Jordan* (Amman), vol. XXXVII (1993)

Rycaut, P., *The History of the Turkish Empire, 1623-77*, London, 1680

Sahillioğlu, H., 'Slaves in the Society and Economic Life of Bursa . . .', *Turcica* (Paris), vol. XVII (1986)

Sanderson, J., *The Travels of J. Sanderson in the Levant, 1584-1602* (ed. Sir William Foster), London, 1931

Sarı Mehmet Pasha, *Ottoman Statecraft: Book of Counsel* (trans. W. L. Wright), Princeton, N.J., 1935

Scarce, J., *Women's Costume of the Near and Middle East*, London, 1987

Schvon, F., *Dimensions of Islam* (trans. P. W. Townsend), London, 1970

Scott, J. C., *Weapons of the Weak: Everyday Forms of Peasant Resistance*, New Haven, Conn., 1985

Scott-Stevenson, Mrs, *Our Ride through Anatolia*, London, 1881

Sergeant, R. B., 'Miḥrāb', *BSOAS*, vol. XXI (1959)

Shaw, S. J., and Shaw, E. K., *History of the Ottoman Empire and Modern Turkey*, vol. 1, Cambridge, 1977

Sheykh-zada, *The History of the Forty Vezirs from the Turkish of Sheykh-zada* (trans. E. J. W. Gibb), London, 1886

Sieroshevski, *The Yakuts* (trans. W. G. Sumner), London, n.d.

Simbar, M. A., *The Wakfiyah of 'Ahmed Pasha*, London, 1940

Skilliter, S., 'Three Letters from the Ottoman "Sultana" Safiye to Queen Elizabeth I' [*Oriental Studies III, Documents from Islamic Chanceries*, 1st series] (Oxford, 1965)

——'Catherine de Medici's Turkish Ladies-in-Waiting', *Turcica* (Paris), vol. VII (1975)

——'The Letters of the Venetian "Sultana" Nūr Bānū and her Kira to Venice', *Istituto Universitario Orientale* (Naples), vol. XIX (1982)

——'The Sultan's Messenger, Gabriel Defrens', *Wiener Zeitschrift für die Kunde des Morgenlands*, Band 62 (Vienna), 1976

Slade, A., *Records of Travels in Turkey, Greece, . . .* , 2 vols, London, 1833

Soorma, C. S., *Islam's Attitude towards Women and Orphans . . .* , Woking, 1929

Spandugino, T., 'La Cronica Italiana di Theodore Spandugino, 1513', in C. Villain-Grandossi, *La Méditerranée au XII–XVIIe Siècles*, London, 1983

——*I Commentari . . .* (transl. L. Domenici), Florence, 1551

Stephan, St H., 'Endowment Deed of Hasseki Sultan', *Quarterly of The Department of Antiquities in Palestine*, vol. 10 (1944)

Stephens, J., *Incidents of Travel in Greece, Turkey . . .* , London, 1841

Stirling, P., *Village in Anatolia*, London, 1954

——*Turkish Village*, London, 1965

Stirling-Maxwell, W. (ed.), *Solyman the Magnificent Going to Mosque*, London, 1877

Talbot Rice, T., *The Seljuks*, London, 1961

Tarfur P., *Travels and Adventures, 1435–9* (trans. M. Letts), London, 1926

Tavernier, J. B., *Nouvelle Relation de l'Intérieur du Sérail du Grand Seigneur*, Cologne, 1675

——*Les Six Voyages de . . .* , Amsterdam, 1678

Tenenti, A., *Piracy and the Decline of Venice, 1580–1615* (trans. J. and B. Pullen), London, 1967

Thevenot, J. de, *Travels of M. de Thevenot into the Levant* (trans. D. Lovell), London, 1687

Thornton, T., *The Present State of Turkey*, London, 1809

Tietze, A., *Mustafā 'Alī's Counsel for Sultans, 1581*, vol. II, Vienna, 1982

Titley, N., *Detailed Catalogue of Islamic Miniatures in the British Library (Turkish)*, London, 1981

Toledano, E. R., *The Ottoman Slave Trade and its Suppression, 1840–1890*, Princeton, N.J., 1982

Tournefort, J. P. de, *Relation d'un Voyage du Levant*, Amsterdam, 1718

Trimingham, J. Spencer, *The Sufi Dervishes in Islam*, Oxford, 1971

Tritton, A. S., *Materials on Muslim Education in the Middle Ages*, London, 1957

Tugay, E. F., *Three Centuries: Family Chronicles of Turkey and Egypt*, Oxford, 1963

Ubicini, A., *La Turquie Actuelle*, Paris, 1855

Ubicini, P. de C., *Roumanie*, Bucharest, 1853

Unsal, A., *Chronique d'une Famille Anatolienne*, Paris, 1989

Urquhart, D., *The Pillars of Hercules*, London, 1848

Vaka, D., *Turkish Women*, Boston, Mass., 1909

——*The Unveiled Ladies of Istanbul*, Boston, Mass., 1923

van Crayesteyn, J., 'Letter to Jacob David' in H. Roseveare (ed.), *Markets and Merchants of the Late 17th Century*, London, 1987

Van Millingen, A., *Constantinople*, London, 1906

Vryonis Jnr., S., *The Decline of Medieval Hellenism in Asia Minor . . .* , London, 1971

Walpole, R., *Memoirs Relating to Foreign and Asiatic Turkey*, London, 1815

Walsh, R., *Journey from Constantinople*, London, 1828

Walther, W., *Women in Islam*, Montclair, N.J., 1981

Watt, W. Montgomery, *A History of Islamic Spain*, Edinburgh, 1965

Bibliography

Welch, A., *Shah 'Abbas and the Arts of Isfahan*, New York, 1973
Weston, S., *Persian Recreations or New Tales*, London, 1812
White, C., *Three Years in Constantinople*, London, 1845
Wilkinson, W., *Moldavie et Valachie*, Paris, 1821
Williams, C., 'The Mosque of Sitt Hadaq', *Maqarnas* (Leiden), vol. XI (1994)
Woods, H. C., *Washed by Four Seas*, London, 1908
Zachariadou, E. A., *Roumania and the Turks, c.1300–c.1500*, London 1985
Zubaida, S., and Tapper, R. (eds), *Culinary Cultures of the Middle East*, London, 1994

Girl returning from a vineyard, Raphael, mid-eighteenth century. Note Cupid's bow (Sotheby, 1984)

Index

Index

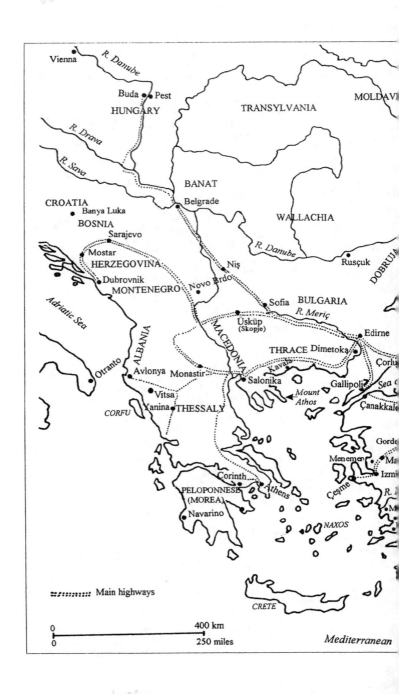